A PAINTER'S

Eljay Dickins

A professional graphic designer and artist, Eljay began her career as a paint and trace girl in the Bob Godfrey Animation studios in Soho, working on Godfrey's major cartoons and, on even, on one occasion providing the voice over for a particular saucy production.

After this "funniest job ever", Eljay moved on to children's educational books and magazines, then worked for several publishing houses designing reference books, including many relating to cookery and wine. She also worked on both animated films and books for Disney, the BBC and Thames Television.

After purchasing the Old Stone House in Turkey in 2006, Eljay and her husband Phil set about devise a way to be able to spend as much time there as possible, as the result of which Eljay's painting holiday business, Turkish Painting Holidays, was born. From this Eljay has formed the view that painting and cooking is the best possible combination for life enhancement, having provided non-stop fun and adventure, whilst allowing her to make many new friends over more than twelve years.

In July 2019 Eljay was diagnosed with an inoperable Grade 4 brain tumour. In most cases this will prove fatal within 18 months. However, after a year of radiotherapy and chemotherapy, Eljay's doctors confirmed with delight that they had shut the tumour down and that, while there can never be guarantees as to the future, their advice now was that she "get on with her life". She has taken them at their word.

A Painter's Palate is testimony to Eljay's positivity, sense of humour and inextinguishable optimism about the future. It is a celebration of her success in the face of seemingly insurmountable odds, to be taken as an inspiration to all.

A PAINTER'S PALATE

Tastes and Tales From a Turkish Art House

Written and Illustrated by

Eljay Dickins

BODRUM BOOKS!

❖

FOR PHIL

❖

Published in the UK in 2022
by Two Click Press

ISBN 978-1-7392204-0-2

Text design by Terry Woodley
Cover design by Laurence Blume

Printed and bound by in Great Britain
by Clays Ltd., Elcograf S.p.A

CONTENTS

INTRODUCTION

I am a Turkeyphile! This book will hopefully give you good reason to become one too. I am also a designer and artist and, along with my partner Phil, live part of the year in our 200-year-old stone house in a village moments from the turquoise waters of the Aegean sea, on the Bodrum Peninsula in southwest Turkey. I have lived in this area on and off for the past 25 years and have seen many physical and political changes, but nothing changes its heart.

When I am not in Turkey I live in London, miles away in distance, time and culture, but once I have landed from my flight in Bodrum I take just one breath of the warm air at the top of the plane's stairs, one glance at the incredible beauty of the pine-fringed coastline as we drive along the airport road, one glimpse of the lush green wooded mountain, one wave to the old pot seller at his stall before I turn into our road and these familiar sights all remind me that I now belong, I am accepted as part of their world, I am '*yarim, yarim*' as they call me in the market, 'half and half'. I am home.

We did not mean to buy The Old Stone House, it was a sort of an accident, I just happened to be accompanying an estate agent friend as I needed a lift, and we popped in to see a property that he was thinking of adding to his books. It was the most romantic and unusual property I had seen since I first came to Turkey, I was awe struck. Phil was in London and in conversation later that evening via Skype, I mentioned this lovely idyll.

'Why don't we buy it?' he said.

'But you haven't seen it!'

'No matter, YOU have and that counts for a lot, I think we should buy it.'

The cost of buying a house in Turkey was pretty cheap at that time – it still is – but it was a bit of a stretch to find the money, however we scrabbled about and sent lumps of varying size to the estate agent over a period of a few days and held our breath… within weeks the stone house was ours. Part of me was screaming, OH MY GOODNESS WHAT HAVE WE DONE? But we never regretted it for a moment. The house is a constant joy and nothing gives us more pleasure that adding bits of this and titivating that as and when we find the cash.

Although there are many more buildings now, and the roads are wider and busier below our village, Gokcebel still retains its charm. The women of the village still bake their own bread in the traditional clay ovens at the end of their gardens; Ishmael still stands behind the shop counter, brewing strong black tea, as his father and grandfather did before him. The children play on the dusty roads with their balls and makeshift toys, the dogs still bark and the cats still stretch out in the sunshine. Everyone has time to chat, time to sit and time to stare. I can feel myself slowing down and sloughing off London's rush. There are no deadlines here and no grabbed lunches on the run. Who could want more than to be able to take time out from daily chores to drop down past the old castle to the sea and sit at their favourite restaurant on the harbour, watching the humble fishing boats bob amongst the enormous 'gin palace' yachts moored up in the spanking new marina. There are no time constraints, no stress; I can sit, dream, sip on an Efes beer or a glass of tea and just *be*.

We have a lovely set of friends and helpers and it was very easy to make friends. When we first arrived here I was bemused to keep finding little saucers or plates of delicacies deposited on our dining table (we never locked the door).

I discovered that our two immediate neighbours were vying with each other to gather me to their bosom as their new friend – a real honour apparently. We tasted and enjoyed all their dishes, but only much later did I realise that one is supposed to return the plate to its donor, not only washed, but filled with your own offering. Now of course I am the first to rush to newcomers with my plate, elbowing away other ladies of the neighbourhood to be first in line.

With all this gastronomic treasure we hardly needed to cook at all the first week or so and it was these interesting and tasty dishes that spurred me on to learn more about our local delicacies.

Learning the language certainly helped, although I am not by any means a brilliant linguist. I managed by dint of listening and looking at adverts on the side of the road to get the gist of the everyday language required. I can pass the time of day and ask appropriate questions when dealing with the tradesmen. 'How do you get your whites so bright?' and 'Migros has cheap mince on offer at the moment'! I'm a bit better than that, but it did take me a long time, Turkish is a very complex language and not from a Latin root, so not a hint of meaning from my schoolgirl classics classes.

Sometimes, whilst shopping, I don't let on I understand until the last crucial moments when prices have been agreed. The look on their faces!

At The Old Stone House we have kept the original features and style – it would have been sacrilegious not to – but a great many renovations had to be made. I'm not a health and safety maniac, but some mind boggling electric wiring and unfenced roof terraces had to be rectified. Thankfully at that time the prices were very reasonable, *fer forje* (iron work) was cheap and we railed off the suicidal roof terrace, made fancy iron banisters for the outside steps and a beautiful wood-burning stove for the winter months too. We have fought leaking roofs, deathwatch beetle, water shortages and constant power cuts. We waited days and weeks for tradesmen to arrive 'tomorrow', and were often surprised in our beds by those who chose to turn up late at night, but now we can look back on the adventures with humour, knowing the house is dry, warm and safe. A really characterful home from home.

My career as a graphic designer and my interest in all creativity, including cooking, led us to decide that after finishing 'proper' work, we could combine all these talents and stay in this lovely environment for longer, so in the Spring and Autumn months we run painting holidays from this venerable house set in its delightfully secluded garden. We have room for only eight or nine guests, who stay in the main old house and its newer satellite extensions. Along with my trusty friends and cohorts, Sandra and Orhan, who also live in the village, we make glorious art, go on trips and eat delicious Turkish food prepared by me – maybe not always in that order, as sometimes I get the distinct impression that our guests are keener on their knife and fork than their paintbrushes.

Turkish food is rated as some of the best in the world. All of our guests agree after only a couple of days of meals at The Old Stone House. We pride ourselves on the freshness of our locally produced fruit and vegetables. Our olive oil is sourced from a local village, as is the superb honey and yogurt used extensively in our recipes. Our menus are interesting and varied, and we take special care to ensure that the meals are carefully balanced as well as titillating to the taste buds. We have even found some people lose weight after a week with us, yet they say they always feel completely full up – this is great news as we don't stint on portions either!

I cannot GUARANTEE everyone will lose weight on this diet, as who can resist the platefuls of Turkish Delight, Helva and clotted cream-covered wild strawberries? And don't get me started on the Baklava and freshly roasted almonds and walnuts and the luscious figs grilled in honey with the thickest creamiest yogurt and the oh, so buttery pilafs served alongside home made *köfte*! Turkish cooking is so generous-hearted, just like its people.

I have been asked on so many occasions by my guests, painters and friends, how I make the dishes I serve throughout their stay. I am always delighted to garner their enthusiasm and accolades, giving out the odd list of ingredients or methods, but I never really bothered to write it all down. Eventually I was persuaded by my partner Phil to finally put it all together almost as a meal diary, so we cover an entire week's worth of menus – breakfast, lunch and dinner – just as I do to serve to my guests on a daily basis. This way you will be able to do a few days' worth yourselves, without having to think too hard about it.

The recipes in this book are all authentic Turkish daily family fare and not the food of restaurants or fancy establishments, it is good nourishing food of the kind that has been made and enjoyed by families for many hundreds of years. Most recipes have been taken verbatim from my ex mother in law or from my caretaker's wife, as well as from some of the women of our village. Some I have acquired by asking judicious questions when dining at cafes and *lokantas* from around and about or the village. Others, I must confess, are the result of a bit of guesswork and experiment. All are delicious.

For the most part the recipes come from the warm climes of the southwestern area of Turkey, which has a sort of fusion of Turkish and Greek food; the argument will continue about whose came first and who copied whom, rather like the chicken and the egg. But it is probably just evolution from this whole area, regardless of the incumbents, drawing on the ingredients that grow best in the locale and using what is naturally available to its best advantage. Without much prejudice I must admit that I do find the Turkish food more varied and more flavoursome, but there are many similarities. It is all wonderfully varied *mezzes*, the freshest fish, salty green and black olives, deep khaki olive oil and a little beef, chicken and lamb. These recipes have been adapted by both communities over the centuries, with input from Arabia, Persia and even the Far East when the Silk Route was a conduit for ideas, food and crafts and Turkey sat in the middle. It is the perfect healthy 'Mediterranean diet' except we are in the Aegean, of course.

Turkish cooking is mostly very labour-intensive. I'm not sure if it is because the women, who do most, if not all of the domestic cooking have more time or because they are persuaded by tradition that this is how it must be. Indeed, I have never seen an ordinary Turkish village housewife with too much time on her hands, it is quite unbelievable how hard-working they are. From girlhood to old age they are working: cleaning the house, looking after countless children, grandchildren, nephews nieces etc, plodding down to the fields or gardens to see to the crops, feeding the chickens, washing clothes and large quantities of bed sheets, perhaps sewing or carpet weaving and above it all serving three substantial meals a day.

Apart from breakfast and evening repasts, in our village of Gokcebel more often than not the children come home at midday for lunch and my local shop owner has his midday meal delivered hot in a billycan by his wife and solemnly eaten on freshly-laid newspaper whilst watching the continuous news bulletins on his extremely loud TV. Recently though, I was staggered and not a little impressed to find a gaggle of neatly turned out schoolchildren aged around ten or so standing in the middle of the road that encircles our village. Curious as to what they were up to, I lingered – hopefully discreetly – until a small scooter arrived and I watched in amazement as the driver unloaded from the box on the back freshly made Italian-style pizzas, which were pounced on and divided up amongst the throng. Progress, I suppose.

Anyway, you get the gist of it, life for the average Turkish housewife is pretty full, even in old age. The same cannot be said for the men, who always seem to have time to hang out together for hours on end. Young men go out for meals or a drink or two, arms draped across each other's backs, equally affable, out for a good time in their freshly pressed shirts (mum again). Those of middle years, and the older chaps, never seem to be out of the tea gardens or cafes, playing tablet, backgammon or some such game and drinking endless, apparently totally free, glasses of tea. I am constantly amazed how the same guys can sit alongside each other day in day out, year after year and still have lots to say to each other. Most are pretty old, so perhaps they have forgotten the previous week's exchanges, but honestly, you'd think they would run out of conversation.

So, from the women's perspective it takes hard work and time to produce a Turkish meal, but also lots and lots of love, which is why I cook too. To cook is to create, just as in Art: a cook deals with tastes and smells as well as colours, he or she presents her plate as an artist would a canvas, therein lies all their love and care and indeed their very soul. To show no interest in one of my meals is the same as dismissing my art as 'rubbish'; it cuts me to the quick.

I am starting from the very basics, what you need in your kitchen to make a good Turkish meal, the pots and pans the correct surfaces, the ingredients and, most of all, the care that is put into every meal. I have tried to emulate all of the old ways in The Old Stone House kitchen, but after five years standing at the sink at midnight I finally got a dishwasher – to hell with tradition!

Funnily enough, I was taught to wash up 'correctly' by a Turkish man, who insisted on making two piles of dishes, first washed in soapy water and stacked, then rinsed copiously in hot clear water and left to dry from that heat. No tea towels. This took an age, but respect where it is due, the glasses were immaculate.

TURKISH HOSPITALITY

In Turkey, hospitality is everything. Nothing is more important than welcoming family or complete strangers into your home, sitting them down and offering them marvellous cooked snacks or meals.

Once upon a time, Phil and I decided to go for an exploratory walk from the back of the village, through the woods to the neighbouring sister village of Dagbelen. I had spotted on Google Earth that there was a connecting track and as we had never been to Dagbelen it seemed like a good idea. We set off through the undergrowth and low branches and past the odd tortoise until we reached the top of the hill, where a breathtaking view over two bays on either side seemed to be the high point (literally) of our trip, but we battled on, for another hour or so, past extraordinarily opulent villas with guard dogs, venturing under and over wire fences, until finally reaching a more obvious road.

Ahead of us on the road, advancing on his motor bike festooned with white plastic bags, came the first human we had seen in over three hours. I hailed him and enquired if we were anywhere near Dagbelen. He gesticulated to the road behind him and told us it was just round the corner. 'But, but, but', he cried, 'first you must come to my house for refreshment, you must be so hot.' Now I am used to Turkish ways, so readily agreed, but even so we were bowled over by his generosity. Firstly, he explained he had to feed the cats. He untied his plastic bags and led us to a small white garage beside a wooden house. Through a gate were waiting about ten or so white cats all shouting and jumping for their evening meal. Ibrahim, as so he turned out to be, fished out large quantities of, well, fish from the bags. He explained that he worked in a local hotel kitchen and salvaged these remains to feed his ever-increasing group of strays. He could not turn them away he said, not while he had food to give them.

Job completed we were ushered into his hallway, where he shouted for his wife. She came bustling out and immediately took control. After introductions, shoes were taken off and slippers (way too small) were proffered and so we were ushered onto a small wooden balcony overlooking what seemed to be a smallholding with a small number of fruit trees and vegetables growing in neat rows.

Glasses of tea and cups of coffee came, then their son was introduced to us. Shyly he spoke a little English whilst his parents beamed with pride. Ibrahim's wife disappeared to return with a tray laden with fresh fruits, cherries, apricots, peaches and apples, a plate of small cakes and four bowls of ice cream! We chatted and chatted and time slipped by, until almost dusk.

'Look at this view' Ibrahim said, 'What a lovely sight, the hills and the trees, the birds singing, I have a beautiful wife and a clever young son, I have a lovely house and food on the table, I must be the luckiest man in the world.' It was at that point I had a revelation. How humbling the man was. What more, indeed, did we all require? I remind myself of this encounter constantly when I find myself 'needing' things.

As we made to depart well after dark, Ibrahim insisted he drive us back to our house, as it was far too dangerous to go back the way we came – wild boar, apparently roamed the woods covering the hill between us. So we returned to the stone house, the whole family and us stuffed into his ancient car, rattling along the road clutching bags of fruit that we had been urged to accept.

We never got to Dagbelen.

MY KITCHEN

So here I am, in my old kitchen cooking for lots of painters the Turkish way. What do I have and what do I need?

UTENSILS

Turkish cooking utensils are mostly simple; large, ugly and cheap tin or aluminium pans. Teflon is considered a great invention, and kept with pride alongside the blackened, venerable fryers and boilers probably handed down through the generations. I bought everything I needed from the still ubiquitous local *bakkal* (shop that sells everything), which also serves as an ironmongers and animal feed store, as well as a purveyor of farming utensils, outerwear and the largest and most vilely-coloured yellowy brown wellies, which are the uniform, along with a woolly hat, of everyone who lives in the countryside.*

There is a man down the road, who I swear never takes his hat off the entire year, I suspect he even sleeps in it. The Turks are massive hypochondriacs and are in perpetual mortal fear of catching a chill, so I am implored to wrap up and wear a woolly vest and anorak the minute the clock strikes September! Sema, our caretaker Sazili's wife, is never without her woolly sleeveless cardigan except on the hottest August afternoon. I suppose you get used to it.

So back to the cool dark interior of my stone-floored kitchen. When we first moved into The Old Stone House, the previous owner had left behind some rather odd looking black pots, which appeared to be made of Bakelite. Thinking these were cheap and unlikely to survive a hob or oven, I used them in the garden as plant pots. Silly me! They are traditional earthenware cooking pots called guvec, excellent for imparting the best flavour to casseroles, I didn't discover my mistake for several years. It's too late, now. I will have to look for some new ones. He also left a legacy of a large slab of marble, its cool surface is used to make the gossamer-like pastry, yufka. Sadly, lack of space forced me to re-vamp my kitchen slightly, but the slab is now in the revered spot as a serving counter above our newly installed Ottoman Bar on the roof terrace. It looks incredibly

*Post August and sometimes even then!

authentic* sitting above the small fridge and shiny glasses in the cupboards below and ideal for hot summer days, when a cold drink is so welcome.

I have pared down my utensils to one VERY large frying pan with a couple of smaller ones, a griddle, five saucepans of varying sizes in stainless steel, two huge casserole pans with double handles (one has fallen off) and glass lids, and two or three *tepsi* or large aluminium trays, these are invaluable for cakes, roasts of all sorts whether vegetable or meat, and wonderful for *moussaka* and *borek*.

I do not possess a food processor, nor a whisk, but I have recently bought a hand blender, which has made my life a good deal easier when making the purees and soups so beloved of the area.

Instead of the processor, I still use a grater, a lemon squeezer, potato peeler, a selection of ancient knives and a large number of hand-carved wooden spoons. These have deep bowls so can also be used for serving, and I find them invaluable for crushing chick peas for *hummus*, before whizzing with my stick blender.

Of course, I don't expect you to eschew the wonders of the modern kitchen, but I rather like the change of pace whilst pottering about in my old-fashioned Turkish haven, so different from the uber-bright, white sleekness of my North London home. I have also developed some rather well-defined upper arms too, a win-win situation.

INGREDIENTS

Must be fresh! Turkish ingredients are very simple, but they rely totally on being the freshest of fresh and thus have to be purchased on the day or at the very least within 24 hours of the dish being prepared. For the most part fruit and vegetables sold in our local markets are unadulterated, hormone-free and organic. I cannot vouch for the supermarkets, but certainly one does not see the uniform shapes and sizes of our European produce and the taste is so different. Tomatoes taste like I remember them, cucumbers are – well, cucumbery! You do not buy or cook unseasonal produce, which makes it all the more exciting to plan menus. I pounce on the first artichokes and broad beans of the season, likewise the first strawberries, figs and nuts. Luckily, the May art holidays coincide with artichoke season, while the September holidays herald figs – such plump delicious fruit, so exotic to us in the UK, yet stacked up on groaning stalls alongside the entire length of the market and sold by the kilo, not in bulbous blister packs of one or two. I buy them by the crate, it makes me feel thoroughly extravagant. There are three markets I use every week, so I can be certain of the freshest of fresh fruit, veg and dairy produce. One up the road, one down the road and one in Yalikavak itself. Our own tiny local Gokcebel market I refer to as 'two old ladies on a blanket' as very often everyone is squatting on the ground with their produce arranged neatly on a piece of fabric. We like to take our groups up to make sketches of the great commercial activity there. I can combine my fruit and veg shopping with showing the painters good

*In truth Ottomans didn't have bars as such, but I fantasise that if they did, this is how they would look!

sites for sitting and making sketches. The Sunday market in lower Gokcebel is much larger and busier, so any artist would find themselves crushed or mown down by gimlet-eyed women festooned with plastic shopping bags, thus I travail alone at that one.

The main market is in Yalikavak, it is the BIG brother, mother, father and auntie of all the other local markets. You need a great many bags. I have now purchased a red and white spotted bag on wheels. I swore I never would have one of these 'ankle bashers', but finally I decided that looking 97 was marginally better than feeling 97, carrying all the stuff I cannot help buying. So off I go to Yalikavak Pazar, in order to feed all those hungry painters.

Yalikavak Pazar is held on a Thursday and a completely different kettle of fish from the tiny one of our village. It is ENORMOUS! It seems to stretch on forever. A feast, a banquet for the senses – and also a bit of a battleground. The colourful fruits and vegetables, the salads, the melons piled high on carts, every conceivable shape, size and colour of pepper, aubergines – fat and stripy, long and purple or just squat – courgettes still with their soft yellow flowers intact, the flowers separated from their courgette parent delicately arrayed in boxes like something out of a florist shop, an undulating pile of pale green and deep-saffron-yellow shiny apples, quinces, strange red berries, sharp bitter, green unripe plums (I have never understood their popularity), piles of hand-tied vine leaves, all shades of honey, all shapes of cheeses, village eggs, milk and stiff thick home-made yogurt sitting in vast tubs.

Although I usually have firm plans for my menus for the week, who can resist something extra, when you spot a seasonal vegetable or special offer? I find myself reviewing the meals and substituting ideas on the hoof, or worse, I buy things that I have no real use for and have to really think hard as to how I can weave them into my lunches and dinners. Well, there is always the Still Life class to think of! Everything is very cheap, but I have been told that Yalikavak is more expensive than some other markets off the Peninsula, because it is mostly rich Turks from Istanbul or Ankara who come down for weekends or summer holidays who buy here, they don't care about cost. I try to think of the lira as being worth £1 (in fact it's about 20 pence*), but when I slip into this way of thinking I too can express genuine dismay at heightened prices. '3 lira for those tomatoes? NO WAY!' I do love a haggle. In fact I tend to haggle everywhere now, and have been known, much to my family's consternation to give it a go in John Lewis – believe me it can work.

I arrive at the Pazar early. The first sale of the day is greeted by the stallholder hurling the money to the floor, then picking it up. An old tradition. This method too is used when you have achieved a massive bargain in a shop, and the shopkeeper may be doing a cash deal. You drop the money to the ground and the shopkeeper picks it up. See! He

* Always changing!

found it, it did not come from you at all. Is this is a mild form of laundering?

Here in the market most women are addressed as '*abla*' 'sister', which is a friendly, yet respectful greeting. My big fear is when I transition from *abla* to Auntie. You then know you are really old. And I dread being called mother – it will happen.

So we start with one end and gradually work our way up and around and then back again. The fruits and vegetables, herbs and other greenery are at the first point we arrive at. We amble past the fruit and veg and turn into the tented area, where the cheeses, dried fruits and nuts, onions, potatoes and pulses are sold alongside detergents, cleaning equipment and pet food. Spices are on the opposite side, in colourful troughs with boxes of *lokum*, sweets and dried chillies, aubergines and peppers.

A quick sojourn at the carpet seller, past the animal husbandry section (did you know they dress their cows in pretty beaded bridles?) and back to the melons and basket wear. I look to buy some and probably end up purchasing all of the following items on my grand market tour.

HERBS

In all the markets there is a multitude of different herbs on sale, all bunched up with the dew of freshness still glistening on their leaves. Always buy fresh, always use fresh, except when the recipe says otherwise. The staples are: dill, mint and parsley, these are regularly found in Turkish dishes. I am never without these in my cooler. They can turn the simplest fare into a glorious concoction. Other useful herbs readily found at market are:

Basil I use this in salads for flavouring and in tomato salads, not really typically Turkish, but it tastes so wonderful with those lush, fragrant Turkish tomatoes.

Bay Leaves Great for all flavouring of soups and stews, and rocket, which jazzes up salads with its sharp almost bitter taste. Huge bay-leaves set alongside a beautifully charcoal-grilled sea bass are an absolute must, I often ask for more.

> **TURKTIP** *I just love bay-leaves stuffed inside a grilled fish, also fennel, which has an aroma similar to aniseed, and leaves resembling those of dill, which is also tasty and pretty as a garnish. The bulb can be used sliced and braised and served as a side dish. It can be found wild all around our village, along with the pungent wild garlic.*

Talking of wild herbs, all around the village and up along the pathways leading to the woodland and the mountains, one can meet older men and women foraging for wild herbs. I think this is now a dying knowledge and I am making it my business to understand it.

HERBS USED IN DAY-TO-DAY COOKING, WHICH CAN BE FRESH OR DRIED ACCORDING TO AVAILABILITY.

Marjoram A very similar plant to wild thyme, marjoram is used in salads as well as meat and vegetable dishes. It is generally added toward the end of cooking. As it is supposedly an aid to digestion, it is especially used in harder to digest dishes, such as game.

Rosemary The narrow, thick needle-like leaves of this bush are used in meat dishes and sauces. It is lovely picked fresh as twigs and stuck into lamb with lots of garlic. Also delicious with sautéed potatoes and fish, especially sea bass. Everyone has a rosemary bush in their garden, we have three!

Sage is used in the Aegean and Marmara regions to make tea. Turks don't eat pork, but it can also be wonderful in pasta dishes or with liver in a butter sauce.

Tarragon Its aromatic leaves are used in certain sauces and meat dishes as well as eggs and salads.

Wild Thyme This herb grows throughout Anatolia, mostly in mountainous regions. It is dried and used pretty much in all dishes.

Of course all of these come dried and for the most part, apart from the staple fresh herbs bought at the market, are far more convenient to use dried. In fact, mint is more often used in its dry form when making *cicek* and stuffings. Remember to use fewer dried herbs than fresh when substituting in recipes.

TYPES OF HERBS AND GREENERY TO BE FOUND FOR FREE

The trend of cooking with wild herbs has spread from tourist restaurants in Turkey to the home front. Though many of these wild greens and herbs are ones we would pass by on foot or in the car without thinking twice, they are now (once again) beginning to be seen as vital sources of health and nutrition. While shoppers used to be satisfied with just learning the names of wild herbs never before seen at the local bazaar, more and more Turkish cooks are starting to experiment with the tastes coming from these relative foreigners to our tables. Of course, the recent news about the benefits of nettle extract in the war against cancer may have played a great role in the resurgence of interest in wild herbs and greens generally.

In truth, Anatolian cuisine has for ages now featured greens and herbs from all over the countryside, gathered under the logic that dictates 'We pick any and all greens that the billy-goat eats.' Though the last quarter century of fast food habits has done much to overshadow these traditional herbs and greens, a renewed interest in healthy eating has heralded their return to people's minds and kitchens. Turkish markets are beginning to carry wild herbs and greens. These greens are used in *börek* fillings, soups and stews, as we would use spinach. Nettles are popular and considered to have health benefits too.

Even in the UK nettles are considered a useful foil for arthritis.

Wild Asparagus (*tilkisen*) is one of the most interesting and tasty wild edible greens found in local markets if you are lucky. These thin shoots are sold in bunches in local bazaars. It is time-consuming to collect and therefore pricier than other greens, but well worth it. In Turkey, it is generally sautéed in oil and cooked with eggs in the way you would a frittata.

Mallow (*ebegumeci*) is another popular green that is cooked in a similar way to spinach, with sautéed onions, lamb and tomatoes. Large mallow leaves can also be used as wrappers for *dolma*. Mallow is known to preserve the respiratory and digestive tract and it can be brewed as a mouthwash to heal mouth sores.

Poppy Greens (*gelincik*) resemble rocket and are edible before the flowers' pods form, as afterwards the leaves become a slight opiate. Its infusions are used for breathing problems, in particular asthma, bronchitis and whooping cough, and it is known to have skin healing properties. While the greens are used in *böreks* or served sautéed in olive oil, the flower petals produce a stunning red jam.

Wild Fennel (*arapsaci*) has a sharp anise-like flavour, is good for stomach cramps, digestion and increasing the production of breast milk, and is generally prepared with either eggs or lamb.

Greens such as **wild radish greens** (*turp otu*) and wild mustard (*hardalotu*) are delicious, boiled or in salads. Wild mustard is known to be a laxative, and a bath in water steeped with the herb is said to be good for rheumatism.

Golden Thistle (*sevketi bostan*) is a yellow-flowered fleshy thistle that is commonly cooked with lamb and chickpeas. Its tea is good for stomach aches and digestion and the leaves can be rubbed on wounds for faster healing.

Stinging Nettle (*isirganotu*) Although the handling and preparation of it is daunting, once blanched it has a flavourful, distinctive taste and is prepared like many other wild edible plants, either sautéed in oil, cooked with eggs or used as a pastry filling. Its tea is widely brewed and consumed for its many medicinal benefits, including as a diuretic and an anti-inflammatory.

Wild Chicory (*hindiba*) is served in salads and steamed, and is an antiperspirant, diuretic and diaphoretic and is said to help get rid of gall bladder stones.

Sorrel (*kuzu kulası*) is regularly served in salads, has a tart flavour and is high in vitamin C. Brewed, it has a number of medicinal properties, including acting as a fever reducer, as a gargle for toothaches and as a skin tonic for acne, psoriasis and eczema.

Slim amaranth (*sirken*) is incorporated into pastries, meat dishes and eggs and is known to be a blood purifier.

Lesser Water Parsnip (*su kazayası*), also referred to as wild celery, is a member of the parsley family and is prepared in a variety of manners such as sautéed and cooked with bulgur, or in omelets and meat dishes.

Wild Garlic Stalk (*körmen*) Last, but certainly not least, is a type of ?????, which is delicious in *börek* and breads. This is just one of the dozens of wild onion and garlic species growing in Turkey.

To be perfectly honest, I'm not entirely sure I would pick herbs from the side of some of our roads as my neighbours do. Far too much carbon monoxide and other emissions to counteract the freshness, in my view. I'd rather pop out to the woods growing on the mountain behind our village. Only the wild boar to contend with so no bending over without checking what's behind you! I should add at this point that I am ridiculed by some folk regarding my calling it a mountain, it's a very high hill I am told. Well, how dull is that? It has jutting rocks, gets misty in the winter and what is more, gives me a crick in my neck looking at it. QED mountain!

HERBS OR FLOWERS USED FOR TEAS AND TINCTURES FOUND IN OUR PAZAR

I have only ever seen them stuffed into bags, so seeing the real mccoy was a revelation.

Melissa (in our garden) For getting a decent night's sleep. Smells lovely.

Sage Used to flavour butters and oils and supposed to be good for asthma in a tea. Obviously not used with pork!

Bergamot Delicious as a tea or candied, delicious and bogglingly expensive in the UK.

Mesir Macunu (Turkish Viagra) I just had to put that in! Untested.

Hibiscus Sort of brown and sticky looking (stick as in twig, not honey)

Camomile So very pretty little white and yellow daisies.

SPICES

Contrary to common belief, Turkish cuisine is generally not spicy (though this varies throughout the seven regions, the further East the spicier). Seasonings and sauces, although frequently used, are simple and light and do not overpower the food's natural taste.

The spread of spices used since antiquity in China and India to all corners of the globe began nearly 2000 years ago. One of the oldest of these areas is Anatolia, where spices began to be brought from various regions of Africa as flavour enhancers. Turkey relies on a great many different spices in its food and although recipes seem to use a large quantity, the taste is never out of balance.

These are the spices used traditionally in Turkish cuisine, as well as those which have entered its food culture from others:

Allspice (*Yenibahar)* it is used in meat dishes, *köfte* and sausages as well as various *dolma* and sweets.

Anise Originating in Egypt, anise is the seed of a fragrant, low-growing member of the celery family (*apiaceae*). It is used in baking and *raki* and is supposed to help children go to sleep (not in the *raki* form, I hasten to say)

Black Pepper (*Karabiber*) The dried black fruits of black pepper give a fragrance and heat to foods. It may be used in almost any dish, and is one of the most basic ingredients in Turkish cooking.

Cardamom (*Kardoman)* This small, white pod of a tropical plant in the ginger family enhances the appetite and relieves stomach upsets.

Cinnamon (*Tarci)* A spice obtained from the aromatic bark of a tree native to South and Southeast Asia. It is used both whole and ground, in pastries, cakes and cookies, as well as sprinkled on drinks such as *boza* and *salep*.

Cloves *(Karanfiller)* The dark-coloured dried flower buds of this plant are ground to powder, crushed or used whole to add flavour to compotes, syrups, cakes, ice creams and certain stews.

Cumin Usually used powdered *kimyon* is mostly cultivated in Anatolia. In Turkish cuisine it is mostly used in meat dishes, *köfte* and in the making of *sucuk*. It eliminates the smell of uncooked meat.

Coriander *(Cilantro*) coriander is mostly used in syrups and liqueurs, as well as certain meat dishes. Candied coriander seeds are sometimes used in pastries. The leaves and shoots of the plant are chopped and added to soups and salads in some regions. Now that it is used more often I can find it in the big Yalikavak market.

Ginger (*zencefil*) In Turkey this is used chiefly in its dried form, though fresh ginger is now becoming available.

Juniper (*ardic*) is an evergreen tree bearing fragrant, blackish round berries. These are used in poultry dishes and in marinades for meat.

Köftebaharı This is a spice mix comprising coriander, black pepper, cloves, bay leaves and wild thyme. It makes for an easy way to flavour *köfte* and I sometimes use it in meat-stuffed peppers.

Nigella Sometimes referred to as black sesame or onion seed in the West, it is actually the seed of a plant related to the common garden flower Love-in-a-mist. It is sprinkled on *boreks* and breads and it may also be used in salads. Scattered on the top it really dramatises a simple dish

Nutmeg *(Hindistan cevizi)* The fruit of a tropical tree, it is ground to powder and used with meat dishes as well as *dolma* and *sarma*, and in bechamel sauce and cheese dishes.

Red Pepper Flakes (*Pul Biber*) obtained by grinding hot red peppers. I buy it in large bags from the market as I use LOADS of this. It is the perfect spicy spice, a sort of sweet, hot-ish pepper, oily in texture, which perks up everything.

Saffron Saffron imparts an intense yellow colour to foods to which it is added. It is used in some soup and seafood soups, in pilafs and in desserts made with milk and rice. It does not dissolve in olive oil, so you will need to use water. It grows in Western Asia and in Northern Anatolia.

Sesame (*susam*) The oil-bearing seed of a meter-tall plant, which is grown chiefly in India, China and Sudan but also in Southeast Anatolia. The seed is used in *simit* and other baked goods, and ground to make *tahini*, which in turn is used in hummus, soups and some desserts.

Sumak This spice is made from the ground berries of a small tree which grows in Southeast Anatolia. It has a sour citrus flavour and is used as a souring agent in kebabs and some salads. It is good with chicken and any dish in which you would use lemon. A syrup made by boiling the berries is also used in salads. I like it sprinkled on hummus with olive oil poured on top.

Turmeric (*Zerde Áal*) This dried and ground root is used in meat, fish and egg dishes. It imparts a strong yellow colour and is sometimes used in place of saffron., I have never found the flavour useful as a saffron substitute, but it can impart a subtle mellow flavour.

Vanilla (*Vanilya*) Originating in Mexico, this spice is extracted from the seed pod of a vining orchid. In the UK it is used to add flavour to pastries and confections, cakes, ice cream, compotes and milk puddings. I have the devil's own job getting decent vanilla in my local shop. They only seem to have vanilla sugar, which is greatly inferior so I bring it from the UK.

White Pepper (*Beyaz Toz Biber*) This is ground, hulled black pepper. It has a more pungent aroma and lighter flavour than black, pepper. My village ladies seem to use white pepper far more than black, and rarely ground black pepper, but that may be down to lack of availability.

TURKTIP *I have bought saffron in our local Yalıkavak market, but do not find the Turkish saffron as aromatic or delicate as the Iranian or Spanish variety. However, if you sniff and sneak a taste before you buy and find it good, it can be a useful addition to your spice cupboard and far cheaper than the European type. Go for the strong variety or you will be disappointed.*

Not spices, but used extensively in a great many recipes:

Pine Nuts These small nuts are extracted from the cones of a species of pine, and used, for example, in meatless *dolmas* along with *kus uzumu* (tiny black currants).

Poppy Seeds The seed of the opium poppy plant, it may be blue-black or white. It is used in baking as well as sautéed in oil and added to salads, canapés and appetizers.

When you are halfway through the market, wheeling your trolley or lugging your overstuffed carrier bags, one in each hand, rather like a camel with his panniers, there you smell it, Nirvana: *gozleme*! Hot, aromatic, pale piles of pancakes stuffed with herbs, cheese, aubergine, tomatoes, meat or spinach, on sale for the hungry – or in my case greedy – to enjoy and relish as a reward for one's shopping fortitude.

So, let us choose our snack. The ladies sell *gozleme* along with the unfilled flatbreads and other sorts of bread, dried biscuits and most flour-based produce. There is plenty of choice of fillings – aubergine, cheese, spinach, meat, potato to name a few – and after making our choice, the huge round pancake base is generously spread with the chosen filling plopped into the middle of the circle of dough, cooked on the hot domed metal and the whole deftly folded into a rectangle ready to eat. For lunch a whole one is perfect, for a snack half or even a quarter will suffice. I eat a whole one in easy stages, half now, the rest saved in its paper wrapping for later. Now, replenished by a snack, let us continue ingredient shopping.

VEGETABLES IN SEASON

The first vegetable, well actually a fruit, is the basis for almost every savoury dish you can think of, and if it isn't, it's used in an accompanying salad. The TOMATO. If you don't like tomatoes or yogurt then Turkish food is not for you.

In the summer the stalls are groaning with them, so cheap and so tasty, they are sweet and aromatic and certainly straight from the grower. You will definitely have tomatoes that have only travelled a few miles to arrive on your plate and I never ever seem to buy enough. I'm always running out and rushing to the shops to buy more, when I was sure I had bought at least a ton of them. Never keep them in the fridge. I always peel them – labour-intensive but so, so much better when you do. Turks peel them with a knife and I realise now that this is far better than the boiling water method in certain recipes because the tomatoes are so juicy, once they have lolled around in the heated liquid they almost turn to mush and the juice runs off the chopping board, down my trousers and sits in pools at my feet. And I once thought smugly that I knew better.

Artichokes I stuff them with pea or broad bean puree, the villagers stuff them with oily potatoes and peas, either way delish.

Aubergines Again, the aubergine is a staple. It is a great substitute for meat in a vegetarian diet and smoked it makes the most delicious dips and sauces. [cut line]

Courgettes No more soggy courgettes! Never boiled, they are instead cooked in olive oil or fried or charcoal-grilled and dressed with garlicky yogurt.

Garlic Ubiquitous. Ordinary veg such as potatoes, carrots, cauliflower celeriac, onions can be used in unordinary dishes to great effect. You will see.

Okra Needs lots of lemon, but a great ingredient in tomato sauce in a veggie casserole.

Peppers Red, green, long and pointy, round and fat or teeny tiny, they are cooked, skinned, pickled, puréed, stuffed and generally added to lots of sauces and soups.

Radishes I have never in my life seen radishes so HUGE! Or so peppery. I love to show our guests the size of them, it's like winning in the village fête for best radish, but all the time.

Salad Stumpy crisp cucumbers, frilly lettuce, fat spring onions, fiery rocket, the longest celery, bulbous beetroot, all delicious with dressings, yogurt, oils and pomegranate 'soz'.

Spinach Delicious in *borek*, with rice and meat, in soups, floating on a casserole of chickpeas, fresh as a salad. All that iron and no grimace, it's so tasty. We even use up the stalks, previously discarded by me before I was enlightened by Sema the gardener's wife. Braised with olive oil and garlic, they make a tasty side dish. Takes a lot of washing, though, at least three or four rinses. No salad bags here. No sirree.

Swiss Chard Can be used in *borek* or any other vegetable casserole dish, stuffed with rice as in *Yaprak Sarmi* or delicious cooked down and stripped of leaves in garlic and oil with a touch of nutmeg, salt and pepper and served on flatbreads. Save the stalks – they are great cooked as a vegetable on their own. I never waste anything.

Vine Leaves I have not yet mastered the slim stuffed vine leaves of Sema but I'm getting there. We grow our own but vine leaves can be bought in the market in small, leaf-sized bales tied up with red twine in weights of 500 grams. Or you can buy the packet variety in brine sold at the supermarket but these are very salty and need a great deal of washing. Like supermarket *yufka*, they are not as good as the fresh variety. The leaves are mostly used in *Yaprak Sarmi* (stuffed leaves) but there are plenty of other ways to use them: wrapped around goats cheese, brushed with olive oil and grilled is very tasty.

TURK TIP for buying market fresh aubergines *When buying, choose aubergines with a bright green cap and stalk – not faded or brown-looking – smooth, shiny skin, heavy for their size, and having no blemishes, tan patches or bruises. Wrinkled, loose skin is an indication of age, and the fruit will be more bitter. Smaller eggplants have fewer seeds, thinner skin, and tend to be sweeter, more tender and less bitter. Press your finger lightly against the skin. If it leaves a light imprint, it is ripe. If it is too soft, it is too old and will be bitter. Looking for fewer seeds? Check the blossom end of the fruit. A larger scar generally means fewer seeds.*

FRUITS IN SEASON

It is still the norm to see only what is readily available seasonally in our local market. I see no point in buying fruit that has been flown thousands of miles before it has ripened. We should be in harmony with our environment and nature. Here endeth the first lesson.

THE GLORIOUS FIG AND THE SUMPTUOUS POMEGRANATE

A story of the ancient orchards in Stratonikea

Early this year we decided that our painting holiday guests might need a few new places to visit, we are always thinking of ways to ring the changes for repeat visitors and to show our guests more of the real Turkey. To be perfectly frank, we have a great time exploring and finding out all about our local area and generally manage to fit in a decent meal and bevvy or two on the way; what we do for our painters is totally selfless and grueling as you will see! So, with the car packed and maps unfurled we set off in the direction of Mugla, the principal city governing the Bodrum Peninsula, in search of Stratonikeia.

After the rather unpromising looking Milas, we hit some lovely countryside lush with pine forests, where almost every kilometer of the highway offered us a honey and/or strawberry stall. I succumbed, naturally and bought a kilo of dark brown woodland honey for £3.30. Result!

After an hour we got a bit nervous, no sign at all for this mysterious place. Bright chalky quarries were slashed out of the hills on either side of the road and there had obviously been some coal mining in the area. We drove on, checking out the mines and quarries and wondering if perhaps they could be Roman. Something caught my eye as we bowled along, I thought I spotted something 'columny'. We had missed the sign, only a tiny one, small and brown, but definitely the place. After making a u-turn at a probably highly inadvisable place we trundled down the dusty track towards a very unprepossessing, well, was it a car park? We drew to a stop and paused to look about. What a sight! There we were all alone on a patch of cleared land amongst the most amazing ruins of a Roman city we had ever seen, and we had seen quite a few.

Now, I have not mentioned why we had singled out Stratonikeia, apart from being close at hand, that is. It is a site of many sites, from Hittite to 14th-century Ottoman, all built one on top of the other – and all of it visible. Some of the old inhabitants' families are still living there today, albeit not many. They farm smallholdings of fruit trees and ground crops on this ancient soil. Thus you get more ruin for your money, except it's free, so far.

HISTORY

According to Strabo, it was founded by the Seleucid king Antiochus I, who named it after his wife, Stratonice. It lies on Kadskule Hill in the west of the fertile Yatasan Plain at the crossroads of main routes that connect western, central and southern Anatolia with each other. Stratonikeia, inhabited continuously from the Late Bronze Age (1500 BC) to the present day, is one of the most important city-states in inner Caria. From the Early Byzantine Period the population started to decrease and continued to shrink further throughout the whole Byzantine period. Over time it came under the control of the Ottoman administration, which constructed many magnificent architectural buildings. Although Eskihisar Village (the latest incarnation), along with most of the inhabitants, has moved to a new area after an earthquake in 1957, four families still remain in the historical village houses within the territories of the ancient city.

Enough culture. Stratonikea is now on our programme of trips. We come not only for the wonderful vistas to draw, but the figs and the pomegranates! When we first came we realised just how many abandoned orchards there were dotted about the site, unfortunately the figs and the pomegranates were just on the wrong side of ripe, just a couple of weeks were needed, so we determined to re-visit within that period along with the painters, and so we did; armed with appropriate carriers. Oh my, what a glut, the fallen fruit surrounded by buzzing wasps was everywhere, those on the trees were plump, golden green figs and bursting fat juicy pomegranates. Everyone took a bag and before too long, both the bags and the artists were stuffed. Quite obviously someone had got there before us, as the best were mostly too high for us to reach. But we had enough heavenly fruit to see us through several meals and a couple of still life projects.

Trekking back to the ancient coffee shop, more on that below, we came across an elderly couple setting up tables laden with figs to dry outside their tumbledown house. We were offered some to try and even though we were completely full, who could resist? Delicious dry or fresh, these truly are the sultans of fruits. Not sultanas!

OTHER FRUITS AVAILABLE TO BUY OR SCRUMP

Green Plums The start of spring is heralded by the arrival of sour green plums known as *erik*. The plums are tart and crunchy and madly refreshing. In early April when *erik* first start appearing, they are especially sour, and for many, including me, they are an acquired taste, often resulting in a pucker on the first try. Families will enjoy plates of *erik* after dinner or as a snack, and in late spring, they are served together with fresh apricots. The plums can be eaten as is – pop the whole thing in your mouth and (elegantly) spit out the pit. Another favourite way to enjoy them is to sprinkle with salt before eating. When we first came to Turkey with some friends from Muswell Hill, we chanced upon a fruit stall on the main drag in Bodrum still open after midnight. The most gregarious of the group enquired what was the name of the diminutive, hard green fruit piled up in small cones to the front of the stall. 'Eric', the night owl salesman responded, letting his cigarette droop in emphasis from the corner of his mouth. 'ERIC!' She screeched and then collapsed in mirth, slowly sliding down the supporting poles of his stand. 'Eric!!' Everyone else in the group caught her hilarity and we all buckled with laughter. The owlish Turk stared in disbelief at the band of mad foreigners. No obvious sale was coming his way. We must be drunk. We probably were.

Persimmons Known as *hurma* in Turkish, these are Autumn's pleasure. Starting in November, large, dimpled persimmons appear in our markets and grocery stores. In Turkey, persimmons are enjoyed extremely ripe, so be on the look out for fruits deep orange-red in colour and exceedingly soft to the touch. To eat a persimmon, twist off the green stem at the top and use a spoon to scoop out the fragrant flesh. Since the ripe fruit is extremely fragile, one must be careful when selecting persimmons. The ideal persimmon is without too many cracks in the skin, and don't put them in the bottom of your shopping bag!

Quince In January and February, quince start flooding the Istanbul food markets. When eaten raw, quince have a dry, woody texture, making them almost difficult to swallow. They are tough and difficult to core, but well worth the effort. Such a distinctive taste; fragrant and exotic, remarkable its transformation when cooked, from a pasty creamy white to a beautiful rosy amber hue. Quince are delicious when poached or made into a jam, like a sophisticated pear that has been to finishing school. In Turkish cuisine, the most common way to enjoy quince is *ayva tatlısı* (sweet quince). For this dessert, quince are poached in a generous amount of sugar, spiced, and then served with a dollop of Turkish-style clotted cream known as *kaymak*. It's also common in Turkish cuisine to use quince for jam, and even quince wine can be found, which is especially good in the summer months.

Lemons and oranges, mandarins and mandolins All of these citrus fruit belong to Bodrum. The coast is strung out with mandarin groves, but sadly not so many now since the big building surge started in 2005. Twelve years of new villas have taken their toll but you can still see hectares of these square patches of shiny green in Yalikavak, Gumusluk, Gundogan, Turkbuku and more especially in Bitez, famous for its groves of citrus. Mandarins, mandolins and the tiny Bodrum mandolin are fresh and juicy. I asked what use the tiny Bodrum mandolins had – only the size of a large marble – and was greeted with arched brows, 'gin and tonics' was the swift response, and indeed, therein they are extremely good. We grow all of these in our garden – how exciting it was to reach up and pick my own lemons! When first picked, the smell is so perfumed, it smells more lemony than I can recall a lemon smelling. We once brought back 20 kilos of lemons in our baggage (will I be put in jail?), the result was several jars of lemon curd, two Kilner jars of preserved lemons and some marmalade. They made wonderful Christmas presents. I was so proud.

Strawberries Strawberries are best between the beginning of May and mid-July. The very best-tasting ones in our markets come from Gumusluk. They are on the whole smaller than our English strawberries and go to mush a bit quicker, but this could be because they are not treated with whatever concoction enables them to be sold in our supermarkets. You can pick your own too, or buy from the numerous roadside stalls.

They are deliciously sweet. Lovely with a spot of *nar* (pomegranate molasses), black pepper or just popped straight into your mouth whilst filling your basket.

Cherries (*kiraz*) Cherries and Sour cherry. OH, when the cherry season is with us, we buy them by the kilo. Sour cherries make the most delicious jam. We always go for the Napolyon *kiraz* – slightly more expensive than the others but really big and juicy and worth the extra lira or so per kilo.

Apricots (*kayısı*) fresh, these are a real treat eaten on their own, or lightly braised in sugar syrup. Dried, I prefer to buy the darker brown untreated apricots. These small pockets of fun are delicious, stuffed with *kaymak* (Turkish clotted cream) and a walnut or almond rammed in for good measure. Great snack or a light dessert with coffee.

Watermelons/Melons Never touch a watermelon before July! During the summer months the watermelon man (remember that song?) trundles along the village roads shouting out his wares, '*KARPUUUUZ, KARPUZZZZZ, KAVUUUUUNNNN, taze, taze*'. His lorry is laden to the gunwales with big round dark green watermelons and paler green honeydews, some of them helpfully cut open to reveal grinning pink and yellow flesh, glistening and dripping with juice. On arrival he is surrounded by local women eager to have their choices weighed on the ancient brass scales, such as in statues of justice, and carted home. These women are strong, believe me, a couple of watermelons under each arm, no problem!

Peaches Turkish peaches from the market are massive, soft and juicy. Choose the most blemish-free by sorting through the piles, but they are still best eaten on day of purchase or at least the following day. No problem there I can assure you.

Turkish bananas or ***muz*** (pronounced MOOZ) I only buy these when I fancy saying the name, it makes me laugh.

TURK TIP for buying market-fresh watermelons

It's pretty difficult to tell if a watermelon is ripe unless it's examined. A really good indicator is the colour on the spot where the melon rested on the ground. A green watermelon will have a white or pale green bottom, a ripe melon will have a cream or yellow-coloured bottom.

Look for uniform shape. *Look for a firm, symmetrical watermelon, if the watermelon has any lumps or bumps, this may mean that it received irregular amounts of sunshine or water during growing, causing dryness or inconsistency.*

Inspect the colour. *A perfect, ripe watermelon should be dark green in colour and dull in appearance, rather than shiny. A shiny watermelon will usually be under-ripe. The market seller will thump the melon rather like patting a fat bottom to check on ripeness. It seems that when you thump, if the melon sounds hollow it is usually ripe, and an unripe melon will have more of a thud-like sound. However, I am still to perfect this method and rather prefer to rely on his expertise, In our village the watermelon man comes around in a lorry piled high with fruit and an ancient set of iron scales on the drop-down platform.*

Grapes Black, deep burgundy, pink and green; some seedless some not. There's nothing like a large plate of washed grapes at the end of a meal.

Mulberry White and black, they attract wasps so the ones in our garden are barren. Our next door neighbour has one by his front gate, everyone plunders them as they pass or even use a ladder to reach, he doesn't stand a chance.

Apples All sorts, but I have never seen a Bramley.

Pears Not to be confused with quince. Pears soften when you least expect it, quinces don't. However, I have a lovely recipe for pears in syrup with a tickle of sweet white wine.

THE LOCAL *CAMI* (pronounced JAHMEE)

Although I have been inside a few nearby Mosques, I have never been inside the one in the middle of our village. It has the usual spiky blue spire and can be reached by laboriously climbing up a long flight of concrete steps. It has a large blue door, but actually I never see anyone going inside, though I know they must. It seems to me that most of our village are what I call 'C of E' Moslems, going to mosque on high days and holidays, funerals (weddings are not held in the cami) and for holy teaching by the Hoja, which are the Moslem version of a worthy sermon, I suppose. I became more convinced of the rather lackadaisical approach to religion when I realised that the supreme *Hoja* was none other than S**, the husband of H**, who owns the breakfast place at the top of the village. A more prolific drinker, smoker and general good timer, you could not wish to meet. Absolutely charming, dwarfed by his wife, but a bit of a rogue.

But back to the architecture of the *Cami* and those *Camis* all over Turkey. As you may know, there is a little circular balcony running around the base of the spire from where the Imam makes his call to prayer. Five times a day. From VERY early dawn to sunset. And it is very loud indeed.

When I first came to Turkey, I was very confused to be awakened by some faint singing, I was in Istanbul at the time, in a block of flats and stumbled out of bed at 5 a.m. – yes, that early – convinced I had left the radio on, even though we did not have a radio. It gave my friends a big laugh when I told them about my early morning quest later that day.

Once I was appraised of the *Cami* call and got used to it, it never woke me up. Nor the rest of the village it would appear. Except Fridays; all the men seem to be there. Friday is a sort of News catch up day, when announcements are made about what has and will happen in the area. We are solemnly informed about deaths and marriages and memorials to come. All in stentorian tones via a large microphone and speakers from the spire.

Nowadays, it is very rare to have a real live *Imam* singing his ancient Arabic songs from on high, mostly it is all taped and automatically switches on via a computer. Indeed, a friend once saw a very portly *Imam* sitting in a coffee shop near to the *Cami* wall on Bodrum harbour, cappuccino in one hand and a red switch on the end of a long cable in the other. My friend, curious, watched this man of the cloth check his watch and press the button, whilst seamlessly sipping on his frothy coffee. The wailing order to pray started reverberating from the speakers as he calmly ate a biscuit and wiped the froth from his mouth. Good job!

About 14 years ago, when we first arrived in our village, the *Imam* was really up there in his minaret and what a voice he had. It was positively operatic! I actually looked forward to him climbing up those stairs and booming out another call to prayer. I became increasingly proud and boastful about him, telling all my friends in other villages that their *Imam* was vastly inferior, too squeaky, too piping, too faint, too, well, not ours. I even suggested a competition to discover The Voice of the area, a good idea for a Turkish game show, I thought. But all good things come to an end and sadly one day I noticed we had a different voice faltering over the rooftops, not our own Turkish Pavarotti, but a, dare I say, very ordinary voice. Upon enquiries I discovered that our man had retired, aged 45, Gokcebel had been his first and only job, or calling or whatever *Imams* do, and he was off to the countryside for a life of contemplation. I like to think he at least will join the amateur dramatic society, or frankly, he is wasted.

WHEN PRODUCE IS NOT IN SEASON...

KONSERV

Konserv (conserves) Sazili's wife, along with most of the older village ladies, spends many hours during the summer glut cooking and packing delicious vegetables and fruits in jars. The huge plain glass or plastic bottles are racked up on the supermarket shelves as soon as spring has sprung and the fresh produce reduces in price. Tomatoes are first up closely followed by medleys of green vegetables, carrots and peppers. Vats of pepper both sweet and hot and tomato paste are made too. Dried peppers and chillies as well as aubergines and all sorts of herbs are carefully strung out and dried for future consumption during the winter months. They take on an intense flavour, which is very different to that of the fresh produce. They also make great decoration for the kitchen, and you will see them suspended from the beams in a haphazard tangle.

Recipes for maintaining the summer months in jars or cans can be found in my recipe section from page 60.

DRIED FRUITS

Turkey is famous for its dried fruits and nuts. You will notice that in European supermarkets or delicatessens the dried fruit is labelled 'produced in Turkey'. Nuff said, they are the best.

Figs, apricots, sun-dried tomatoes, dates, prunes, apples, pears, candied bergamot and cherry tomatoes, raisins, currants and peppers – you name it. I recently brought home my entire Christmas stash from Yalikavak market: dates, figs, bergamot, walnuts, hazelnuts, pistachios, almonds and pine nuts. I spent so much that the stallholder thought it was his birthday, but it would have been twice as much, if not three or four times more in the UK.

I made fabulous stuffings for the poultry, compotes in brandy, chocolate dates, almond soup, walnut tart and so much more. I will give the recipes later. I also dragged over several kilos of quince, the suitcase weighed a ton. I had to look very brightly at the check-in lady to get away with it. It was definitely worth the struggle.

The most glorious sight is seeing the acres of red chillies drying in the sunshine on family balconies, roof terraces, patios and yards. These will eventually be made into *biber salcasi* (hot pepper paste). They also dry the sweet red peppers too, for, you guessed it, sweet pepper paste.

Figs should not be messed about with. They speak for themselves, the sweetness and texture and, particularly the colour, make them so special in their own right. They are also wonderful to paint, as countless artists have already shown.

Fresh or dried they go particularly well with soft curd or goats cheese, either stuffed or in a salad nestling together on a bed of pale green salad leaves. I will grill the fresh ones too, drizzled in the best honey and that's it. Just serve with *kaymak* or delicious thick *kamakli* yogurt. Food for the creative mind.

The story of my mis-reported suicide

Whilst on the subject of figs, something very strange and funny happened while I was preparing this particular hot fig dessert.

One of our guests from Australia by way of Bali, was a rather odd character and, to be honest, tried our patience considerably. She must have known this, although we tried very hard to untighten our lips when she was around. I had just bought a new oven which had many and myriad unfathomable knobs and dials. I had departed the dinner table to grill the figs in honey, placed the upturned figs in the large tin tray, dolloped lots of honey over them and placed under the grill. But which knob for plain grilling? The kitchen is not the lightest of rooms and the knob graphics were not clear. I turned one and waited, nope, so I tried another, nope, I could detect no perceptible heat. Knowing that my painters were waiting outside for their promised pudding, I panicked and stuck my head well inside the oven in order to see when the coils of the grill glowed red, indicating that it was time to turn up the correct knob. At that point Miss Australia passed by the open kitchen door. She said nothing to me, nor did anything so I was not aware of her presence, but apparently she then rushed back to the table and announced to the assembled company that 'Eljay may need some help as she is trying to kill herself'! I realised later on after the laughter subsided, that had I been intent on such I would never have been saved.

HOMEMADE TOMATO/PEPPER PASTES (recipe on page 160

I have not made these, but I am assured it is easy. I buy mine from a wonderful woman who runs the *gozleme* stall in the market. She scoops out this deep red paste from huge plastic vats, all of it freshly made. I asked her what time she had to get up in the morning to not only make the *yufka*, which any Turkish housewife will know HAS to be fresh daily, but also the tomato and pepper pastes and the stuffed vine leaves too. She rolled her eyes, 'very early', she said. She looks remarkably fresh herself, bright-eyed and cheerfully bantering with all and sundry.

CHEESE, MILKYOGURT

There are now bespoke cheese shops in Yalikavak, run by charming girls in crisp white aprons, standing in front of row upon row of interesting cheeses, but I am still loyal to the *pazar* stalls: I get lots of tastings and nobody quibbles about my buying small amounts. Once, a stallholder threw in a bottle of his mother's olive oil as a '*hediye*' present. It pays to be loyal.

Dairy produce is a very important part of the Turkish diet, and yogurt is most important of all, but cheese comes a close second.

It's believed that the first cheeses were made not in Switzerland as many people think, but in Mesopotamia. This region is considered the 'cradle of civilisation', and covers the strip of land between the Tigris and Euphrates rivers in southeastern Turkey and Iraq. I am a great lover of cheese and find it invaluable during our weekly holiday menus, the flavours are so varied it doesn't seem like the same product. I use it in *boreks*, toppings for *pide*, in courgette patties or *mucver*, and so much more.

THE GOLDEN MILKMAN

There used to be a back road to the village, which ran from the main road between Yalikavak and Gundogan and past all the good supermarkets. Now one is no longer allowed to turn left, it is not really so useful any more. A few years back I was returning from my usual supermarket run and I saw an elderly man struggling to walk up the hill on the way up to the village. As is the custom, and almost expected, I stopped to offer him a lift. He gratefully sank into the adjacent front seat. It was only a short ride, but I made light conversation, 'Where have you been?' He responded with a broad grin revealing a full set of golden teeth, upper and lower pair gleaming in the setting sun.

'I went down to get some milk.'

So amazed was I by his dentistry, that I barely let loose a mumble before he went on;

'I came from Tansaş' (the name of the supermarket at the bottom of the road.)

We had by this time arrived at the village and at his appointed place he slid out of the car along with his shopping bag.

A few days later, on the same road, the same man was walking along, I stopped again,

'Merheba' I pronounced cheerily, 'You been down for milk again?'

'Oh, yes,' he replied as he once again clambered aboard, tucking his bag under his knees. We chattered on about the weather and general stuff that my Turkish would allow until he departed at the same place.

I didn't see him again for a couple of days, it was the *Bayram* (religious holiday period) and most people were with their families, feasting. The Turks love a feast.

I was working in the studio, when I was assailed by a cacophony of the hanging metal bells at my front gate! Most unusual. I went to open it and there was my old man, clutching a massive Fanta bottle filled with milk.

'Oh, I have been looking for you everywhere,' he told me breathlessly, 'I wanted to give you this – it's from my cow, fresh today. The one grazing behind Tansaş. Happy *Bayram*!'

He proffered the still warm bottle. I had hardly said more than a couple of demurring words of thanks, when he turned on his heel and left.

Well! I cannot begin to explain the anxiety this gift caused. Phil was most concerned, he thought we should boil it, or maybe throw it away or perhaps give it to the cat.

'It must be full of bacteria, or smallpox, or is it TB?' Lengthy discussion ensued along with much riffling through the internet. We left it in the fridge to give time to think.

The next day I remembered how the old carpenter we used to make our furniture once brought his cow to work with him to graze in the garden, he too had a nifty set of Fanta bottles. He looked healthy enough and his four children. I took the bottle of milk and poured it on my Muesli – it was, I have to say, the most delicious milk I have ever tasted.

It goes off very quickly, so don't leave it for a day if you are ever offered any, by the man with the golden teeth, sadly I never saw him again and I never had the chance to ask him who his dentist was.

TURKTIP *When buying yogurt, there are several types,and are offered in tubs, boxes, jars and earthenware dishes. Usually you will find;*

***Homogenised**, which is supermarket-type yogurt and can be low fat or normal. This is usually the cheapest and can be bought in enormous tubs that would not disgrace a paint store.*

***Kaymaksiz**. This is yogurt without the kaymak or thick cream.*

***Suzme yogurt** is the perfect substitute for sour cream.*

***Kaymaklı**. This is the real deal with cream in it and a nice crust on the top.*

***Tava yogurt**. Sold in boxes, again with the thick crust and you can almost slice it.*

***Labne**. This is a sort of cream cheese made by straining the yogurt through muslin or some such, and what is left is a perfectly yummy cream cheese, used in desserts.*

Beyaz Peynir

The most common cheeses in Turkey are fresh white cheeses, or *beyaz peynir.* These cheeses are most similar to feta. White cheese is a staple at breakfast, as a filling in layered pastries and other baked goods, on salads and as a meze or starter. It can be made with cow, sheep or goat milk.

There are endless varieties and brands of white cheese to choose from. As a general rule, the higher the salt content, the harder the cheese will be.

You can buy white cheese everywhere in Turkey, from the grocer on the corner, to the largest supermarket. You can also buy it in bulk at the local bazaars. It's available in blocks, slices and crumbled, usually stored in brine or water, in boxes, packets and even cans. I generally buy a huge block from the *pazar* and then a couple of packets or tubs, which keep better in the fridge as they are immersed in brine. I can't tell you how many times I have stabbed the pack whilst hurrying to get lunch on and immersed myself in brine as well! There is a lot of it!

TURKTIP *When cooking with beyaz peynir wait until the end before adding salt, the cheese can add enough of its own.*

Another popular cheese common in Turkey and Greece is *taze kasar**, which means 'fresh' cheese that hasn't been aged. Fresh *kasar* is a smooth, firm, light yellow cheese usually made from cow's milk. It's a very versatile cheese, good for slicing, melting, grating or alone. As with white cheese, you can buy fresh *kasar* in the supermarket, or in large rounds or slivers at the bazaar

Eski Kaşar

The city of Kars, in the northeastern region of Turkey, is most famous for producing Turkey's best aged *kasar* cheese. The Kars variety of this beloved cheese is usually made with pure cow's milk or a mixture of cow and goat milk. I love the flavour of this cheese. Strong, nutty and sharp. Unlike fresh *kasar,* which must be eaten quickly after production, aged *kasar* is stored for about six months inside a burlap sack before it's consumed. It is ideal for grating.

Tulum (TOO'-loom) is the general term for a pungent, soft, sometimes crumbly form of white cheese made from goat's milk that varies greatly between regions. *Tulum* is made from pure goat's milk and left to mature for two to three months inside a goat skin. Throughout Anatolia, it's common to see *tulum* on display still inside the hairy goat skin. There are many types of *tulum* that vary greatly throughout Turkey's different regions, *tulum* from the southeastern part of the country is different than those made in

*Pronounced KASHAR

the Aegean regions and in inner Anatolia. The most coveted *tulum* is from Erzincan, a city in the East. *Tulum* is best served as an appetizer before meat fare. The traditional way is to serve crumbled *tulum* with walnut halves, sweet butter and flatbread.

Helim (HALUMI)
Rinse and dry the halumi then slice into 5cm pieces. Dredge with flour and some paprika or chilli flakes. Deep fry until golden. Serve immediately. I like to serve this squeaky cheese* with a salad of watercress, lettuce, rocket and grilled tomatoes.

Another way is to wrap the Halumi with a slice of oiled aubergine and roast in the oven. It looks more interesting that way as a canape or appetiser.

We had a painter in one of our groups who didn't eat vegetables, any vegetables. We were at our wits' end, until by chance we discovered that she loved halumi cheese. She got it every day after then, she didn't seem to mind at all.

Smoked cheese is produced in the areas surrounding Düzce and Hendek in the Marmara region of Turkey. This cheese gets its robust flavour in special smokehouses that burn pine. This cheese has a wonderful aroma and rich, smoky flavour. It comes in wheels covered by a light brown, textured hull.

Köy peynir is a soft new cheese resembling Mozzarella; mild in flavour, it varies in saltiness, but always delicious, it must be eaten within days as it will go off.

Lor is used in making ***sigara boreği,*** all ***boreks*** etc.

Plaited and stringy cheeses Odd, stringy and salty, conversation pieces!

Cokelek Same as ***Lor.*** This is especially for fillings, *borek*, pies, *mucver* or some such. [presumably not literally identical or you'd put it with the Lor altogether?] Crumbly like cottage cheese, but without the wetness or squeaky consistency. Must be fresh, doesn't last long before descending into old flannel taste but, I have discovered, freezes well!

We should lump butter into this cheese category too. Butter is important in Turkish cooking. It is used in frothing sauces, pastries, and to drench rice pilafs with its delicious golden liquid. Butter is still sold in the markets fresh from the farms, piled up in high cones or as huge lumps sitting under the glass domes. It is thick, soft and a deep yellow, just like I remember it used to be in 1950s Britain. My mother used to buy butter paddled into shape on marble slabs in ancient Sainsburys shops, now just a distant memory revived when I buy from the market place.

Anyway, what goes with fresh cheese and butter better than anything else…

*It really does squeak!

BREAD!

Many ladies from my village bake their own bread and there is usually an ancient old clay bread oven at the bottom of every garden. Here is made *bazlama,* a sort of puffy flatbread. The village women also make their own *yufka* – thin whispers of flour, water and oil, cooked over a curved iron plate on an open fire.

One day about four or five years ago, I'm far too old to be precise about time, Şazili's wife Sema asked me if I would like to join her and her friends making *yufka.* An invitation too good to miss. She indicated that if I brought a couple of eggs and some cheese they would make me a treat. I know only too well what a Turkish food treat is, something remarkably tasty. We had painters from America at the house, so I made my excuses and left.

Apparently, Sema and her friends sit and make *yufka* every alternate Sunday and it is quite a social occasion. We agreed to meet at the top of the village as I did not know the way to this *yufka* 'factory'. Sema and I walked along the top road past the newer smart villas until we reached what I can only describe as a ruin. It was an almost roofless outbuilding attached to a very down-at-heel house, but there were children running about the yard and shoes by the door so I knew it was occupied.

Sema led me to a small flight of steps to the ancient wooden door, behind which I could hear chatter and laughter. A plume of wood smoke rose from a hole in the roof above us. The door creaked open at a ridiculously jaunty angle and I was greeted by a sea of beaming faces, all women young, old and ancient, wearing country head scarves and sitting on the ground with their round *yufka* boards astride their laps. I blinked in the semi darkness and could see this was a really tumbledown old stone house, thick walls with the light seeping through, several rather large holes in the roof and the earth floor completely covered by sheets of transparent blue polythene. In the corner, slightly apart, sat a lady at an open wood fire, in front of her a convex metal dome in which she was deftly flipping over a large sheet of *yufka* with a long stick. Once cooked, this wafer-thin veil would be floated onto a pile of ready-made rounds, to settle and cool.

The process was simple. Each woman started with a small ball of dough the size of a golf ball, which would be rolled out and out and out with a thin rolling pin. Once almost transparent the rounds would be wafted over to the fire and the woman would cook each piece, turning them over with her stick. The room was smoky and dim, the women's chatter loud and probably full of licentious gossip and there I was, right in the middle clutching my cheese and eggs. They made me a special pile of cheese *gozleme,* which they kept warm for me on the metal dome, whilst I, having politely asked if it was OK, took photos. I understood later that because there is so little water in these crispy rounds, they can be stored for weeks on end and reused in many dishes or reconstituted as a softer version with the addition of that lost water.

After a while my *gozleme* was wrapped perfectly cleanly in newspaper and I returned home with my booty. I offered the still warm pastries to the Americans as a food parcel for their journey home that afternoon, but was very disappointed to hear from them that they were far too greasy and difficult to travel with. I actually think it was the newspaper that did it, I can't imagine how they would have reacted had they seen the 'kitchen' from whence they came! Nothing lost, we ate them ourselves later on. Delicious!

THE BAKERS, or *FIRIN*.

Well I just LOVE the local baker's shop, or *Firin* as we call it. It is open 24 hours a day seven days a week and bakes with a traditional wood burning oven. You can see the towering piles of wood to the side of the old rickety building and the heat is extreme. Shift workers beat and pummel and bake and retrieve on long wooden paddles the different kinds of bread and buns. There is a constant swishing sound as paddles slide in and out of the oven. The bread slides down a chute in front of the fire and is stacked on the shelves all around the shop. It's never there for long, mind you! It is the staple food of the Turk, builders and businessmen on their way to work, housewives, small children all wait patiently for their turn to grab armfuls – yes, I mean armfuls of the hot bread almost before it has finished tumbling from the oven. You must be careful to remove it from the plastic bags as soon as you can or else condensation will spoil the crustiness. Who can resist tearing a small lump off the tip of the long oval-shaped delights on the way home? Not me!

I usually get to the baker's at 7a.m. prompt, sometimes earlier. We have fresh bread every morning for breakfast, if I arrive any later I may miss the special pastries and buns we all love so much. It happened once, never again!

I buy *boca*, a sort of brioche; *acmi*, a stuffed and glazed bun; *borek*, a cheesy pastry (you can have meat or potato fillings, but cheese is my choice); *simit*, sesame-coated rings of firm crisp bread; *pide*, flat rounds that look button-backed with Nigella seeds; plain *ekmek*, the usual oval log; flatbreads, thin breads, puffy breads, round and square, sweet pastry, sesame and cinnamon twists, brown breads, seedy breads and anything you can think of made from dough and pastry. There is even a wonderful brown seeded bread shaped like a large flower.

I pad out with my bags piled high. 'I have a lot of guests.' I explain.

The baker asks me to marry him.

Meals made from bread dough are many and myriad. We have met *gozleme*, but there is also *pide* – Turkish Pizza, *Lhamucun* and many many more, you can find the recipes on pp00.

So we have almost finished the Yalikavak *pazar* shopping expedition. But before we go home, one more stop. It has to be the last one. Onward to the fish market!

There are three fish shops in Yalikavak. One is the main market on the harbourside, one in a kiosk by the old marina and one right by the *Pazar*. They are open most days without a break, but sell out early. It is enormous fun to arrive early in the morning to choose your fresh wild sea fish from the market place, jostling with other contenders for the best pieces, whilst batting away the over-insinuating cats that know what's on its way. The supermarkets sell fish in the larger branches, but these will be farmed, still perfectly fresh, but wild is better. Sadly all too rare these days.

FISH

Some fish is from the sea 'wild' and some is farmed, in our area you can choose. The Aegean is famous for its fish, so if possible I ask for sea fish or *denizde*. Usually you find, *levrik* (sea bass) *cupri* (sea bream); tiny pink *hamsi* (anchovies) when in season are considered a real delicacy and there is also red mullet, whitebait, barracuda, monkfish and so much more.

We must not forget too the calamari, octopus – best grilled with garlic in my opinion – and plump moist prawns. Our local restaurant makes superb griddled prawns in brandy sauce, although I'm pretty sure it's not a Turkish recipe. Everything can be cooked in casseroles, plain grilled or fried, but whatever the season fish are at their best stuffed with rosemary or bay, cooked on charcoal and served with the freshest rocket, grilled tomatoes and if you insist, chips! I do.

There is a fish market directly on the harbour where the fishing boats are moored and the men sit mending their bright orange nets. Here both farmed and sea fish are for sale and a pretty good variety caught on that day. You have to get there quite early in order to get a good choice. I usually have to ask the name of some of the strange looking fish, lying glittering on his piles of mini arctic ice floes. Everything is worth a try.

FUNNY HATS, COLUMNS AND NOMADS: A TALE OF ENDLESS WANDERING AND EVENTUAL REST.

Mostly, I have to admit, we prefer to eat our fish in the local restaurants and one of our favourites is in Iasos, about an hour's drive from Yalikavak. This haven of tranquility, save for the new, extremely large television installed, is one of the best situated restaurants in our area. Long wooden tables and benches set under a wooden pergola surrounded by old olive cans stuffed with bougainvillea right slap bang on the water's edge. Bobbing fishing boats slap gently to the front and side, a tiny row of shops behind, one selling the finest pastries this side of Saturn, a Byzantine church above and the cream of ancient Greek ruins a hundred yards away. We can sit with a beer or the ubiquitous glass of tea and survey the views, the old Ottoman castle, the crusader fortress, and the historic stone harbour gate, which was shaken loose by earthquakes a millennium ago, looks romantic and eerie in the distance. All this and fabulous fish and roasting hot real chips. Sandra, who is as slim as a whip, always orders an entire serving plate of these golden treasures, just for her. I wish I knew her secret. Who could want more? Amazing ruins, wonderful food, an ice cold beer and the sea. Almost no time to paint.

Regarding the wonderful seaside restaurant, the story goes that a nomadic family with four young boys wandered into Iasos one day, the family were tired and decided to stay for the summer. The four young boys eyed the village, the pretty harbour and the antique ruins and decided to cease their wanderings, stay and open up a shack *lokanta*. This *lokanta* grew larger and became more established, it got a proper roof, an indoor kitchen, a jetty and a loo (of sorts). The older brother looks after the money, the middle brother is the jovial host, the younger brother became the chef, and the other one, well he must do something, but I have yet to find out. Our jovial host is called Cayar, pronounced JR. So he bought himself a stetson, had his photo taken in it and now grins gap-toothed from these billboards hanging off every tree on the way to Iasos. That's marketing for you, albeit from the '70s. We are now firm friends and we always get the warmest of welcomes when our painters come to eat at this wonderfully situated place. If you make special overtures in advance they will prepare soft shelled crabs and other delicacies, but Sandra would be happy with her chips!

Iasos has a special atmosphere that you cannot fail to feel as you first enter the Agora through the arch and past the curious cows and goats on either side. The warmth, the peace and smell of dried earth and thyme fill the air, it is breathtaking to emerge from the shaded archway into the bright light of the day and see before you the senate, the white marble roads and the soaring apricot-coloured columns proudly pointing upwards, welcoming us to this deserted haven.

Hardly a soul visits this place except in high season, so we have the perfect place to paint and draw. Personally, I find the sense of history and adventure eerily pressing on me from all around. How could it not? So much has happened here.

This ancient Carian city has had an extraordinary and eventful history and once fully-excavated will prove to be as huge a discovery and as important as the great city of Ephesus, or even more so, as my friend the Italian archaeologist told me as we chatted during one of his 'stone numbering' sessions.

Caria was a Bronze and Iron age region that covered most of the Aegean and part of the Mediterranean coasts during the 11th to 6th century BCE and seemed to be a force for good (all things being equal in the ancient world). Situated alongside the newer harbour of the present village of Kiyikislacik (a name to conjure with!), Iasos was once an island and a member of the Delian league of 468 BCE whose main aim was to fight invasion by the Persian Empire. It is easy to see how the geography of this location made it so strategically important and how the natural harbour, although since changed and silted, would have made it a great commercial port. It eventually came under the rule of the Byzantine empire but by the 15th century, when the Ottomans ruled the city, it lay deserted.

Iasos was most famous as an exporter of the beautiful pink marble quarried nearby, which can still can be seen in the form of columns and walls of some of the most well-known Roman municipal buildings. There are also examples of this marble in the incredible Iasos museum set into colonnades around an ancient temple. This is not a museum as you and I know it, no glass boxes, no 'do not touch' signs – the sole curator is a stern young woman who will open up for you on demand whilst still chivying her young children, who enjoy the museum corridors as an extension of their playground. It is a pleasure to amble around and encounter youthful exuberance among the ancient headless statues to revered forgotten grandees of long ago.

This place never fails to make me happy.

BUYING AND COOKING FISH

If we do decide to cook at home we grill our chosen fish in the garden on our purpose-built barbecue (*mangal*). Most Turkish gardens have one and if they don't there are dozens of picnic areas with stone-built BBQs so nobody misses out. I don't cook the fish inside for obvious reasons. These are the more usual fish we find in the market, along with some teeny tiny ones that look as if they should have been thrown back. In my opinion all fish, especially as fresh as what we get in Yalikavak should be very simply cooked, either grilled, fried or BBQ'd.

Sea Bass (*Cipri*) **Sea Bream** (*Levrek*) Both these fish are pretty well served everywhere and easily available. Mostly they will be farmed fish, although sometimes as you can find *Denizde* 'from the sea', but of course more expensive.

Monk Fish wonderful to buy one whole fish and divide up between a group of friends. As everywhere, it is an expensive fish, so this works well.

Barracuda Sometimes see this elegant fish in pride of place on the fish restaurant's ice cabinet. Strictly an open sea fish, but occasionally found closer to land.

Red and **Grey Mullet** Red mullet is highly prized and the best are caught in the Aegean or Mediterranean seas, so stroke of luck there! Best fried.

Sardines again popular Aegean fish, especially during early Autumn, which means October, November time.

Pandora (*Mercin*) Known in Turkey as The Fish Of Summer.

Octopus in my opinion the best way to serve octopus is char-grilled on the BBQ with garlic sauce.

Squid the only way is freshly prepared battered and deep fried and served with lemon, or grilled with garlic as the octopus.

Prawns grilled, braised in sauce, or cold in a salad, they are often served on long metal skewers that have been placed on an open fire, with just butter swished across them.

I also love to make fish soup and a delicious recipe with rolled fillets of whatever fish you can get hold of, sitting in a tomato sauce made with *raki* and dotted with *bayaz peynir* (feta cheese). See page 70

This dish is made even made more perfect when served in individual copper dishes, which I purchased in the market (haggled him down to £4 each); hand-beaten and complete with handles, they come straight from the oven to the table and look fantastic.

Hamsi A Turkish delicacy and national fish, *hamsi*, or anchovies are cooked at a larger size than the ones we are used to in cans with roll tops. Caught in the Black Sea, and best in the winter months, they are even expensive in Turkey so a speciality in fish restaurants. Served with pride.

So, there you have it, my morning's work at the Yalikavak Pazar and beyond, and I haven't even mentioned the clothes, shoes, carpets, pots and pans, dangerous-looking garden tools, crockery, linens, plastic, jewellery, antiques, toys, underwear, textiles and knickknacks just begging you to follow the strident cries of the salesperson – Come on, take a look, pick me up, BUY ME!'

I return home to disgorge my goodies before they spoil and I still have that other half gozleme. Where was it?

THE STAPLES OF MY LARDER

TEA , TEA AND MORE TEA

You can't go anywhere without being offered a glass of Çay or tea in Turkey, no commercial transaction, however small is unaccompanied by that amber liquid. No friendship uncemented, no gathering complete without it.

You would have imagined that tea was always in Turkey, so ubiquitous is it nowadays. I had thought that tea was a part of the Turkish culture for thousands of years, but no!

TURKTIP *Larder essentials in my Turkish kitchen*
These ingredients are an absolute must for any authentic Turkish meal. If you have only these on hand, you have the culinary world by the throat!
Onions, tomatoes, peppers, parsley, dill, mint, cinnamon, olive oil, nar, yogurt, lemons, rice, bulgur, pulses (beans or chickpeas), flour, salt, black and white pepper, pul biber. sumac, tomato paste, sugar. *These ingredients plus any staple such as* ***minced beef*** *or* ***lamb, cheese,*** **pulses,** ***eggs*** *etc. can be turned into hundreds of delicious permutations.*

You would have imagined that tea was always in Turkey, so ubiquitous is it nowadays. I had thought that tea was a part of the Turkish culture for thousands of years, but no!

In truth, tea only came into Turkish culture in the late 19th century. I had always presumed that tea came to Turkey along the Silk route from China. It did get some air time, but Turks were coffee fans and it was not until the late 1870's that it became more and more popular throughout the newly-opened tea houses in the Sultenahmet area of Istanbul, purely because it was cheaper than coffee. Wasn't it ever thus.

Sadly for me, the coffee served in most locations near us is still the Nescafe powdered sort, or the sedimented Turkish kind, neither of which I care for. The cappuccino and mocha, flat white etc are slowly becoming more available in the trendy (and very expensive) coffee shops in Bodrum – and don't the cool Turks love it – but never to be found in our village. I stick to tea, NEVER with milk and always '*aci*' or 'light' tea for me, brewed or steamed in a *cay demlek* and mixed to preferred strength with boiling water. I can drink litres of the stuff. The glasses are small and at three Turkish lire a glass worth every penny of the time spent in langour over a *cay* watching the world go by.

Tea is now grown in Turkey, in the Rize region, which has the perfect climate and soil. Black tea comes in huge packets the size of two-kilo flour bags and yes, I can taste the good from the bad now. Tea is the Turkish people's staple drink, one of the biggest facets of their life. The tea garden and the mosque were and are the main social gathering points for the Turkish male and dare I say the *cay bahcesi* (tea garden) seems to be winning.... so far.

DRIED GOODS, PULSES, LEGUMES AND NUTS

My shelves in the kitchen at the Old Stone House are groaning with jars of dried goods. I used to have far more decorative miscellanea perched there, but they have been banished in favour of various sealed jars, plastic or glass, with all of the following. I prefer not to encumber myself with cans of beans, they take up far too much room, although I concede that the canned chickpeas make a smoother hummus, when you don't have a food processor. All of the following are well used in many different guises; all you have to do is plan ahead as most need pre-soaking. I don't bother soaking the lentils, a bit of boiling water for five minutes will suffice if you're in a hurry.

Turkey is one of the preeminent exporters of nuts and dried fruits, just check your packages next time you buy in the UK. In consequence the choice and freshness and taste are so much better without the journey, so I buy kilos in the market and quite often pack them up myself and give away as Christmas presents in hampers.

Chickpeas, so, so useful as a bulker for meat dishes and a substitute for those eating vegetarian. They also make great dips and mezzes, along with all the beans and lentils.

Haricot Beans great in vegetarian and meaty stews.

Lentils Red, Green and Yellow All brilliant for soups, falafels, with fish for stuffings, you name it.

Fava Beans For one of my favourite mezzes. Also great stuffed into artichokes with dill.

Rice There are several types of rice, short and long grain, but luckily it is carefully labelled as PILAF or DOLMA rice; you can use all the short grain rice for puddings.

Bulgur (fine and coarse) I use the finer type for mixing in with the raw meat for *köfte* and the courser type for pilafs and *kisir* (bulgar salad).

Semolina Used in puddings and confections such as *helva*.

Macaroni Used as in the rest of the world.

Orzo This is very often mixed in with the rice in pilaf and looks interesting as well as adding a nuttiness to the texture and the taste.

Pine Nuts Absolutely essential in non meat *dolma* and scattered on mezzes or toasted on salads for crunch. I use them liberally when I think a dish may need a boost. Luckily they are cheaper in Turkey and I buy them by the kilo!

Almonds For sweet or savoury dishes, although I had the devil's own job finding ground almonds for my lemon cake. I went to the patissier in the end and he had some specially ground for me. The consistency was good, but it was a little damper than our packet stuff in the UK so storage would have been difficult. However, as it tasted so much better I used it all up.

Walnuts Smashed and mashed, whole or broken into pieces, these home-grown beauties are an essential part of Turkish cooking. As we live on Walnut Street well….

Hazelnuts Lovely roasted with vegetables such as squash and kale.

Pistachio Nuts The queen of Turkish nuts, used extensively in *baklava* and decorations on many baked sweetmeats. They are especially good made into an ice cream or surprising you in a cube of Turkish Delight.

SEEDS

Sesame, Pumpkin and Sunflower

You always know where a Turkish man has been sitting as the surrounding area of ground will be scattered with lots, and I mean lots, of sunflower seed husks. I was taught how to extract the seed from the husk in one neat movement of the tongue, but could never master it, always finishing up with husk fibres wedged between my front teeth. Not a good look.

Strictly speaking the following are really fridge not larder. I also have two freezers now.

MEAT

Meat is very expensive, especially in our region of the Aegean coast, where animal husbandry is mainly for dairy, so it is used quite sparingly in some local dishes, which does not in any way detract from the taste. At the *kasap* or at the supermarket, you can buy most cuts, and you can ask for bones to make your beef broth stock. But you need to know what you are doing.

I quite enjoy going to the butcher's or *kasap*, they are the old fashioned sort we used to have on every high street, small, with one hearty butcher in his apron, a huge wooden block and a lady in a separate kiosk with a glass front to take the money, There is always a dog on the pavement outside. Ever-hopeful, and guarding his territory, one ear cocked in case a generous soul drops him a bone as he snoozes by the door.

I usually find it more convenient to get my meat from the supermarket, shame on me, but with so many people to cater for I have little time for these niceties, but I will go occasionally, especially for a special dish. I have noted some recipes here and further on in the main recipe section.

I plan my menus well in advance in order to maximise my use of what is left for soups and salads, so I do buy large quantities of beef and lamb mince, chicken and casserole mutton in advance, then prepare and freeze, *köfte* being a good example. These can be spiced and seasoned, formed into patties and frozen between sheets of foil, to be taken out on the prescribed day and much time that saves. Casseroles, too, freeze well and moussaka, as well as, surprisingly, the stuffed peppers, NOT aubergine though, except if within a stew. Also a word of caution, always taste the defrosted dish, as sometimes the distinct flavours get muffled during the freezing process.

Cuts of meat

Mainly beef, lamb, mostly minced or cubed for economy, and shoulder or neck cuts for the yummy *guvec* or stews; fatty cuts for BBQs and stuffings or anything that requires cooking on an open fire. Shin is good. No pork, obviously.

Offal, better known in Turkish as *sakatalar* (sah-kah-TAHT'-lar), are the edible parts of the animal, usually beef or lamb, apart from the meat itself, such as liver and kidneys, for example.

Feet and heads of animals are often used for stewing or roasting, rather like we used to do in the old days, calves foot jelly, for one example. Many varieties of meats are prized for their high nutritional value and are considered delicacies. Calf and lamb brain are considered a delicacy in Turkish cuisine. They are served fried or boiled and sliced as a salad with a dressing of olive oil and lemon or vinegar. Now, I knew what this was when a doctor friend from Kusadasi served this up to me, and I am afraid I rather upset him, because this was where I drew the line, even though I remember my own mother preparing brawn in the fifties, it was a no-no. It was a genuine compliment to be served it as it is considered to be a real treat with a mild flavour and smooth texture, I have no idea one way or the other.

KELLE OR SHEEP'S HEAD

In Turkish cuisine, *kelle*, or sheep head, is used to make soup and roasted and served with Turkish spices I did try it in a local restaurant, and actually once you get over the rather difficult prospect of being served a skull on a plate, it is very tasty. If you want to try it and are not so brave, you can have the meat removed from the head and served on a plate without those eyes staring at you. Rather like a thinly cut, crispy roast lamb.

Turkish Tripe Soup
Are all my food memories offal-based, I wonder? We used to eat this in the local Turkish café in Stoke Newington called the Istanbul Iskembeyesi (the Istanbul Tripe Soup). Well, I only tasted it and everybody else drank several bowls full. Usually at around 2a.m. after a great night out in Soho, as it was considered a good cure for a hangover. The smell of garlic was profound. My abiding memory was moving as far away to the other side of the bed as I possibly could to avoid the stink.

CHICKEN

We use a fair amount of chicken and I have many decent recipes for our painters, with lots of fresh veg or pulses cooked together. Chicken with artichoke hearts, lemons and green olives, yum! Chicken with chick peas, chicken with aubergines, you name it, we've had it. You can buy whole chickens in the market and butcher* yourself, which means of course lots of lovely stock from the bones, or you can buy it ready prepared as breasts, thighs or wings, etc. Strangely, wings are relatively expensive, considering their status in the UK. Some sort of fashion I think here in Bodrum. We love it marinaded overnight in various spices, yogurt and honey then cooked on a high heat to caramelise. Always a winner, especially with hot roast potatoes with garlic and rosemary – you may as well use up the oven's heat economically, electricity is hugely expensive in Turkey.

BEEF

There being no pork available, beef is paramount. Cheaper than lamb and less fatty, it can be added to all dishes with pulses, beans and vegetables; or on its own in casseroles or minced for stuffings and kebabs. Once away from the coastal region it is more likely that fish and crustaceans will be supplanted by meat.

* I mean cut up, not kill!

On our famous reccie to Stratonikea, I had to remain for a while by the ancient coffee house to rest as I had a bad back at the time. Ever eager to practise my Turkish, I started up a conversation with Dursan, the proprietor. The conversation over a glass of tea went like this;

'Lovely tea, I see you cook it over an open fire.'

'Yes, everything tastes better on a fire.'

'Do you cook any meals here?' (thinking how useful that would be for our hungry painters).

'No.'

'Oh that's a shame,' heart sinking to my boots, wondering how I was going to feed the troops.

'...but you should have been here last night, when I had my friends over, oooooh! We had fish and meat and mezze and raki....' He smiled his toothless smile.

'Well could we be your friends too?'

'Yes!'

We arranged a meal to be served the following week and it was delicious. So simple, a mezze of pointy green peppers and aubergines and courgettes in garlic yogurt and spicy butter, followed by *Sac Kavurna (beef stew)*, bales of bread served from huge plastic bin liners(!) and fresh water and honeydew melons to follow. All washed down with copious amounts of raki and wine.

And he cooked the lot!

Find the recipe for the *Sac Kavurna* on page 115.

LAMB

Lamb can be fatty, so even when I use mince I mix with some beef as well, you can buy this combo at the supermarket so I am not the only one that thinks this. Mutton can also be used, sometimes the flavour can be very strong, so often I heave in the *yeni bahar*, mixed spice and other flavourings and plenty of lemon juice to cut the fattiness.

I use lamb, or a lamb and beef mix, in *Karni Yarik*, moussaka, and stuffed peppers Lamb makes excellent *köfte* and cubed and cooked and served on aubergine puree it is sublime as in *Hunkar Begendi*, a famous Ottoman dish. Recipe on page 116.

Delicious with mint, cumin and citrusy sumac, serve it with fruits and nuts, dollop some red wine in or cream it up with yogurt, it is very easy to mix your flavours and radically change each dish.

> **TURK TIP** *When making köfte the more you kneed the meat the better – it will stay formed into its chosen shape, without the use of an egg.*

CURED MEATS

Beef Socukuk (dried, cured, fermented beef sausage)

Dry and spicy, flavoured and coloured with copious amounts of paprika. These are the *chorizo* of Turkey. They can vary between being mild in flavour to really spicy all depending on the paprika added. I love it served with *menemem* and mixed in with chicken casserole.

Pastirma Pastrami, speaks for itself, it is very popular in Turkey and on sale everywhere. There are many different types of sausage, some perfectly decent, but always rather alarmingly pink. Tiny so-called cocktail '*koktel*' sausages are sold in packs in our local supermarket, and I use them as snacks for the local dogs, which tells you a lot!

There are also sliced salami-type offerings, with or without pistachio, and not unlike Italian mortadella. They can be useful for cold salad lunches, but I don't use them much.

TURK TIP *The cheaper cured meats tend to leak fat like a Dutch dyke without that finger. Buy the best you can afford. When solidified, this fat can give you a heart attack just by being scraped out of the pan.*

KINDNESS TO ANIMALS AND MY RABIES JAB

There was a lovely big dog in our village, he was old and did not belong to anyone, but he was obviously not well. Contrary to what is thought about the Turkish attitude to animals, the villagers are on the whole very kind to their pets as well as those not their own. There are exceptions, but I suppose that's the same the world over, there are good guys and there are bad guys.

So, a few people were feeding this dog as he lay in the porch of an empty house. He worried me, there are so many stray dogs around and not all of them get a fair crack of the whip, I wanted to make sure that he was getting the best treatment. I went to the vet and got him some 'dog tonic' and I checked he did not need worming etc. He was pretty lethargic, but perked up no end when a sausage was produced. I produced many sausages. So many in fact, that I had to return to the supermarket for new supplies, the cheapest on offer were the aforementioned 'Koktel' sausages, a glorious shade of Barbie pink, but nevertheless most acceptable to the dog population. I bought a party pack (!) and stopped off by our sick friend.

Now here is where I was really stupid. Instead of putting the sausage in front of him, I held it between my finger and thumb, he excitedly reached up with his mouth and clamped his jaws over my hand. Not his fault, it was more of an overbite than an attack. The skin was broken on my little finger, but no more than that. I went home splashed on some Tea Tree oil and continued with our art course. The next day my finger had swollen to its own sausage size, but not pink, yellow, that sort of grim, 'oh dear it's blinking infected', yellow. Thereby followed local clinic, Tetanus injection and antibiotics. I was then ushered into a room where I was questioned heavily about this dog, did I know it? Was it sick? Upon the affirmative I was given an appointment for rabies injections. I knew the dog wasn't rabid, but they told me I would not be allowed to travel back to the UK without the certificate to say I had been inoculated.

Mournfully I went down to the local hospital and presented myself. A course of three injections was prescibed. Well, I can honestly say it was very unpleasant indeed. It felt like they were injection golden syrup. Three times in one week I went, ruing the day I fed sausages to a dog. Sadly the dog died, not of rabies, of course, but I still carry my certificate.

OILS

Olive oil, both virgin and clear, Turkey manufactures its own and as with any other ingredient, you should always use the best available, or at least the best you can afford. Rather like wine, it is useful to taste before you buy, though I grant you this is more likely in Turkey than in the UK or any supermarket-driven country. I don't buy my oil from the supermarket in Turkey, although of course there are lots to choose from, I go up to my favourite hilltop village where I get honey, eggs and oils and sometimes their local wines, purchased in a 4-litre bottle with handles. To be honest, to call it value for money is the best I can say for this particular beverage, but I digress.

The village oil is pressed in a co operative, run by the village for the village and comes from huge olive groves surrounding the hamlet. Some goes to local markets and some is sold in the local shops. It is delicious, green, fruity and thick with a slightly spicy undertone. It too comes in massive bottles, which when finished I return to be refilled. I use it unsparingly and can get through one of those huge containers in a fortnight! There is something rather decadent in glugging out the olive oil in such quantity, but it makes such a difference to the taste of our food.

Our caretaker, Sazili, like many of the villagers near us, has about three olive trees. Every November the nets go underneath and the shaking begins. Beating with sticks and sometimes climbing amongst the branches, he manages to retrieve every last vestige of olive fruit. This is where I come in: he asks me to take him and his load to the local *fabrika* or olive press, where everyone goes. This is not really a request, it is my duty! So I load up his few bags and drive to Gundogan, where he delivers his bounty. What seems like a few minutes later, hardly enough time for me to conduct my five-or six-point turn in the muddy forecourt, he returns, beaming, with three large old water bottles filled with olive oil. I presume that it may not necessarily be HIS own olives that have produced this green liquid, but what you put in you get out in kind. Rather like a crematorium I've always thought … well possibly.

We also use sunflower oil and hazelnut oil, this time from the supermarket, the hazelnut oil has a high burning temperature so ideal to add to other oils when deep frying and you want a pleasant flavour.

Butter is often used for frying too, and you cannot escape the deliciousness of rice with large knobs of butter mixed in, or the bubbling melted golden liquid poured over your kebabs and pastas – this is definitely the key to the best pilafs. I'm afraid it is not possible to be on a low fat diet in Turkey.

WRESTLING IN OIL

Another use for olive oil is exceptional to Turkey. Wrestling!

I have been a couple of times to watch this weird and frankly occasionally homo-erotic sport. Although my Turkish male friends reject this hypotheses. The aim is to get your opponent on his back so his navel is exposed to the heavens. You can also carry your opponent aloft and walk five paces. I'm pretty sure there are lots of other ways to win, but to be honest I find the whole sport baffling, though hugely entertaining.

The wrestlers are abundant, there are masses of them, all assembled in a field surrounded by traditional drums and horns as well as stalls selling canned drinks and various foodstuffs. Families encircle the arena on tiered seats along with picnics and their own club's colours draped around their necks.

They are paired off according to weight and/or size. However, the most amazing thing about this sport is the oil lathering! Oil and water mixed are slathered all over the body of the fighters, even inside their cut-off leather trousers. This is to avoid being caught by their opponent. So, at the start, the wrestlers march onto the field cheered on by their fans, they stride like Greek army officers, whilst slapping the thigh of the alternate leg as they march. Slap, thwack, slurp! One of the most macho displays I have ever seen. They are not great physical specimens, some have distinct bellies and flab, but are obviously very strong indeed. Then at the word of the referee they start grabbing at each other, the hands trying to get a grip on the glistening foe. They are even allowed to get their hands inside their keks! And I mean RIGHT inside, no actual fiddling allowed, but I daresay it's a near thing. I heard later that there are 'handles' within the trousers that the opponent can use as leverage. The winner goes on to fight the winner of the next pair and so on. There is a winner's purse and the winning wrestler is much feted. These men have been practicing the art from a very early age and they are very well respected. I was relieved to discover that the olive oil they use is not deemed suitable for cooking, however it does wonders for their skins!

CUSTOMS

THE FULL PLATE AND THE EMPTY PLATE, TURKISH TABLE MANNERS

Something that is still hard for me to get used to in public eateries is the 'eager waiter'. I am rather a quick eater, although trying to slow down more nowadays. I suppose it comes from being a mum and always having to snatch meals on the hoof, or being constantly interrupted during mealtimes. Whatever the reason, I used to be one of the first to clear my plate; instead of waiting for the rest of the party to complete their meals, my plate was whisked away, sometimes before I had even replaced my knife and fork! I would be left, utensils still raised, mouth still full staring at the white tablecloth. However, within seconds a clean plate would appear, clean cutlery and I would be made ready to replenish with whatever I wished for later. The Turks, rather like the French, like to linger at meal times, sometimes to extraordinary degrees, but your place at the table must always be clean and tidy. When smoking was not considered unpleasant or antisocial or even unhealthy, Turks smoked – well, like a Turk. Even doctors smoked whilst attending their patients. In aeroplanes, they were allowed to smoke at the rear. Once, I was seated at the front of a plane going to Istanbul when the rest of my co-passengers in that row lit up. I complained, but was sternly informed by the hostess that as there were more of them than me I should be the one to move. She didn't reckon on me, though. Six puffing men were finally sent to the back of the class. But I digress. Turks like a between-course cigarette, indeed, they like a between-mouthful cigarette. I have been fascinated by women (usually women, do they think it is less fattening?) taking a mouthful of mezze, a slurp of wine, then lighting up one of those ultra-thin long cigarettes, chatting, flicking ash and not touching another morsel for maybe 20 minutes, meanwhile I have consumed my mezze, scraped the last piece of fish from the bones, had my fruit and asked for the bill.

My favourite harbour-side restaurants are laid side by side. I try to be even-handed, using one for cheaper, plainer meals and another for pricier, more elaborate dishes. When I say pricier, I mean about 70 Turkish lire for a wonderful meal of two or three courses with wine. That's £7 a head*. I mean, £7! Most of the owners have become friends and it's difficult to pass by without being invited in for a glass of tea, sometimes a beer and a mezze, absolutely FOC. It can take several hours to pass down our main street, even if I have something pressing to do, nothing can get in the way of a glass of tea.

SPECIAL OCCASIONS

Wedding fare, funeral fare, circumcision fare, it's always chicken porridge, probably best avoided.

Keskek is a traditional wedding dish made mostly in Central Anatolia and the Aegean region of Turkey. Weddings in these regions can last several days, but wherever the ceremony the main criterion is the same: feed everyone well! Our village is not an exception to that rule and we have been invited on several occasions to participate in the noisy banter, the mass of plastic chairs and tables, filled with elderly aunts and grandmothers, eyeing up their main chance to sink a bowlful of this or that. The weddings I have been to in our village usually take place in the main square, although there have been some on the land of the bride's or groom's parents. Vast piles of those white plastic garden chairs and tables arrive and several cauldrons are set up over open fires under some sort of makeshift shelter. These are manned by burly women of a certain age, who boss everyone else around, but are fiercely proud of their kitchen skills and determined to offer the best food ever. Everyone is invited, passing strangers, unknown locals, all the family including distant cousins third times removed, the imam and the local tradespeople. No one is left out. At first I felt guilty pitching up without

* At time of writing.

a present and drinking and eating at an almost complete stranger's table, but you are made to feel so welcome it really would be rude to refuse. Our local café owner's son got married two years ago and there were 3000 guests. Yes, that isn't a typo!

Quite often the bride will be taken to her new home on the back of a camel loaded with all her trousseau, surrounded by family and friends banging drums and blowing horns. The camel is festooned with ribbons and a woven headdress and saddle fringed and baubled with brightly coloured wool and embroidered cloth. These camels used to be owned by the families, but now more often than not they are hired for the occasion.

Before the ceremony, it is typical that first the groom's parents or the elderly members of his family visit bride's parents to get to know each other. Traditionally they should bring a gift of some sort of confection, such as chocolate or *Lokum* (Turkish Delight). After welcoming them, the girl makes Turkish coffee and serves it to the guests. Parents introduce themselves and then the boy's parents state 'the reason for their visit'. They say that their son wants to marry the daughter of the family and ask if they give permission to this marriage or not. The girl's family wants some time to think about it and the boy's family leave. In some regions, this event repeats a few times. Even if the girl and boy already have a relationship, this is a strict tradition before marriage – a Turkish girl should have the permission of her parents to get married.

The wedding comes in two stages: the betrothal and the actual ceremony. These events occur within two days and I have been told that once the betrothal has been celebrated, there is NO turning back! At the betrothal the girl wears a red dress and veil and the *Imam* holds his hands over both their heads whilst covered by this cloth. After which comes much macho dancing by the men and a lot of fluttering by the women. The dancing comprises a great deal of stamping, arm linking and swooping downwards so the knee touches the ground. Stirring stuff indeed. During the civil ceremony the girl wears what is known as a 'meringue' and my goodness it is just like one. Wide and white with every embellishment you could order.

They always look stunning in a wildly over the top way. No matter how lowly the village, the rest of the women at this ceremony do their very best, teetering on outrageously vertiginous shoes, with flouncing feather concoctions on their heads, they really throw themselves into it. The older women usually don't bother much and come in the usual long dark floral skirt and tightly wound headscarf. They sit in shaded hunched groups checking out everyone else, and get very well served by the youths of the family, who are ordered to bring them copious amounts of the celebration porridge at very regular intervals.

Should you want to risk it, the recipe for *Keskek* is on page 44. To me, and frankly almost all of my friends, it is an acquired taste and best avoided!

You may think differently.

One small anecdote regarding weddings: I was due to have some friends over to stay for a week or so at The Old Stone House. As we were arriving from the UK on the same day but via different airports, they got to the house several hours before us. Being of an adventurous disposition, they decided to potter out to find a bar and get themselves a beer. Along the road they spotted a bar with people drinking and sitting around at the usual plastic tables. The husband called the waiter over and asked him in English for a drink.

'Certainly', he replied, 'what would you like?'

'Well, two beers would be nice,' replied the husband.

'OK', the man said and rushed off.

As they settled down at their table they noticed that he was haring across the road to the local supermarket; puzzled, they followed his route, he then returned with two cans of Efes beer, nice and cold. 'Oh dear', said the wife, 'have you run out of beer?'

'No, this is my brother's wedding party and we don't drink alcohol at this time,' he said. Crestfallen, my friends apologised profusely and made to leave. 'NO NO NO!' he cried, 'please drink your beer, it is our pleasure and do come tomorrow at this spot because then it is the party and we will be serving everyone alcoholic drinks.' Now, that is hosting at its best.

Lokma

A sort of deep-fried tiny doughnut steeped in sugar syrup. Fried *lokma*, given away on the anniversary of a death, or *Mevlit*. These sweet little doughnuts are the epitome of the maxim 'a moment on the lips a lifetime on the hips', and there is plenty of underscoring of that point amongst our ladies of the village. Who can blame anyone for indulging in these gooey, fatty confections? Quite often you will come across a *Mevlit* or anniversary of a death. There are rules regarding funerals and remembrance, anniversaries are celebrated rather like weddings, Yearly, tri-yearly and more. During this period it is common practice to cook or have caterers in to provide food for the family, friends or anyone else who should be passing by, even sometimes spilling out on to the streets. *Lokma* is often offered as it is not too costly to produce and you can hire a street cart for the occasion, whose proprietor will cook, and serve the *lokma* in paper cones. Easy, quick and relatively sticky-finger free.

The *Mevlits* at home usually take place in the afternoons and are followed by a big meal. It is a tradition to serve *Akide Sekeri* (Akide Candy) and *Lokum* (Turkish Delight) in paper cones after the *Mevlits* take place. It is considered very rude to refuse this offer, therefore it is advisable to take it by saying *'Allah kabul etsin'* ('May the God accept'). Unfortunately, I had no idea about this affront and did not attend my neighbour's *Mevlit*. I thought she was just being polite and that the occasion was meant to be a family gathering. Luckily for me, she was a very generous soul and insisted that I take a large plate of food the following morning. This is when I understood the slight. After that I attended every wake and *Mevlit* in the village. So, whether *Mevlit*, weddings or funerals, you will see me there, stuffing my face. Not such a bad tradition; sort of life-affirming and very sociable.

RAMADAN

Ramadan Festival after a whole month of fasting and the Festival of Sacrifice are two of the oldest Islamic festivals in Turkey.

Ramadan is a time for visiting relatives and paying one's respects to the elders. People give away sweets, coffee and desserts during the festival and children watch free Turkish shadow plays.

The main characteristics of the Ramadan Festival are that neighbours, relatives and friends pay visits and go to see each other. Young people kiss their parents' hands and receive best wishes and blessings from them. It is a tradition to give money or little gifts to those children who kiss one's hands, it's a sort of Christmas celebration when families want to be together to celebrate.

The symbols of the Ramadan Festival

- A new moon
- Sweets and traditional desserts
- Delicious traditional foods
- A cup of Turkish tea or coffee
- Best wishes and blessings
- Visiting relatives and neighbours
- *Karagoz* and *Hacivat* shadow plays which are flat puppets hand worked by sticks behind a sheet lit by a traditional oil lamp.

On my very first visit to The Old Stone House in order to complete the paperwork for its purchase I was all alone and had never slept there before. Surprisingly, I was not at all fazed by this as I considered that the house had a warm and friendly feel to it. I was concerned, however, to have my sleep interrupted by the smell of smoke. I leapt out of bed like a wild woman. How could I have been so stupid? I must have set fire to our just-bought house and it was about to be burnt to the ground! I rushed into the kitchen, nothing bad going on there, so then prowled around the house, like some two-legged hound taking sniffs at every turn and corner. It wasn't until I went into the garden that I realised the smoke and smell were coming from a garden just adjacent to ours. It turned out that it was just before sunrise during the fasting period of Ramadan, so my neighbour had lit a small bonfire in the garden in order to cook up some last-minute cauldron of hearty fare to see them through until sunset. What a relief!

KURBANLIK

The Festival of Sacrifice is a four-day religious event. Traditions include sacrificing an animal in a special ritual, visiting relatives and helping the poor.

Traditionally, on the first day of the Festival of Sacrifice, men of each family go to a mosque for a special morning prayer. Then the sacrifice ritual begins. Families share about two thirds of the animal's meat with relatives and neighbours, and they traditionally give about one third to the poor.

I am not at all keen on this as you can see herds of mournful sheep on the side of the road waiting to be bought and then slaughtered and the meat distributed. This is supposed to replicate the time when God ordered Abraham to sacrifice his son, to prove his love, but at the last moment he was allowed to kill a sheep instead. Thankfully more people are now giving money to charity instead, or just going to the butcher's shop, buying as much meat as they can and giving it away. I cannot, however, persuade Sazili that this is a good idea. I usually stay indoors for this day.

The symbols of the Festival of Sacrifice

- Sacrificial sheep
- Morning prayer in the mosque
- Delicious traditional foods
- A cup of Turkish tea or coffee
- Best wishes and blessings
- Visiting relatives and neighbours

Small aside on picnics and barbecues. These are very popular with the Turks, there are special places set aside for families to go to make and share their food. We have one such place behind our village, replete with wooden benches and tables, a *mangal* (barbecue), a Tandoor oven, and hopefully enough rubbish bins. Typically they will barbecue chicken and meat, as *köfte* or chops, simple and easy to handle outdoors. Plenty of bread and fruit naturally.

Before we move on to the proper recipe section here are some observations on Turkish life.

HEALTH AND SAFETY!

There is not a lot of H&S in Turkey, although smoking is now forbidden in public buildings and restaurants, much to my relief.

Seat belts in cars are supposed to be worn, but how often have I spotted a family driving in a positively dilapidated car with the youngest on the lap of the mother in the front seat? And sometimes on the father's whilst driving! And don't get me started on the number of people you can get on a scooter.

Lorries are often filled with workers on the open backs, rolling around as they puff their black smoke up a hill. I get nostalgic for 50's England when I spot the dustmen clinging to the back of the cart as it bowls along, and unless you are suicidal you don't ride a bike!

To be frank, the Turks are rather sniffy about H&S, especially the men, who seem to regard it as some sort of reduction of their manhood, but gradually things are improving and to my surprise and to be honest, disappointment I noticed the road leading up to our village now has two freshly painted yellow lines down its centre.

We once asked our gardener to prune our very, very, VERY high pepper tree, only to come back home to find him in brown wellington boots (ubiquitous) with a fully loaded chainsaw roaring away on the end of a stretching garden hose. He completed the task, but not before the main branch was felled, landing on the main electricity pylon and putting the village in blackout for a few hours. He mended the wires, carefully replacing them one by one. No one seemed to mind a bit.

NEVER ADMIRE ANYTHING A TURK HAS, FOR EXAMPLE, CLOTHES, JEWELRY, CHILDREN (NO I'M JOKING HERE!)

I did this once by mistake. We were at a carpet village, drinking wine and dancing. There was a wandering girl from the East, who was out and about looking for work of any sort to get money to send back to her kids, who she had left behind close to the Iraqi border. Her husband beat her, so she had ran away. She was a pretty woman and danced beautifully, once she had overcome her natural modesty. She was fascinated by us and especially me with my strangely (to her) coloured hair. In order to make her feel welcome, I chatted to her about her life, her dancing and her traditional attire. I mentioned how nice her bracelet was, a simple nickel band. She immediately took it off and gave it to me. I was horrified and tried to give it back, but the more I protested the more adamant she was. I had to keep it. I felt bad. Everyone felt bad, but it is considered insulting to return a gift once given. Several people had tears in their eyes. I still have the bracelet.

FAMILY LIFE

Turkish families are for the most part very traditional; mum stays at home and dad goes to work. Although you will notice that once retired the rural man does absolutely NOTHING but play tablet and backgammon all day. Mum does everything, and willingly. I have never seen a child, teenager or even adult, if they are at home, still without the cleanest of white shirts, crisply ironed. They are mostly well fed, well nurtured? and well behaved. They take joy in the smallest things and, although kids do want their smartphones, I have seen little children playing cars in the dirt using bits of wood as the toys. They are also hugely appreciative of education and consider it a privilege to go to school, let alone a *Lise* (a sort of A level college) or university.

Turks are generous to a fault and will always share what they have with anyone. Indeed, my old builder tells me that in his village they set aside a house with rooms made up with comfortable beds and cupboards filled with food in case a stranger in need should wander through. Can't see that happening in Walton-on-Thames*.

Food is important to the Turkish people and they take great pride in presenting me with wonderful dishes concocted from the most humble ingredients. As I said before, freshness and quality of ingredients is key, along with centuries of passing down recipes from many cultures and across the generations.

SWEETIES

One cannot possibly go to Turkey and not try *Baklava*, Turkish delight or *pekniz* sweeties.

Lokum

The story of the creation of Turkish Delight (*lokum*) begins in the late 1700s. Ali Muhiddin Hacı Bekir had come to the imperial capital of Istanbul from the Anatolian mountain town of Kastamonu in the late 1700s to cook for the *emperor.* He had been

* Apologies to residents of Walton-on-Thames.

ordered to prepare a soft confection for the poor Emperor's teeth were tired of the hard sweets of tradition. After much thought he arrived at the answer. *Rahat lokum* ('comfortable morsel'), nowadays called simply *lokum,* or Turkish Delight, was an instant hit, especially at the palace. Ali Muhiddin became a celebrity overnight as what seemed like the entire population of Istanbul traipsed down the hill from Topkapı Palace to Eminönü on the Golden Horn to buy boxes of Comfortable Morsels to thrill the jaded palates of Ottoman potentates.

I have never tried to make it myself, but I make sure I get mine from only the best suppliers. Don't be fooled by the marshmallow type sponges covered in coconut flakes and set into boxes with pictures of harems or curly toed sandals. NO! Plain simple, straightforward, sticky, nutty and a light caramel in colour. SO yummy. You cannot be satisfied with just the one. Since writing this, I have come across pomegranate *lokum*, so I revise my opinion to include this.

Apart from the tiny shop in the carpet village up near Mumcular, where I get my supplies, there is only one place that sticks in my memory – an old-fashioned sweetie shop in Ankara, where only the best *lokum* is sold. It was a fascinating place, rather like an old-fashioned draper's emporium, the whole back wall lined with dark wood drawers, a glass-fronted counter surmounted with one single sweep of marble to the front separating? the white-coated assistants and the customers and upon which are displayed samples of the confectionery. We were allowed, no, encouraged to taste as many as we could without bursting or running into a diabetic coma. Oh, my days, about one hundred different flavours – orange, rose, hazelnut, pistachio, mandarin, strawberry, caramel, pomegranate and, when the choice was settled, all laid out in tissue-lined boxes wrapped in gloriously over the top ribbon and presented to me with beaming smiles as if it were a Hollywood Oscar. Dusting the sweet white powder from my mouth, I accepted my prize and departed.

Cezerye (carrot sweets)

A speciality from Mersin region in southern Turkey, *cezerye* is a delicious confectionery made of carrots, nuts and sugar, coated with desiccated coconut flakes. They are utterly delicious, healthy and also known to be an aphrodisiac. Mind you, I can't vouch for that!

Tahini *Helva* or 'bomb' *Halvah* (or halva)

A sesame snack, this is delicious and can be flavoured with chocolate, coffee, vanilla, rosewater or orange oil. You can add pistachios, almonds, hazelnuts or black sesame seeds for more crunch and flavour.

Often you will be offered 'bomb' at the end of a meal in a restaurant, this is usually merely Tahini *helva*, wrapped in foil and cooked in the embers of the open fire. Very simply delicious. There are the types you can buy in the supermarket, in 500g packs, which are hard and crispy or the softer home cooked version, which although they share the same name are completely different.

Semolina *Helva*

'Helva' really means sweetmeat, so a general term. This is what sometimes arrives on my dining room table from a neighbour by way of welcome. Sazili's wife makes excellent helva. Why he is so wiry beats me. See page 149.

Pekmez

Pekmez, this versatile and natural grape molasses has been a part of Anatolian culture for centuries. It is not only a staple part of the Turkish breakfast, but also a health remedy that increases the body's blood content and is rich in vitamins, minerals and antioxidants.

It is a molasses-type substance derived from pressed grape juice, mixed with a special sandy earth and boiled and strained and boiled again until it reduces right down to a thick dark red syrup. Traditionally, no sugar or additives are added, making it a natural sweetener. It is commonly made from grapes, but can also be made from different fruits, including mulberries, plums, apples, pears, pomegranates and most recently, carob.

The thick, sweet syrup is a staple item on every Turkish breakfast table. The delicious extract is either served alone, or more commonly poured into a dish with tahini and then swirled to create a marbled effect. Eaten with fresh bread it a real treat.

Pekmez can also be enjoyed in forms other than syrup. It is commonly used in desserts and tastes great as a substitute for sugar in baking.

Grape juice jellies stuffed with walnuts

My children called these long thin lumpy delights 'old man's willy.' Sorry, but that's how it is.

In Turkish it is called *pestil cevizli sucuk*, literally 'walnut sausage' because of its shape. It is made rather like candles by stringing walnut pieces together and dipping into the syrup until thoroughly coated and then dried.

***Nar* or pomegranate molasses**

Nar Eksisi or Nar *Eskili* (not so prized, but cheaper!) pomegranate molasses, is produced by boiling down pomegranate juice, in a similar fashion to Pekmez, but this time with added sugar, resulting in a thick, rich, deep red and fully flavoured liquid. Turkish pomegranate syrup is a remarkably versatile product similar to, but so much better than, balsamic. It can be used simply as a syrup for desserts, especially those containing strawberries, but it is absolutely outstanding as a dressing for tomato or carrot salad.

GOKCEBEL AND OTHER MARKETS

In spite of my best intentions and after heaving kilos of fruit and veg back from the main market in Yalikavak, I still run out of things. I also prefer to use the freshest of ingredients so usually go out again mid-week to our own village market to get new supplies. Our painters often come with me for the experience.

Tuesday mornings until 1.00 p.m. is our village market day. We like to take our groups to make sketches of the great commercial activity there; actually two old ladies and a blanket covered with home-grown produce and one stallholder! However, in high summer we sometimes get an extra table or two with crocheted woolly hats and vast Turkish bloomers on display.

The stallholder takes great pride in showing how enormously large these pantaloons can expand to become, stretching them sideways to the limit while at the same time eying up our backsides with a practised gaze. We try not to be too insulted, a trader has to be a pragmatist.

I can combine my fruit and veg shopping with showing the painters good sites for sitting and making sketches, but it has to be said that mostly they too are waylaid by the excitement of it all and end up buying those vast bloomers and the head scarves. I often wonder if they ever wear them.

The prodding and the squeezing, not always fruit and vegetables, continues for a couple of hours, all under the undisputed paternal gaze of Ishmael the shopkeeper, who, arms behind his back, surveys who is buying what, who is selling what and who is the one with guests or relatives to feed, who is too late to get the firm tomatoes (a heinous crime hereabouts) and who just doesn't turn up at all.

All this excitement is to be reviewed later whilst serving bread inside his dark and cool shop. I will reveal more about his shop – the ONLY shop – later.

This is a day the villagers look forward to, time to natter and exchange views, time to discuss who has got married or engaged, whose grandchild has achieved scholastic greatness, what is the state of health of their family cow or donkey, recent deaths, animal or human, and all the latest gossip on the 'bad' people of the village. (I know of one lady of easy virtue who was sadly drummed out of the village only recently, more of that later too.)

Surprisingly, in this day and age, there are still folk in Gokcebel who do not travel outside the village, the thought of going as far as Bodrum City, about 20 minutes away is already adventurous in the extreme, but further, Milas or even Mugla? NO way!

If you do want to push the envelope and have a small adventure, Bodrum town is not far away in kms, but centuries away in its character .

GETTING OUT AND ABOUT IN BODRUM

Getting around is a real experience here in Bodrum. We organise our own transport for our groups, from small people carriers to coaches, all depending on the size of the group attending our holidays.

This makes our guests' lives far more comfortable and worry-free: gazing out of the window at the passing views of forests, high wooded hills and beautiful coastline require all your attention. However, for a real taste of authentic life we reckon on the Dolmus (pronounced DOLMOOSH) for a true adventure.

These small crowded minibuses are frequent, quick and very efficient and stop anywhere and everywhere en route, so long as you have got the hang of hailing one.

The word *dolmus* comes from *dolu*, meaning 'full', the bus will wait until it is completely full before embarking on its journey and it certainly can get crowded! Not everyone will get a seat, but you will be fine – the Turks are very polite and well-mannered, so you may often be given a seat if you are a foreigner, or a woman, or over 40, or all three as in my case!

We probably take at least one *dolmus* trip during the painting holidays. Reaching Bodrum Town takes 20-25 minutes and from our village it is a scenic route, going over the mountain that separates Bodrum from Yalikavak, past the old windmills and through the Ortakent valley.

Once within the city outskirts, the stops will be more frequent and more people will squeeze in: returning from Bodrum on market day can be a real sardine-tin journey as you will be sharing with countless bulging bags, sacks and baskets crammed full of produce.

It is probably best, if you don't want this experience, to take an earlier bus, or take time out in one of the many bars or cafes on the waterfront, then travel back after the rush hour. Taxis are expensive on long journeys, yet local ones are surprisingly reasonable; bright yellow like in the USA and saloon cars or jolly squat van-like vehicles, they can take up to five people.

I have been known to get eight into a taxi going to the driver's fiancee's mother's restaurant (don't ask, but the food was worth the bruises). Other modes of transport used frequently in our area are donkeys, tractors, and occasionally when celebrating, camels. There are few trains in Turkey and none where we live.

If walking, which is the predominant mode of transport around our way, watch out for the elegant ladies from Ankara and Istanbul who drive large 4x4s, smoke endless cigarettes whilst constantly talking on their mobiles, are too small to see over the steering wheel and in consequence are some of the worst drivers I have ever encountered.

STREET FOOD

Whilst we are still wandering the streets of Bodrum, perhaps we should investigate Turkish street food, which offers so many varieties and tastes according to the seasons and the location. Street food is very popular and one should never be afraid to try it as the turnover will be quick and thus everything will be fresh on the day, if not the hour!

In Bodrum during the summer you can find barrows loaded with green-lipped mussels stuffed with saffron rice, served with fresh lemon wedges, freshly roasted corn on the cob and the ubiquitous *Simit*, slung like a Sultana's necklaces around a slender pole perched on the vendor's shoulder. Sometimes I wonder why I bother to cook at all, when all you have to do is pop out to the street and grab something fresh, cheap and utterly delicious from the friendly vendor of your choice. Here are some of the other delicacies of the open road.

Mussels/*Midiye*
Green-lipped mussels in little glass-sided trolleys, stuffed or not, but usually stuffed with saffron rice, a Turk does not believe in half measures when it comes to food. We sometimes are a little too concerned about health and safety and miss out on these treats so go on, be brave, we've never been hurt yet. SO yummy.

Simit
In Istanbul you will see droves of men with poles looped with *simits* hawking their wares. I was fascinated when I first saw them, freshly made and still warm is the best way to eat these treats, they are something between a bagel and a crusty roll. Not so dense as a bagel, they are twisted before being formed into a circle then dipped in molasses and then sesame seeds and baked with no prior boiling. *Simits* vary in size, density and colour all depending on the baker. For instance, the *simits* from our local shop are thinner and harder than the ones bought at my favourite bakers in Yalikavak; these are softer, and crisper on the outside. Do not be tempted to save your *simit* from breakfast for the afternoon, or heaven forfend the following day, they will be dry husks.

Ice cream/*dondurma*
Dondurma typically includes the ingredients milk, sugar, *salep*, and *mastic*. It is believed to originate from the city and region of Maras and hence also known as Maras Ice Cream. *Salep* is a thickening agent, a flour made from the root of a type of orchid. *Mastic* is the resin of a type of shrub, related to the pistachio tree, with a piney scent and flavour (it's this that's at the heart of mastika liqueur). These give the *dondurma* its stretchiness and oddly seem to slow down the melting process, great for those summer days by the beach. It is often served by a man in full Ottoman costume brandishing two sticks, which he uses rather like one of those bobbin on a string toys stretched between his open arms. He bangs a bell, when a sale has been made and he has completed his task. We have a seller in Yalikavak who performs the complete theatre, very entertaining.

Pide
A Turkish flatbread smothered in ground meat, with cheese. Originally from the Black Sea region, you can find '*pide* houses' everywhere in Turkey. *Pide* dough is kneaded then rolled out and shaped with the fingers to make a long oval or round shape. Various toppings such as cheese, ground beef, spinach and vegetables are spread over the top, then the sides are brought up to half-cover the filling and the ends are pinched closed. You can choose from many different meat or cheese fillings and even have an egg baked on top. I have a terrible story about *Pide* from one of my painting holidays:

Sometimes a girl needs a break and when the going gets tough the tough get a *takeaway*.

And so it came to pass, I decided to get *Pide* in for dinner one evening. I had it down on my menu in advance and was exultant that I would be able to join everyone for cocktails on the terrace, instead of being hunched over my stove. The reasons were twofold, 1. I was a bit tired and 2. it was a cultural experience not to be missed as *Pide* is excellent fare. I had arranged the cooking and delivery of the *Pide* with military precision several days prior to the allotted evening. A *lokanta* a little way down the road from us sold excellent food, both '*Alo paket*' (takeaway) and in-house. I had ordered ten *Pide of* mixed flavours, cheese and meat, to be collected at 8 p.m. A few minutes' drive, I thought and Bob's your uncle, instant dinner. Our guests were settled on their first G and Ts and I set off down the road. I arrived in front of the *lokanta*, carefully reversing up to the doors so I could load straight into the boot. I went in, the place was empty. 'Is my *Pide* ready?' I enquired. The lonely waiter rose from his newspaper and looked blank. 'My *Pide*', I repeated.

'Sorry, the chef has gone to Bodrum,' he said. I stood open-jawed in disbelief.

'But what about the *Pide* I ordered?' He slumped back into his original position.

'I don't know about that,' he said, 'he will be back in an hour or so, then he can make it.'Turks have no conception of time management.

My heart sank through the floor, I thought of the guests oblivious of their impending hunger at home.

'Anywhere else I can go?'

'Gundogan?', the waiter proffered, '...maybe'.

I turned on my heel and headed back home. Now I have not mentioned that we had one very particular guest from America, who did not like to be kept waiting, she would be in her seat at the table, knife and fork clutched in her hands bang on 8pm. 'Oh, Lord, I prayed, 'let Edna be in a good mood.'

'Psst!', I hissed at my helper back on the terrace, 'pour them another gin and keep them happy , I have to go to Gundogan.'

'What, what? I don't understand,' whispered the helpmate.

'Is anything the matter?' quizzed Edna with narrowing eyes. 'Is the *Pide* ready?' I avoided her gaze.

'Just keep them happy, I have to go to Gundogan.'

And so I did, ten minutes of gear crashing and wheel screeching and I was in Gundogan, looking for this supposed saviour of my sanity. I circled Gundogan then tried a few side streets, PIDE SALONU burst upon my eyes in bright neon. At last. 'Quick, I need ten *pides* with salad and pickles please, five cheese, five meat.' The man at the counter was laughing at my agitated state, rolling his eyes at his mates who appeared to have nothing better to do. 'That will be 20 minutes.' OH, how I cursed the Turkish zeal for freshness that evening. Twenty minutes?! What to do? I paid up and darted back to the car, charged home to check on the incumbents, probably quite wobbly with gin by now. Edna was at the table, napkin tucked in, her fingers tapping the surface. Inwardly groaning, I achieved a semblance of brightness. 'Not long, now everyone, so sorry for the delay, If you would all sit down and make a start on the mezzes and wine I will be right with you.'

But I wasn't. Oh no.

I returned to the car and rubber burned back to Gundogan to collect my prize. Could I find the Pide Salonu? NO. I must have circled Gundogan several times, delving in and out of what I thought was the side street where it was hiding. I cried to myself, I hit the steering wheel, I groaned and I pleaded with the deity to help me, then, at last, I saw it on the corner. Abandoned the car and rushed in.

It was about 9.30 p.m. when I returned to the drunken rabble that were my guests, who had, not unreasonably turned on me, whipped up to this level of self righteousness by Edna. I had lost all vestige of decorum by that time and flung the polystyrene boxes to each and all. No plate, no niceties. The lukewarm *Pide* was devoured along with its rather soggy salad. It still tasted good, but I will never, ever do that again. Back to my hunched-over-the-stove stance every night; far safer.

Kokorec

Grilled intestines, better known as '*kokoreç*,' are among the most popular street foods in Turkish cuisine. Sheep intestines are thoroughly cleaned then wrapped around a mixture of offal and spices and grilled until crispy. The grilled rolls are then either sliced and served sprinkled with oregano or chopped up together with tomatoes, parsley and spices and served inside flour tortilla-like flat bread. When I first came to Ankara my husband and his Turkish friends insisted that I try *Kokoreç*. I had no idea then what it was but they assured me, with wide eyes and smiles, it was delicious and a delicacy. So I was taken to a tiny and extremely humble stall on the side of a busy Ankara Street where my treat was delivered. It was, I have to say, perfectly tasty and certainly I could have managed more. They then amidst a great deal of mirth told me what it was. Oh, I was not at all happy about it, I am not sure whether it was the subterfuge, the worry about stuffing places where erstwhile something rather more unpleasant lurked, or whether it was that I, in fact, rather enjoyed it that concerned me the most. I spent the rest of the afternoon worrying about contracting some terrible food poisoning, despite assurances that the intestines were sparklingly clean. I was, dear reader, fine.

Dürüm

A durum is a wrap that is usually filled with typical doner kebab ingredients. The wrap is made from lavash or yufka a flatbread made with flour, water, olive oil and yogurt. Kumpir stuffed, baked potato, usually huge, filled to the gunnels with any permutation and condiment. Best from a stone or wood oven.

Mısır

Freshly boiled or grilled corn on the cob. This popular snack is almost exclusively sold during the summer months by the real street sellers with their push-cars.

Kestane

Due to the lack of corn in winter, the street vendors mentioned above shift to roasted chestnuts in winter time.

Balık ekmek
Literally translated as 'fish bread'. And that's basically what it is — fish, grilled or fried in front of your eyes and stuffed inside a large piece of bread. Fans of this fast-food can have a blast in Eminönü, on the shore next to the Galata Bridge, where it is usually made with mackerel caught before your eyes. I could never get my head around why the open fires set in the middle of the boats selling this sandwich didn't burn a hole in the bottom and sink the cooks!

Kebab in Turkish refers to any type of meat or poultry that is cooked over a coal fire. One of the most common and delicious street foods is *'Döner Kebabı'*, which means 'turning kebab'. This is because, in case you did not know it, the large spit on which the meat and spice mixture is pressed, turns around vertically in front of a charcoal fire. As the surface of the meat gets brown and crunchy, the chef shaves off very thin strips with a giant knife. Most people know it stuffed inside the thin pockets of pitta bread, but I just love it thrust inside a large chunk of split Turkish bread with salad and pickles.

Lahmacun
Comes from the Southeast, and is made with leavened dough rolled out in a paper-thin, round shape. A thin layer of minced lamb or beef, onions, garlic, tomatoes and chopped parsley is spread over the top before it is cooked on a wooden slab in the oven. They are presented flat, but eaten rolled with a squeeze of lemon and a handful of salad and onion inside. I serve *Lahmacun* for lunch during our art courses, and it is easy, quick and very tasty, somehow all the nicer when eaten in your hands, although sometimes essence of oil paint can get in the way of your enjoyment.

Lokma See page 148.

Sahlep
A comforting hot drink with Cinnamon and Pistachio Nuts. Street food is available in the winter months too: roasted chestnuts, spicy doughnuts and my favourite comfort drink, *Sahlep*. In Istanbul this drink had its own special marble kiosk, which I gather is the traditional place to serve this warming drink. Marble and brass and very grand indeed. If you want your *sahlep* out of the way of marble kiosks, the vendor may bring it to you, via a cart surmounted by a grand brass urn or samovar.

Fresh orange juice can also be bought from street kiosks, not necessarily street food per se, but you take it and sit wherever you can, a massive glass of cold freshly squeezed orange juice, thick and deep in colour, the most refreshing drink you can buy on the street, apart from Ayran.

Ayran
Ayran is the drink of the people! Yogurt, iced water and salt. They are right, it is perfect for the hot weather when you need to cool down and replace your body's salts. This too

can be bought off a cart ladelled out from an urn, but far more likely now, it is sold in foil-top cartons. Ready to go.

TOILET PAPER RATIONING AND MY UNFORTUNATE DESCENT INTO THE BITEZ LATRINES

Street food is delicious we know, but sometimes it's good to get out and sit down to eat at one of the many excellent restaurants and cafes in our immediate location. They serve wonderful food, the service is second to none and you are not regarded as an irritant even if you stay long hours over just a mezze or a glass of beer and some olives. In fact it is not even considered a sin to bring your own food! Well, not everywhere, but I was really surprised and not a little embarrassed when my Turkish pal brought out a packet of bread rolls and *simit* whilst we were drinking the ubiquitous glass of tea at the council-run café on the marina in Bodrum. I raised a wary eyebrow on spotting the packet of floury baked goods. My companion was nonchalant to say the least, 'want some?', he enquired. I became rather English at this point and presented him with the supposition that the proprietor may prefer to serve their own home-grown pastries. 'Nah, it's fine.' he said. And indeed it was.

When I first came to Turkey over 25 years ago, now, the food was as it is now, delicious, and plenty of it, the service was efficient and very friendly, but oh, dearie me, the loos! If indeed there were any, they were grim, smelly (the heat didn't help), and only a choice of the 'crouch and hover'* variety. To cap it all, even in the fairly salubrious restaurants should you wish to use the facilities, you had to explain your destination and amount of loo paper you considered appropriate… then, if this was agreed you were handed out the one, or maybe two sheets deemed satisfactory and off you slunk. This whole act performed in front of an entire audience of diners. In fairness, they didn't take much notice, but I was mortified.

On one horrendous occasion, forever imprinted on my mind, I had to make use of a very rudimentary and particularly odoriferous cubicle by the side of a beach bar in Gumbet. I must hold my hand up. I had consumed a couple of Margeritas, and I slipped. Right in! The screams could be heard in the Greek Islands, and after being helped out of this particular hole – not easy with elasticated swimming costume around your knees, I had to be thoroughly hosed down by my comrades, who unkindly were doubled up with laughter. As I say, thank goodness for progress, that's one piece of Ottoman culture I prefer to eschew.

OPEN ALL HOURS AT TESCO *(music thrown in)*

You may remember me mentioning that I buy a lot of my olive oil and honey from the carpet village up in the hills, about a 40 minute drive away. We go up there with our painters to show them the old style of arable farming life. I always tell my painters that

* I should also point out at this juncture that I was later to learn that the Turks were in fact the first to use the flushing loo, still a croucher though.

Comlekci Koy (pronounced Chemlekchi koi) is a village whose way of life has changed little for decades, maybe hundreds of years. Although now they use cars and tractors, not donkeys. Actually there are some donkeys, but rather old ones. In truth, the tractors and cars are pretty old too, I get a good laugh out of watching my male painters getting all excited over a Ferguson Tractor, looking like something out of an Old Macdonald illustration, taking photos and stroking its rusting wheel arches as if discovering a long lost child.

Anyway I digress. This village, really a pretty humble affair, was and still is a carpet-weaving village, although nowadays the art is fast dying out and very few women are making these carpets any more. Mostly these carpets are now woven for family use, trousseaus, wedding gifts, that sort of thing, but some are still made for sale and distributed via a cooperative in the village; some too are taken to the local surrounding *pazars*. This cooperative is run by the village mayor, he has held this position now for about 20 years, I suspect because no one else wants the job, Hyati is his name and a more generous man you could not wish to meet, nor a heavier drinker! He could drink Raki for Turkey. It never seems to affect him badly at all, no one would guess he had had a few, apart from the one occasion when he fell from his roof terrace and broke his arm. He vowed to lay off the Raki after that incident, but soon drifted back. Mind you, I don't think his generosity is reliant on his drinking, he remains kind and thoughtful, albeit less cheerful when stone cold sober, which is about 20% of the time.

As well as the carpet cooperative, the milk cooperative and the honey and oil cooperative, the village also grows vegetables and fruit as well as farming sheep. The wool, of course, is used to weave the carpets. Hyati owns vast tracts of olive groves too, he also runs the only local shop,

The shop is something like the one on tv's *Open All Hours*: it sells absolutely everything! I mean everything. Pots and pans, Turkish Delight, brown wellingtons, brushes, farming equipment, wine, beer, bread, oddly ornate teapots, key fobs, plastic plates, tangerines, dates, and all manner of strange things on the topmost shelf covered in a fine film of dust, I doubt he himself knows exactly what he's got. The last time I went he chased me down the street brandishing an electric kettle, and despite my protestations, forced it on me to take home. This I added to the honey, eggs, wine, olive oil and wellingtons (always useful) he had already insisted on my taking. It's a struggle with me pressing him to take my money and him refusing. I end up paying for some stuff I never wanted at all, and never giving a penny for the stuff I did. Hey ho.

Last year Hyati proclaimed that he would like to offer my painters a fun night in his new roof bar. He had worked hard on it and was very proud of it. He would give us a barbecue and we would dance to music by one of his ancient musician pals. It would be a treat.

He proudly ushered me up a flight of metal stairs to the roof of his shop. And there it was, a vast square of tiled floor, still with the numbers scrawled in the corners, quite obviously 'left over' from a hotel, with what looked like a telegraph pole cemented in the middle with a small shelf nailed to it! *Saturday Night Fever* it was not. With much trepidation I took our valiant group the following week, he had spread beautifully coloured carpets over the tiles, with plenty of lolling cushions, on the barbecue was sizzling chicken, lamb, vast salads lay glistening green in washing up bowls liberated from his shop, bottles of wine and Raki were lined up on that shelf, his friend with the mandolin* was crooning ancient folk songs and a few hangers-on were dancing. We had the best time ever. It is now a permanent fixture in our programme.

* surprisingly an exact Tony Bennett lookalike.

THE RECIPES

Every painting week starts on a Sunday night and I try to begin with a bang, something that, although more buffet style, takes longer to prepare because at this point of the holiday I have had that oh so important ingredient, time.

I should also mention at this point that thanks to the loan of freezer space by my trusty cohort, Sandra, and a lucky Turkish 'Gumtree' purchase of a small under-the-counter freezer, I have been able to plan way ahead and freeze up my basic components such as minced meat (*kyima*) chicken, lamb and beef cuts, sauces and pastries, and this has been a godsend. Most of the meals cannot be frozen, unfortunately, but at least I can make them faster with this added help.

All breakfasts are a variation on a theme: freshly baked pastries, brioches and breads, yoghurt, fruit, jams and non-Turkish muesli. Sometimes I ring the changes with boiled eggs or *sucuk* (sausage), but I prefer to have the big blow-out breakfasts at the weekends as you need at least two hours to consume this feast.

I will point out at this juncture my golden rules for the tastiest food and should things not turn out quite as expected, how to redeem a supposed failure.

LEMONS! OLIVE OIL!

This works every time, Just that little push with some extra lemon juice, zest or both can lift a plain dish to nectar. Lemon juice in the lentil soup, zest pulverised into the hummus and I have never spoiled a dish by adding too much olive oil. Vine leaves, drenched in further olive oil taste even better, a slurp of olive oil and sumac on to *Baba Ganus* or hummus, extra heat and spice in those meatballs. Job done.

Oh, and have you tried using the oil from your fabulous jar of black olives in a salad dressing? Superb. Although in my opinion Turkish food relies on the freshness of its vegetables rather than additives to produce the delicious flavours, sometimes in sauces and stews the layering of flavours adds a depth to the taste. I experiment with herbs, spices and wines to give this depth. A dash of extra spice: *Pul Biber*, cumin or cinnamon. Some sugar, not much, can lift a tomato dish and combats the acidity. Not much mind you. The Turks are a bit profligate with both salt and sugar. So take it easy.

I am also not a fan of waste, so I plan my meals so that any leftovers can be re-used in another meal the following day: cooked lentils can be added to rice pilafs and roasted veg added to chick peas to make a yummy dip. If I have to separate eggs I make sure that there is an alternative use for whichever, white or yolk is not required. Custard one day, pavlova the next. That sort of thing. Anyway that's where individual ideas can spring in and save a fortune and be good for the planet. Anything else can be given to the chickens!

Some of the recipes will have variations on a theme, either from necessity (ingredients unavailable) or taste, or just for the heck of it!
I emphasise that this deviation from the recipe is not a problem and I urge anyone reading this book to become more adventurous and even anarchic. You will get to understand the flavours of a region and then you can make everything your own.

TURKISH BREAKFAST (*koy khavalti*)

Koy khavalti or village breakfast is the highlight of the week. In our village during the spring and summer months all the 'bigwig' Istanbulites and Ankara folk drive or fly down for the weekends or stay in their well-situated summer houses along the coast. All of them will be partaking of *Koy Khavalti* on Saturday or Sunday. This is a big family event. Rather like our Sunday lunches of years gone by.

It is not really breakfast at all, but rather a brunch. You can sit down any time between 9.30 and 1.30pm and be prepared to stay for two or even three hours, especially if you are Turkish and in a group of friends. I have never had a bad one. The price is on average about £6*.

The meal goes something like this, although obviously there are many variants depending on which place you attend.

First of all comes the tea, a vast *demlek* or double kettle of searingly hot tea, glasses and sugar, no milk, obviously.

Then the fresh salads arrive, pointy sweet green peppers, cucumbers, tomatoes and fresh herbs. Cheeses – several varieties – olives, green and black; stuffed vine leaves and copious amounts of fresh bread, again different varieties, *pide* and puffy bread along with crusty white and brown loaves on which you spread deep yellow butter; *Gozleme*, *boreks* – two types minimum – and then, oh joy, *menemem*, hot and fluffy alongside spicy *sucuk* (sausage).

After wading through all of this, you are offered, eggs: omelettes, or simply fried in butter and served in individual copper dishes, or just plain boiled. More tomatoes and peppers, more breads and then just as you are flagging, a selection of homemade jams and preserves: tomato, strawberry, cherry, chilli, quince, tangerine, mandarin, orange, lemon and drippy, gooey honey. Kaymak completes this serving, which resembles an exotic Cornish Cream Tea. The tea will be replenished several times as the hours roll by. Heavenly.

*The Lira exchange rate changes frequently but the prices never seem to!

There are two *Khavalti yeri* (breakfast places) in Gokcebel. There used to be only one and there was a lot of muttering when the new one arrived, but both thrive so there is no problem.

The first breakfast place is called Hava Hanim or Hava Anna, In fact I lived in the village for over three years before realising it was there. I only discovered it when I read about the famous Hava Hanim in Gokcebel in a *Sunday Times* travel article on Turkey! So I set out to look for her and discovered she was but a few minutes walk from the house.

You could not miss Hava, the owner, what a woman! Small and plump with enormous bosoms, she is larger than life. Cackling and shouting as she flings dough onto an open fire, yanking out great trays of piping hot *borek* and then manhandling these onto the tables for her customers. Everyone yells for more bread and she dumps another lump of dough to cook. There never seems to be enough and it took me quite a while before I was brave enough to shout out for my extra portion. Her husband, diminutive and twinkly-eyed, is the master of the fried egg, and dodges flapping chickens around each table scooping out buttery white and gold ovals from a spattering pan.

All this chaos is going on as the elegant, moneyed women, their grey-haired husbands, and their languid offspring smoke, talk on their phones, drink endless glasses of tea and linger for hours. I loved it!

The second place is much more ordered. The views across the home farm are beautiful. The food is exceptional and run by another husband and wife team, who have become good friends of mine. Everything is home produced, even the butter, their children are the waiters and the buzz is extraordinary as groups of up to ten people descend on their brightly clothed tables. Both experiences are *non nonpareil.*

I haven't put in nearly all of the recipes I use or have come across in my time in Turkey, and for the most part I recognise that my cooking has largely come from the Aegean area and even more narrowed down to our own part of it, Gokcebel, our village. However, I think the dishes I have presented will launch you into the 'feel' and tastes of Turkish cooking, the use of the spices, herbs, the indulgence of using lots of butter and olive oil, and the emphasis on taking pleasure in cooking and serving food to family and friends. Turkish people regard, as I certainly do, food to be a gesture of love and friendship. No matter how poor or rich the person may be, they will offer you copious amounts of food and drink at the drop of a saucepan and not take no for an answer.

Religion is threaded with food as the marker of human life, birth, marriage, death and all those celebrations in between, this is especially noticeable in our community. You will start to recognise a pattern in the recipes, whether sweet or savoury, they all sing out, 'eat me, I love you!'

From these recipes you can see that it is not always necessary to apply the strict letter of the method, or indeed the ingredients, and most certainly the flavours can be doctored to suit your taste, within the regional palette available. You can make each of the recipes your own, as indeed have I to a lesser or larger extent.

The larder is your palette and the platter your canvas. As in any of the arts, be expressive and true to yourself, nothing else matters.

That is the joy of cooking, a sprinkle of this, a blob of that, a curiosity as to how it would taste with something completely different. I have hopefully given you the basic tools and now you can stretch yourself and be creative in your own way to suit your own family, environment or pocket. The finished work of art will be an – albeit short-lived – masterpiece.

Turkish food is among the best in the world, because its roots are from all over the world. Play with it, experiment and – above all – enjoy eating your creations.

AFIYET OLSUN! (Bon appetite)

SOUPS

For obvious reasons we run our holidays in the summer months, so soups are not hugely prevalent, but our guests do like a soup and they are so easy to whizz up and freeze, who am I to deny them?

Good stock is the only base for the perfect soup. Stock cubes just won't cut it. Whenever you have time, make up a few litres in advance and freeze. You will have to adjust the flavouring once defrosted as freezing does muffle flavours. Chicken, beef and vegetable stocks are essential for any good soup.

STOCK RECIPES

To make great stock and get that depth of flavour you need bones and top notch veg.

I was born just after the war and I remember rationing. My mother was a fantastic cook and would conjure up marvellous meals from the most basic ingredients. She never wasted anything and I follow her ways even now in this throwaway age we seem to live in. Turks feel the same way, I'm glad to say.

Whenever we have a chicken or a joint I never chuck the bones. Everything goes into the large stockpot along with bay leaves, celery sticks, a couple of carrots, a large onion and peppercorns. This is the very least you can put in the pot. Add some thyme, parsley stalks, and any other vegetables you have to hand. Set on the hob covered with a litre or so of water, depending on the size of your pot, and bring to the boil. I simmer for about two hours to maximise the flavours. Then strain into a storage pot. This works well with beef or lamb bones, too. You can reduce down to intensify the flavours.

For vegetable stock, put together carrots, parsnips, celeriac and any other root vegetable, celery, a bouquet garni of fresh thyme, sage, bay leaves and parsley, a couple of large brown onions, garlic cloves, a litre of water, and if you like the idea, some non-acidic white wine. Chop all the veg, sauté in some butter to soften, add the water, wine and bouquet garni and simmer for an hour.

FERMENTED SOUP OF TARHANA

My builder gave me a jar of this that his mother had made. He explained how to make it, but I left it in the cupboard for ages. It was still fine when I finally followed his instructions. It was a treasured recipe and he tells me that his mother's is the best. Naturally. He was right.

This is a yogurt and spices dried soup, a staple soup of the Turkish culture. The Turks' answer to Cup a Soup. These are usually family recipes handed down from mother to daughter so may vary in taste and substance.

Invented by the Central Asian Turks, *Tarhana* is believed to be the first ever instant soup mix. Prepared in the summertime in anticipation of the cold winter months, this fermented and dried soup mix can last up to two to three years.

The name '*tarhana*' probably comes from the word for sourdough in Turkish, but there's another story about how it got its name. There once was a Sultan travelling the land, and he stopped at a poor peasant's house. Not having much to offer in her '*dar hane*' (narrow house) she quickly prepared some hot soup from her stash of soup mix for the Sultan. She called it '*dar hane*' soup, and over time, since the words are close in pronunciation, the soup's name evolved from '*dar hane*' to '*tarhana*'. It's also sometimes referred to as the Sultan's soup. You can decide which you prefer.

What is *Tarhana*?

This is how you make it, although once you get to the drying outside bit, I reckon those of us in Northern Europe will nip out for a tin of Baxters!

- 2 onions
- 2 tomatoes
- 2 red peppers
- Olive oil
- 2 tbsp thick strained live-yogurt
- 7g yeast
- 1 tablespoon or teaspoon of dried mint and/or parsley (optional)
- Flour as you see fit
- 1 can chickpeas (optional)

Coat the bottom of the pot with olive oil and add the onions, tomatoes and red peppers and let cook for about 20 minutes on low heat. When the vegetables are fully cooked and softened, remove them from the liquid, leave to cool.

Combine the vegetables with yogurt and yeast and gradually add the flour to make a stiff dough, your choice if you'd like to add dried mint and parsley. It's also optional at this time to add boiled chickpeas into the mix to help speed along the fermenting process. Knead the dough until smooth.

Place the dough in a plastic or glass bowl and cover with wax paper. Allow the dough to ferment at room temperature for about 7–10 days. Be sure to check on it every day, kneading the dough for 5 minutes each day. You may have to add additional flour into the dough if it becomes too watery, or separate the dough into different bowls to make it more manageable. It's the end of fermentation when the dough no longer puffs up. After 4–5 days the taste will become sour, after 7–10 days it will becomes sweet again, that's when you'll know it's done.

Break the dough into small pieces and spread on a sheet to place outside under the shade to dry for 1–2 days, occasionally turning them over. It is essential that the mix is completely dried before bringing inside.

Once dried, crumble the mixture as finely as you can, rubbing it between your hands or pressing through a sifter.

Store in cloth bags or glass jars in a cool place or refrigerator, for up to 2–3 years. Yes, that's what I said – 2-3 years!

Preparing the Soup with *Tarhana* Soup Mix

Simply mix the *tarhana* with boiling water, butter and spices and let it cook at low heat. Told you, Cup a Soup, although considerably healthier. Optional toppings include: dried mint, red pepper flakes and lemon. Obviously it's a no-brainer, get given some, buy it in the pazar then just add water!

OTTOMAN ALMOND SOUP

The old ones are always the best.

- 150g almond, blanched, grounded
- 2 tbsp butter
- 50g flour, all-purpose
- ¼ litre whole milk, warm
- 1 litre beef broth made from bones, no stock cube!
- 1 pinch nutmeg
- A drop or two of quality almond essence
- Salt
- Pepper

Garnish:

- 1 tsp butter
- 1 handful pomegranate seeds

1. Melt the butter in a medium-sized pot. Add the flour, stir and slowly pour the warm milk in while stirring constantly. The milk and flour should blend very well. You can use an egg beater. Then add the almond, beef broth, nutmeg, salt and pepper. Cook for about 20–25 minutes on low heat. Do not cover the pot with the lid!
2. Garnish. Melt 1 tbsp butter in a small pan and add 1/4 cup beef broth. When it starts bubbling, add the parsley and pour this mixture all over the soup.
3. Place the soup into the bowls, sprinkle some pomegranate seeds on the top. Serve immediately while still warm.

RED LENTIL SOUP

This soup is a staple in our house. I can knock up a *mercemek corba* in half an hour. Tasty and warming, it is almost a meal in itself. The tomatoes are optional.

- 1 mugful of red lentils (normal mug size, not the dainty sort)
- 1l water or stock
- 1 large onion
- 3 carrots finely chopped
- 1 medium-sized potato
- Fresh tomatoes or in this case 1 tin of decent tomatoes (or you can leave these out altogether to make a slightly different flavoured soup, both ways are OK)
- 2 large cloves garlic
- Handful chopped parsley

Bay leaf
Pul Biber or chilli flakes
Salt and freshly ground black pepper
Lemon juice of one lemon
Olive oil for frying
Yogurt for topping

1. Fry the onions with a little salt on a medium to low heat to soften. Add the garlic, stir for a minute or so, then stir in the lentils and carrots. Cook until coated with the oil, do not let it burn, sprinkle in the pul biber to taste. Cook another minute. Add a bay leaf, a litre of water or stock and the tinned tomatoes, bring to the boil then set to simmer for about 30 minutes. Check the taste, then add salt and pepper to suit.
2. When cooled a little whizz to a thick creamy consistency.
3. Add the lemon juice and sprinkle in the parsley.
4. Heat to serve, add lemon juice and top with yogurt before serving.

TOMATO SOUP COLD

This is delicious and so cheap and easy to make in the summer months when tomatoes are so plentiful and juicy. Much better with fresh tomatoes in my opinion. Serves 4.

1 red onion
2 spring onions
1 large or 2 small red peppers, de-seeded. I like the thinner pointy ones, they are sweeter
3 large tomatoes or 350g tomatoes
1 cucumber
4 tbsp red wine vinegar
1 tsp sugar
4 tbsp/large glug virgin olive oil
Basil (basil goes beautifully with tomato and our market now serves all varieties in massive bunches, green and purple)

1. Peel the tomatoes, use the boiling water method this time as it softens the fruit nicely and brings out the juices.
2. Chop the onion, pepper, tomatoes, cucumber, salt and olive oil, pop into a large bowl with the red wine vinegar and sugar and leave to marinade in the fridge for minimum of 4 hours, overnight if possible.
3. Whizz until smooth, strain through a colander or sieve lined with muslin or wet cloth over a bowl for another 3 or 3 hours. Serve chilled and garnished with basil leaves and crispy croutons on the side.

PERSIAN HERB AND LEGUME SOUP

Not strictly Turkish, but from the same thought process, plus I love it, so here it is. 4–6 servings, more if you add the meatballs as I do.

65g chickpeas, soaked overnight in water
30g kidney beans, soaked overnight in water
60g dried fava beans, soaked overnight in water, or 1½ cups frozen lima beans
3 onions
3 litres vegetable or chicken stock, the real stuff (make it up to 3–4 litres as you may prefer a more liquid soup. Up to you..
Lots of olive oil
5 cloves garlic, minced
1 tsp ground turmeric
30g dried lentils

Salt
1 large handful fresh mint leaves, torn into pieces
1 bunch leafy greens, such as spinach or chard, stemmed, and coarsely chopped
Small bunch fresh dill leaves, minced
Small bunch fresh coriander, chopped small
Small fresh flat-leaf parsley, chopped small
Dollops of plain strained yogurt to taste, Greek will do.

1. Usually dried noodles are added to this soup, but I prefer to serve it with spicy meatballs to make it more of a substantial dinner dish than a first course soup.
2. Dice one of the onions.
3. Heat a large pan over a medium-high heat and add a large glug of the olive oil.
4. Add the onion and sauté until lightly browned, about 5 minutes.
5. Drain and rinse the chickpeas, kidney beans and fava beans, and add them to the onion along with 4 of the minced cloves of garlic, the turmeric and lentils. Sauté for 1 minute, then add the stock and bring to a boil.
6. Boil the beans, covered, for 1 hour. Tilt the lid so the pot is partially covered and simmer, stirring occasionally, for 1½ hours. Season with salt.
7. Slice the remaining 2 onions into thin half-moons. Heat a sauté pan over high heat and add another glug of olive oil. Add the onions and fry, stirring frequently, until the onions are brown and caramelized. Add the remaining garlic and the mint and sauté for 1 minute.
8. Season with salt add the leafy greens and the fresh herbs and cook for 2 minutes.
9. Serve with meatballs (see pp 000), a large dollop of thick yogurt and a few tablespoons of the sautéed onion mixture.

CUCUMBER COLD

Serves 6. Another great summer soup, which uses up all the local ingredients perfectly.

2 large cucumbers, or if in Turkey 4–5 small cucumbers about 500g
250g of natural yogurt
1l chicken or vegetable stock
A handful of spinach
125g shelled walnuts
2–3 cloves of garlic
4 large spring onions chopped
A handful of fresh mint, chopped
A handful of dill, chopped
Pinch of Pul Biber
2 slices of stale bread (not processed, the chunky type 'artisan' bread is best, crusts removed, roughly torn
A large glug of olive oil
White wine vinegar, a splash
1 tsp sugar
Salt and pepper
Juice of ½ lemon

1. Whizz it all up in a large bowl with a stick blender or in batches in a processor or blender. Check for seasoning, add more olive oil, salt, pepper, lemon juice if desired.
2. Serve scattered with more chopped and peeled cucumber, mint leaves and walnuts.

PEA SOUP WITH PUMPKIN SEEDS

The wonderful thing about the Turkish *pazars* is that the grind of shelling peas is taken away, the stallholder sells his or her fresh peas shelled and bagged up in half kilos. Equally broad beans. Easy peasy! (sorry)

500g fresh peas
Small glug olive oil
I onion chopped
80ml white wine,
500ml vegetable stock
Lemon juice
Salt and pepper
30g pumpkin seeds toasted, zest of lemon, olive oil, mint leaves to garnish

1. Soften the onion over a low heat with some salt. Add the wine and cook on a high heat for a few minutes to reduce the alcohol. Add the stock and the peas, bring to the boil and simmer for 5–6 minutes until the peas are well-cooked.
2. Blend with a stick or put into a blender when cooled a little. Adjust the seasoning.
3. To serve hot, swirl the olive oil over the top and sprinkle with the toasted seeds, leaves and lemon zest.

BEETROOT SOUP WITH PEAR AND FETA

This is a lovely looking soup and can be served hot or cold. Serves 4–6 depending on appetite.

350g beetroot either roasted or boiled. Skins removed and grated
1 onion
I stick celery
1 fat clove garlic chopped finely
2 small ripe pears, grated
300ml stock
A few fresh sage leaves
Salt and pepper to taste
50g feta cheese
40g walnuts, chopped

1. Soften the onion with the celery and a pinch of salt in a pan over a low heat. Add the sage leaves (not too many as they can be strongly flavoured) and cook for about 10 minutes until the celery is completely cooked.
2. Add the garlic, cook for a further 2 minutes then add the pears and beetroot, pour in the stock, stir and bring to the boil. Simmer for a few minutes, then blend and season to taste.
3. Serve with crumbled feta and chopped walnuts with a sprinkling of roughly torn sage leaves.

DAUGHTER-IN-LAW SOUP

Named after the bride Ezo Gelin who tried to impress her difficult mother-in-law with this hearty soup, I never got to the bottom of whether she did or did not, but it is so delicious and simple to make that I would put it alongside Red lentil as among the most popular soups in Turkey. It also freezes very well. Serves 6.

300g split red lentils, rinsed and drained
1 onion, finely chopped
3 tbsp coarse bulgur wheat, rinsed and drained

1 small carrot, finely diced
1.75 litres chicken stock
4 tbsp tomato paste
2–3 tbsp butter
1 tbsp dried mint
2 tsp Pul biber
Red pepper flakes / paprika flakes
Juice of 1 lemon
Salt and freshly ground black pepper to taste
Lemon wedges to serve

1. Put the lentils, bulgur wheat, onion, carrot and the chicken stock (or water) together in a pan. Bring to boil and then on a low heat simmer, stirring occasionally for about 30 minutes or until the lentils and bulgur are tender.
2. Then add the butter, the dried mint, the red pepper flakes and the tomato paste, mix well and simmer for another 10–15 minutes, until the soup has a creamy consistency.
3. Add the lemon juice and more stock if required, then season with salt and pepper.
4. Serve hot with lemon wedges and crusty bread on the side.

FISH SOUP

To make the fish stock
2 whole red gurnard or grey mullet, scaled, cleaned
2.5 litres water
1 white onion, peeled, roughly chopped
1 bunch parsley, roughly chopped

For the soup
1 celeriac, medium size, peeled and cut into cubes
2 carrots, peeled, cut into cubes
1 potato, peeled and cut into cubes
1 tbsp white rice, washed and drained
2 tsp salt
½ tsp black pepper

To thicken
3 egg yolks
4 tbsp lemon juice

1. Boil the fish in a large pot with onions, parsley and 10 cups of water for about 25 minutes, until the fish is cooked.
2. Remove the fish and strain the stock.
3. Remove the head, tail, skin, bones and gills from the meat, cut into bite-size pieces and set the meat aside.
4. Place the strained stock back into the pot and add celeriac, carrots and salt, cook over low heat for about 10 minutes, then add the potatoes. Finally add the fish and cook until the vegetables have softened.
5. In a bowl whisk the egg yolks and lemon juice, together with a ladle full of hot fish stock.
6. Pour this mixture back into the soup pot; cook for another 5 minutes and then serve the soup with chopped parsley and lemon wedges.

PUMPKIN SOUP

You can make this with roasted pumpkin or just add the raw pumpkin to the pot for a quicker method. Both ways are delicious, but don't leave out the spices. I have to confess that I sometimes don't bother with peeling if using butternut squash. Wash it though!

Either 1 whole pumpkin or butternut squash will do, weighing about 1kg
2 large onions roughly chopped
2 large cloves of garlic squished and chopped
1 litre of stock (chicken or vegetable)
Olive oil to roast.
Turkish/Greek yogurt to serve
½ tsp each of powdered cumin, coriander and cinnamon (you can mix the spices how you wish, I have used Ras al hanout *in extremis*.)
Sea salt and pepper.

1. Peel and chop the squash, removing the seeds.
2. Toss with the oil in a large roasting tin; once well-coated, sprinkle with powdered cumin, coriander and cinnamon and the salt and pepper
3. Roast for half an hour or so in a hot oven; 200° C /Gas 6 turning until soft with crispy edges.
4. Meanwhile, in a large saucepan heat up another glug of olive oil and add the onions plus a pinch salt. Soften over a low heat. You want a sweet caramelised taste so take it long and slow, about 20 minutes should do the trick.
5. When the squash is ready add to the pan and top up with the stock. Bring to the boil and simmer for about 5 minutes. At this point you can add some heat: a pinch of pul biber/paprika or chilli powder.
6. Whizz with a stick blender. Adjust the seasoning.
7. Serve with a blob of yogurt, a sprinkling of hot spice and a drizzle of olive oil.

MEZZES

I could live quite happily on mezzes alone. Usually whilst in a restaurant, I will wander over to the mezze counter and choose whatever I fancy, then realise I can't accommodate another morsel. Not really a problem I suppose, however, I resolve to run to the harbour next time, so I can have the fish course as well; probably I will need to run back too, but all in a good cause.

DATE AND BLACK SESAME HUMMUS

A balance of sweet, salty and savoury, it makes a change from the normal hummus. You can get the same effect by whizzing in dates to my recipe below, leaving out the spices and mixing in a spoonful of *Nar* along with the olive oil. Serves 4

400g of cooked white beans or a tin of cannellini beans, drained
1 tbsp olive oil
4 medjool dates, roughly chopped
Juice of half a lemon
Sea salt
2 tbsp date syrup, honey or *pekmez* (grape syrup)
2 tbsp toasted black sesame seeds
1tbsp white miso

1. Put your beans into a food processor with the olive oil, dates, lemon juice, miso and a pinch of salt and whizz to your preferred consistency. Taste, add more salt if necessary, and loosen with a bit of water or more olive oil if it looks too thick.

2. Once the texture is how you like it, scoop it into a bowl, drizzle with the date syrup and sprinkle with the black sesame seeds.

MY PLAIN HUMMUS

If you are dry chickpeas soak overnight, drain, then they must be boiled gently for at least 1 hour, preferably 2. If they are not soft enough when you whizz them, the texture will be gritty. Mind you, plenty of my guests said they enjoyed the rougher texture of the pre-whizzer hummus I prepared. Remember to reserve some of the cooking water, you may need it.

1 can or 125g dried chickpeas
Dessert spoon (heaped) Tahini paste
1 good-sized lemon grated zest and juice of
2 cloves fat garlic
Glug olive oil
Cumin to taste
Pul biber and/or sumac to sprinkle on top

1. Put all the ingredients except the olive oil and spices into a large bowl. Whizz until creamy consistency, if it seems too thick, add some of the cooking water.
2. Add salt, pepper and cumin to taste, Then add a glug of good olive oil and mix thoroughly. Check seasoning. Serve with a drizzle of olive oil mixed with sumac or pul biber on top.
3. I also make red pepper hummus, spinach and nutmeg hummus, artichoke hummus and, actually, 'what have I got in the cupboard' hummus is my favourite.

HOT HUMMUS

Makes a change from the cold variety and much richer, good for the colder months, when you baulk at salads.

2 x 400g cans of chickpeas or equivalent in 'real' chickpeas
2 tsp cumin seeds roasted or 1 tsp ground
2–3 garlic cloves crushed
2 large glugs olive oil
Juice of 2 lemons
2 tbsp tahini paste
6 tbsp Turkish yogurt
Salt and pepper to taste
Handful pine nuts
2 tbsp butter

1. Preheat oven to 200°C 400F, Gas 6
2. Whizz up the chickpeas, cumin, garlic, olive oil, tahini and lemon juice as you would to make Hummus. When smooth, add the yogurt and whizz again until a looser consistency. Season. Pour into a shallow oven-proof dish.
3. Dry-roast the pine nuts and then add the butter and melt, then pour over the hummus mixture.
4. Cook in the oven for about 20–25 minutes until the hummus rises. Serve hot.

CHICKPEA AND POMEGRANATE 'HUMMUS'

Only a 10-minute ride into happiness here. Serve, as with most of these dips, with pitta bread, crudités or even crisps. I draw the line at Twiglets.

400g cooked chickpeas/tin
2 generous glugs of olive oil
1 glug pomegranate molasses
1 tsp cumin seeds
2 green chillies, de-seeded and chopped
1 red onion, chopped
1 handful fresh coriander, chopped
1 handful fresh mint, chopped
100g feta cheese, crumbled
Pomegranate seeds and more pomegranate molasses to serve
Salt and pepper to taste

1. Whizz the chickpeas, molasses and seasoning, keeping it coarse. (as the actress said….)
2. Stir in the other ingredients.
3. Serve with the scattered seeds and some more drizzled molasses.

AUBERGINE SLICES TWO WAYS

The ultimate fruit for mezzes. Second only to onions, oh and tomatoes, the aubergine is the most versatile dish maker.

1 small aubergine
Oil, for greasing
225g pack halloumi
½ lemon, zest and juice
1 handful basil leaves, shredded
Pinch crushed chillies (pul biber)
1 tsp honey

1. Preheat the oven to 200°C, fan 180°C. gas 6,
2. Trim the stalk end of the aubergine, then cut into 5mm slices lengthways using a sharp knife or mandoline, discarding the round end pieces with little flesh.
3. Heat a griddle pan until hot. Spray the aubergine slices lightly with oil and griddle for 1–2 minutes on each side, in batches if necessary, until the slices are charred and tender.
4. Cut the halloumi into 8 finger-sized sticks and place in a bowl with the lemon zest, most of the shredded basil and the crushed chillies; toss gently to coat.
5. Line a baking tray with baking paper. Wrap each halloumi stick in a slice of aubergine and place on the tray, seam-side down. Spray with a little extra oil, season with black pepper and drizzle over the honey.
6. Bake for 10 minutes, then squeeze over the lemon juice and scatter with a little extra basil to serve.

ANOTHER IDEA

3 medium sized aubergines cut lengthways into 5mm-thick slices
3 tbsp olive oil
1 tbsp za'atar
1 large handful of pomegranate seeds
1 handful fresh chopped mint leaves
2 tbsp tahini

1. Heat a griddle pan over a high heat. Brush the aubergines with the olive oil; season. Griddle in batches for 2–5 minutes each side until charred and soft, then remove from the pan and leave to cool.
2. In a bowl, mix the za'atar, 2/3 of pomegranate seeds and ½ chopped mint leaves, then place over one side of the aubergine slices and roll up. Secure with a cocktail stick.
3. Drizzle over the tahini, then scatter over the remaining pomegranate seeds, extra za'atar and mint.

CHICKPEA PANCAKES WITH ZA'ATAR

A quick and easy mezze that you can double up on ingredients to serve more people, or make the pancakes smaller! This recipe serves two greedy people.

120g chickpea flour
¼ tsp salt
1 glug of olive oil, plus some for drizzling
2 tsp za'atar
Oil for frying

1. Gradually whisk 300ml tepid water into the flour and salt in a large bowl.
2. Add the olive oil and whisk until no lumps. Rest the mixture for half an hour.
3. Heat your grill to a medium heat. In a large frying pan heat the oil until it is ready for the pancake mix. I drop a small trickle into the pan to test that it's hot enough.
4. Pour in half the batter and cook as you would any pancake for about 2–3 minutes. You should see bubbles forming on the surface. Pop under the grill to continue cooking the top of the pancake. When done, slip the pancake out of the pan and repeat. To serve, sprinkle with the za'atar and drizzle with olive oil. You can roll and stuff with pickled vegetables (see Konserv p.00) and serve with a side salad.

FALAFELS AND SAUCE

Well I struggled when I read the recipes for these things and to be honest I always thought they were a bit dry and tasteless, but I have sorted out my own recipe and they work a dream. I like them for lunch as a filling for flatbreads with green leaves, some pomegranate seeds, and a lush yogurt and tahini sauce sprinkled with some crunchy *dhukka*. I let the painters make up their own.

You can add all sorts of different spices to suit and also wilted spinach (not too wet) or even frozen peas, to give colour.

400g dried chickpeas soaked overnight and cooked for about 45 minutes in boiling water. (canned chickpeas are easier but not so crunchy)
1 red onion chopped roughly
2 cloves garlic peeled
1 lemon
1 tbsp plain flour (chickpea if possible)
1 heaped tsp pul biber
1 tsp cumin
1 tsp *Yeni bahar* (all spice)
1 dessert spoon of Biber Salcasi

Handful of fresh coriander or mint or half of each
Salt and black pepper to season
Oil for frying

1. Grate the lemon zest, then put all of the ingredients bar the flour into a processor and whizz until well mixed, but not too smooth, as you want a bit of crunch. Add flour to achieve a consistency that allows you to form the mixture into balls, but not too stiff , (that way dryness lies!) Add some lemon juice if it feels a bit too stiff.
2. Form into small round patties the size of a large walnut, they don't have to be spherical, if you are going to put into a wrap better to flatten them slightly so they don't roll back out.
3. Fry in a shallow pan on a highish heat, turning until a golden brown.
4. They DON'T freeze, tried that and they all crumbled into pieces, nothing daunted I served them as a topping to a salad and everyone asked me for the recipe!

CHICKPEA PATTIES

These are really falafels, but the yogurt and cooked onions give them a new softer identity.

225g chickpeas, prepared as above
1 level tsp turmeric
1 x 500g tub thick Turkish yogurt Greek too
Grated zest ½ lemon
1 dessert spoon lemon juice
Salt and black pepper
2 small red chillies, de–seeded and finely chopped
Handful fresh coriander
1 heaped tsp coriander seeds
1 heaped tsp cumin seeds
Glug of olive oil
1 small onion, peeled and finely chopped
1 small green pepper, de-seeded and finely chopped
3 large garlic cloves, peeled and finely chopped

For the frying:
1 large egg, beaten
3 level tbsp wholemeal flour or chickpea flour (gram flour)
2 tbsp groundnut oil

1. Toast the cumin and coriander seeds until they release their oils and fragrance. Grind in a pestle and mortar until a smoothish powder.
2. Put the olive oil in a saucepan and fry the onion and green pepper along with the garlic and chillies for 5 minutes on a low heat until they have softened and begun to turn brown. Then stir in the toasted ground spices and turmeric and continue to cook for a further 30 seconds.
3. Whizz up the chickpeas and the herbs until a crunchy paste as in falafels. Transfer to a large bowl and stir in the softened onions, spices, 3 tbsp of the yoghurt and the lemon zest and juice. Mix well, and season to taste.
4. As soon as the mixture is cool enough to handle, form it into patties about 5 cm in diameter and 1 cm thick, Dip first with beaten egg then toss them around in the wholemeal or chickpea flour. Next heat a couple of tablespoons of oil in a frying pan on a high heat and when it's really hot, fry as in falafels.

LABNEH

A quick and easy mezze dip is *Labneh* (a sort of cream cheese) and za'atar mixed with a small glug of olive oil, salt and pepper.
By adding roasted beetroot on top with a drizzle of good sticky balsamic it's delicious.

Beetroot in the *pazars* are always sold replete with their fresh green leaves: washed and roasted in the oven with their skins on and leaves removed, these red and wrinkled beauties go deliciously with the *labneh*/za'atar mix. I like to just pop the washed leaves onto the roasting tray about 20 minutes before the beets are ready. Tossed in the oils, they will slightly crisp up and look pretty against the deep red and white of the beets and cheese.

The beets should take about 40 minutes in a hot oven (200°C Gas 6), but test with a knife to be sure they are cooked through. Once cooled, rub off the skin, chop into large chunks and pop on top of the cheese.

LABNEH WITH PINK PEPPERCORNS, CORIANDER, FENNEL SEEDS AND BROAD BEANS

We have pink peppercorns in abundance in our garden, they hang like pendulous pink forbidden fruit from our pepper trees, which seem to grow just about everywhere. Not only do they look lovely on the tree, they perk up this dish no end. You can find pink peppercorns in delicatessens or you can buy one of those multi-coloured clear pepper grinders you get at Christmas time and pick out the pink ones, only joking!

1 large pot of *Labneh* (750g)
50g butter
200g broad beans cooked to al dente
4 garlic cloves chopped
1–2 tsp pink peppercorns
1–2 tsp fresh coriander
1 tsp fennel seeds
Salt to taste

1. Place peppercorns, coriander seeds, and fennel seeds in a small skillet; cook over medium heat, stirring occasionally, until fragrant, about 2 minutes. Let cool slightly, about 5 minutes.
2. Crush the seed mixture using a mortar and pestle, or bash with a rolling pin inside a plastic bag. To serve, loosely mix the seeds and salt into the *labneh*, top with the broad beans and drizzle with foaming melted butter.

ALTERNATIVE AND SLIGHTLY QUICKER *LABNEH* FIX

500g *labneh*
1 generous glug olive oil
2 tbsp Za'atar
Salt to taste

1. Put the *labneh* onto a shallow wide plate, sprinkle with the za'atar and drizzle over the olive oil.

Regarding *Labneh*, I can buy the packaged stuff so easily and when the painters are in situ I am usually short on time, and don't have the space for dripping bags of muslin in my tiny kitchen with guests milling about, so I don't bother making mine during the holidays. When I do, it's worthwhile. You can, it's not hard. Here is what you need:

A large sieve
Some muslin (or cheesecloth, or in my case an old clean IKEA curtain)
As much yogurt as you want to use, I suggest for this experiment a 750ml pot.

1. Put the sieve over a large bowl and line it with the muslin. Dollop the yogurt into the muslin. Tie up the cloth and let the yoghurt drip into the bowl for as long as it takes. Overnight is good.

Bob's your uncle, fresh, delicious *Labneh*! I discovered the cat loves the drips so a double whammy.

BEETROOTS ROASTED WITH CHICKPEAS AND ORANGE

4 medium size beetroots
4 tbsp of olive oil
1 red onion cut into slices
3 tbsp apple vinegar
Pinch sugar
Dijon mustard
500g cooked chickpeas or a can of same
A handful of chopped parsley and fresh mint
2 oranges peeled and segmented

1. Wash the beets and cut away the green leaves (you can use them for salad if fresh enough.
2. Coat them in olive oil, wrap in tin foil and roast in a hottish oven (180°C fan 200C no fan for 45 minutes to an hour.
3. Cook the onion in olive oil and a pinch of salt until soft. Do not brown.
4. Turn up the heat and pour over the vinegar and sugar and stir. Once the liquid has evaporated and the onions are a striking purple in colour, take off the heat.
5. Remove the beets from the oven and leave to cool a little before removing the skins. I find gentle rubbing does the trick, you will look like Lady Macbeth for a while, but who cares?
6. Put the chickpeas, quartered beets, onions and the herbs into a large bowl, lightly mix and dress with olive oil and mustard whisked together, plus some freshly ground black pepper.

YAPRAK SARMI

With the addition of a judicious pinch of proper saffron, this rice stuffing can be used in courgette flowers too; so wonderfully delicate. These are steamed to preserve the flower, baked or can be deep fried in batter.

You can also make the same Sarma/Dolma using green or red cabbage leaves, you can stuff tomatoes, onions, aubergines, anything that will hold the rice.

RICE FOR STUFFING VEGETABLES AND VINE LEAVES

If it can be stuffed, a Turkish cook will stuff it! Serves 4–6

30 ml / 2 tbsp currants
185g long grain rice
2 glugs olive oil
2 tbsp pine nuts
2 medium onions, finely chopped or grated
5 ml / 1 tsp ground cinnamon

8 fl oz / 1 cup hot water
1 handful each of freshly chopped parsley and dill
1 tbsp dried mint
Salt and sugar to taste
Freshly ground black pepper

1. If you have fresh leaves, soften them in boiling salted water, drain and rinse under cold running water. If using the preserved variety, wash thoroughly to remove all saltiness. Cut away the woody stalks of the vine leaves.
2. Mix the rice, currents, pine nuts, onions, spices and fresh herbs together
3. Place each leaf with the widest edge towards you and one by one, place a large teaspoon/small dessert spoon of rice stuffing at the base of each leaf. Fold the edges inwards over the stuffing and roll up to form a finger-sized *dolma*. Keep the leaf tight against the filling – a loosely rolled leaf will probably eject its stuffing whilst cooking. Line your pan with some vine leaves. Arrange the *dolmas* in the pan seam side down and tightly packed in layers.
4. Whisk together the water, olive oil, lemon juice, sugar and salt and pour over the *dolmas*.
5. Wet a circle of greaseproof paper lightly and place over the *dolmas*. Place a heatproof dinner plate on top of this, which fits easily and acts as a weight.
6. Cover and cook over a low heat for about 45 minutes or until the *dolmas* are tender. Remove from the heat and set aside to cool. Do not attempt to remove the *dolmas* until they are cooled completely, they are very delicate. I like to pop them in a Tupperware box or dish once cooled and easy to handle, drizzle more olive oil over the top and leave overnight. Serve with lemon wedges.
7. Do not be tempted to leave out the sugar in the cooking, I did for healthy reasons and was tartly told by my neighbour on returning my plate, they were not sweet enough. She was right.

SEBZE KÖFTESI

All forms of vegetable patties are a staple in less affluent areas but I can assure you they are absolutely delicious.

1 carrot, peeled
1 celeriac, peeled
1 small cauliflower
1 small leek
3 potatoes, boiled, peeled
75g peas, boiled
½ bunch parsley, finely chopped
3 spring onions, finely chopped
2 eggs, whites and yolks separated
75g breadcrumbs
1 tbsp butter
Oil for frying
2 tsp salt
1 tsp black pepper

1. Place the carrots, celeriac, cauliflower and leek into the food processor and chop into fine dice. Sauté the chopped vegetables in butter, and then add peas, parsley and spring onions. Continue sautéing until the vegetables have softened.
2. Meanwhile, mash the potatoes, add salt, black pepper, sautéed vegetables and egg yolks. Mix well, and then make patties, you choose the size.
3. Set up the frying station by first heating the oil. Then set two bowls, one for the egg whites and one for the breadcrumbs. Dip the vegetable patties in beaten egg, then in breadcrumbs and fry until golden brown.

4. Transfer to a plate lined with paper towel. Serve hot.

SUN-DRIED TOMATO AND NUT MEZZE

15 pieces sun-dried tomatoes (In Turkey they are split into halves and dried, or you can get them bathed in oil in jars, either will do)
65g hazelnuts or walnuts
1 handful chopped parsley
2–3 tbsp olive oil

1. Put tomatoes into hot water and set aside for 15–20 minutes, and then drain (don't do this if you use tomatoes from a jar).
2. Put tomatoes, hazelnuts and parsley in a food processor and chop until it becomes a paste,
3. Transfer onto a serving plate and pour olive oil on top.

RED PEPPER AND TOMATO MEZZE

2 garlic cloves
1 30g jar roasted red peppers, rinsed and patted dry
85g walnuts
5 inch (12 cm) piece of baguette, crust discarded, bread torn into pieces
1 tbsp tomato paste
Extra-virgin olive oil
½ tsp ground coriander
½ tsp cayenne
Small bunch finely chopped fresh coriander or parsley

1. Mince and mash garlic to a paste with 1 teaspoon salt. Puree remaining ingredients with garlic paste in food processor until almost smooth. Season with salt.

ONIONS ROASTED IN ORANGE AND THYME

6 medium-sized onions, peeled.
250g butter
1 dessert spoon of balsamic vinegar
Glug pomegranate molasses
Juice and zest of 1 orange
Salt and pepper

1. Preheat oven to 200°C / 400 F Gas 6
2. In a saucepan melt the butter along with all the other ingredients except the onions.
3. Halve the onions then cut a slice off the bottom of each side so they sit steady, pour over the flavoured butter, cover with foil and cook for 45 minutes. Remove the foil and roast again, basting with the juices, for a further 40 minutes or until the onions look coloured and crispy on top.

MUCVER Pronounced MOOjveyr, love that word!

This is my go-to dish when on automatic pilot. So easy to make, the only problem is I have so many to make in one batch. When frying off the pancakes, you must be careful not to pile on top of each other or they will steam and go soggy.

3–4 decent-sized courgettes or 2 large ones
Bunch of spring onions
Bunch of dill
Bunch fresh mint, leaves stripped to make a

large handful (dried mint is acceptable, if so, use 1 large dessert spoon)
1 pack feta cheese, crumbled
2–3 eggs depending on size, I use 2 large ones.
2 tbsp self raising flour, you may need a bit more. Plain flour and baking powder is fine.
Salt and pepper to taste (don't add the salt until you know how salty the feta is).

1. Grate the courgettes by hand or in a processor, if you hold by the stalk end you won't grate your hands. Discard the stalks. Place in a colander and sprinkle salt over the top, this will force the water out of the courgettes. Leave for 20 minutes or so.
2. Get a clean tea towel and put the grated courgette in the middle, twist up the towel so you wring out the courgettes. Green juice will run out, you will be left with a dryish mass. Or mess?!
3. In a large bowl mix together the feta, herbs and courgettes, add most of the egg and the flour and mix thoroughly, you should have a consistency of thick batter. If too stiff add the other egg. Season to taste. Watch that salt!
4. Heat a very large pan of sunflower or hazelnut oil until sizzling. Take a dessert spoonful of your mixture and settle in the pan, flatten slightly with the spoon or spatula; don't worry if the shape is irregular, that's part of a *mucver's* charm. Repeat until you have filled the pan, but not too close or they will not crisp. You should get around 4–6.
5. Fry until golden brown and then turn over until both sides are crispy.
6. Serve with a yogurt sauce or on their own as an appetiser.

NOTE: you can use all sorts of veg to make *mucver*, cauliflower and leeks are good.

BULGAR AND LENTIL *KÖFTE* (*MERCEMEK KÖFTE*)

I just love the look of these little orange torpedoes, they always cut a dash at lunches or dinners and my neighbour told me that mine were better than hers. The only difference as far as I could see was that I added the grated zest of a lemon as well as the juice. It really perks up a fantastically economic dish and brings it to a gourmet level. As with the falafels, don't stint on the flavouring. I ring the changes, by adding a dessert spoon of dried mint at the same time as the bulgur.

1 glass* (unit) red lentils washed
½ glass (unit) fine bulgur wheat (*köfte*)
1 small onion chopped
Small handful (about 6) of finely chopped spring onions
1 tbsp *biber salcasi* (red pepper paste)
1 handful of chopped flat leaf parsley
1 tsp ground cumin
1 tsp pul biber – add more if you like it more spicy
1 tbsp olive oil
1 lemon, zested and juiced

1. Place the red lentils into a pan of boiling water
2. Simmer until bubbles come to the surface, then add salt (it needs salt so check again at the end of the cooking process).

*This is a Turkish tea glass, so a small teacup not to the top would be about right so long as they relate the same. It is not that important, just remember to add 4x that unit of water and you're fine.

3. Add the *salcasi*, spices and stir, then pour in the bulgur. Take off the heat, put a lid on and let the bulgur absorb the rest of the water. If the mixture seems to be dry, add some more hot water. It's not an exact science.
4. Put the chopped onion in a pan and soften in the olive oil, add to the mixture and leave to cool.
5. Once the mixture is cool enough (we don't want to cook these), add half of the spring onions, chopped parsley, a glug of olive oil and lemon zest. Check the seasoning. If it still seems too dry, add more lemon juice.
6. Form into balls the size of a walnut or a golf ball depending on how you like it – err on the side of caution with size, though, as they are lovely to eat in a couple of mouthfuls.

The traditional way of shaping these *köfte* is to then place the balls in your hand and squeeze so they take on the shape of your inner fingers, an undulating shape of four indentations around the köfte. It took me a while to master this neatly, so if you are frustrated leave as an elongated rugby ball.

FAVA

I have been informed by many a Turk that my fava is some of the best they have ever tasted! No mean feat. I hope I don't sound conceited telling this, but I get so excited when the teachers praise the pupil.

For my fava I use dried fava beans. You should be able to get these in some of the more interesting grocer shops, but if you find them impossible to track down, then yellow split peas will do.

500g fava beans, rinsed under the tap
1 large onion
2 large cloves garlic
1 medium size carrot topped and tailed
1 tsp sugar
1 very large glug of olive oil
Lemon juice from half a lemon
1 bunch fresh dill
Salt, pepper to taste
1 small red onion

1. In a large saucepan pop in the beans, the onion cut in half, sugar, carrot and garlic plus a small glug of good olive oil. I often add the dill stalks at this point as they are packed with flavour.
2. Cover with water to a level of two fingers above the beans. Bring to the boil and simmer, covered for at least 40 minutes, test the beans for softness and cook some more if necessary. If you find you need more water, then add it, the mixture must not burn or get too dry or thick.
3. Whizz the mixture to a puree with a stick blender until smooth, don't worry if it seems too loose at this point. The texture of thick double cream is fine.
4. Add the lemon juice and a large glug of olive oil, salt and pepper to taste. Then pop on the heat again and stir madly for a few minutes.
5. When cooled down a little add the fresh dill chopped finely, leaving some for decoration.
6. Traditionally this is served on a flattish stoneware plate, I have a large shallow terracotta dish that is perfect, the cooked fava should be about the depth of two fingers.
7. Smooth the puree and lightly mark out in diamond shapes, by using the point of a knife in diagonal lines, no need to cut through.

8. Set aside to cool completely then refrigerate for 12 hours.
9. When ready to serve, decorate with more fresh dill and finely chopped red onion.

The fava should be firm, but not hard and can be served with flatbreads or salad. This will feed 10 people as a starter and is perfect for a summer party when you want to feed lots of people for minimum outlay and fuss.

BOREK (small triangles or squares)

SIGARA BOREK

Rolled like reefers! It is much easier to make the cigarettes from a circle of *yufka* than a square as you need the pointy bit to fold around last and stick down, but you can use *filo* in squares. With *filo* you have to keep it damp, because it is not nearly as moist as *yufka* and will dry out quickly.

6 rounds of *yufka* (see p00).
A handful of chopped parsley/dill/chives or a mixture of all
250g *lor* or crumbled feta cheese
Water to stick

1. Cut your circle of *yufka* like the spokes of a wheel into eighths.
2. At the round end place a small amount of mixed crumbled cheese and herbs.
3. Start to roll the mixture towards the pointed end, tucking in the sides as you go, dip the pointed end into water and stick firmly down.
4. Once all the cigarettes have been made, they can be shallow or deep fried in sunflower oil. I shallow fry as I can't bear to have lots of used oil lying around in my small kitchen. Turn the rolls occasionally to get an even golden brown and drain on paper towel. Serve hot.

These can be frozen before cooking if you like batch cooking as I do, with no perceivable problems.

LARGE *BOREK*

This is cooked in a large '*tepsi*' or tray and cut into squares at the serving point.

CHEESE VERSION

6 large *yufka* sheets
300ml milk
4 eggs
4 tbsp olive oil
1 tsp salt
½ tsp black pepper
500g crumbled Turkish white cheese (*lor*), or feta, which you have to crumble yourself.
4 tbsp chopped flat leaf parsley (you might want to add a few chopped spring onions)
Nigella seeds for garnish

1. Heat oven to 180°C/360°F 160F
2. In a large bowl mix the butter/olive oil with the milk, eggs, salt and pepper.
3. Mix together the cheese and the parsley.
4. Grease a large square or circular baking tray with oil or butter, then lay on your first sheet of yufka, this will flop nicely into the space and you can then squiggle it about so it wrinkles and settles into waves.
5. Add about 1/6 of the milky mixture, then another sheet of dough, covering again with the liquid, then a third flop of yufka. And a slush of liquid, then your cheesy filling. Cover this with your fourth sheet of dough and repeat the process until six sheets? have been used up.
6. Paint the top with the last knockings of the milk and eggs and sprinkle with nigella seeds. I like a lot of these.
7. Bake in the centre of the oven for 25–30 minutes until golden brown.
8. Bake it in a 185 F/365 C oven for about 45 minutes, until the top is nicely browned and the middle is set firm. I have heard it is a good idea to cover the cooked *borek* in a tea towel so the crust softens a little before serving. Mine never last that long!

AUBERGINE *BOREK*

This is quite delicious, especially if like me you are an aubergine fanatic.
The 'rose' shape is a bit of a departure from the usual triangles or squares and looks spectacular when served. You can also substitute butternut squash, which works extremely well if you don't share my passion.

260g or filo pastry sheets, remember you have to work really quickly if using filo
1 large aubergine
1 medium onion, finely chopped
3 small tomatoes, peeled and finely chopped
1 handful flat leaf parsley, finely chopped
60g grated mild cheddar or feta
1 tbsp olive oil
1 egg, beaten and 1 tbsp olive oil for brushing the *boreks*
Black Nigella seeds to decorate
Salt and freshly ground black pepper
Bowl of water to seal the *boreks*

1. Preheat the oven to 180 C / 350 F/ Gas Mark 4
2. Scorch the aubergine on an open gas flame turning occasionally by the stalks until the outer skin is charred and blistered and the inner flesh soft. (Alternatively, they can be baked in a hot oven for about 45 minutes.) Peel away the burnt skin and discard the stalks. Put the flesh in a colander to drain away any bitter juices. As with this method in all recipes, you can prepare this stage in advance, cover with lemon juice and refrigerate.
3. Sauté the onions with some olive oil for a couple of minutes, until soft.
4. Add the tomatoes and cook for another couple of minutes, until most of the liquid has evaporated. Stir in the parsley and season with salt and pepper.
5. Once cooled, add the cheese and mix well. Check if more seasoning is needed, set aside to cool.
6. Place the sheets of dough on a flat surface and cover with a damp tea towel to keep moist.
7. On a dry surface, place 2 filo pastry sheets on top of one another and cut in half horizontally

to form 2 rectangles. Place 1 tablespoon of the mixture in the middle and roll like a cigar. Then, starting from one end, roll the cigar shape round and round the tin starting at the centre into a rose shape sealing the end with a little water. Make sure you seal all the openings/cracks with a little water. Repeat this with all rectangles.

8. Mix the egg with the olive oil. Brush the boreks with this mixture and place them on a greased tray. Sprinkle sesame seeds over the boreks and bake them in the oven for about 25 minutes or until golden.

CARROT MEZZE (*HAVUC*)

This turns out a glorious light saffrony orange colour and takes no time to prepare. No one knows what it is when they first try it.

2–3 large carrots or 4–6 small ones (sweeter)
A large glug of olive oil
3 large cloves of garlic, minced
1 large pinch of cumin (if you roast and combine whole it adds a bit of crunch)
Pinch of sea salt
3 heaped tbsp of Turkish yoghurt

1. Grate the carrot. Warm a sauté pan and put in a glug of olive oil.
2. Add the grated carrots and stir gently for a few minutes so they warm through and wilt a little. Set aside to cool.
3. Grind the garlic to a paste in a pestle and mortar, using the rock salt as an abrasive to help in grinding it down.
4. Stir the garlic into the yoghurt and then add the cooled carrot. Stir to combine.
5. Cover and put in fridge for at least an hour to let the flavours develop.
6. I serve with a black olive in the centre for colour contrast. I also like to add a sprinkling of walnuts, but that isn't the Turkish way.

BEYAZ PEYNIR OR FETA FRIED CHOUX BALLS

I will fill a choux ball with more or less anything: cream cheese and flavouring, baked and puréed squash, cauliflower puree flavoured with nutmeg. Drizzle the tops with that syrupy balsamic vinegar and you have a very presentable savoury profiterole.

I medium leek finely chopped
1 clove garlic
1 glug milk
1 glug water
115g butter for mixing
500–600g flour
6 eggs
170g feta, crumbled
1 tsp nutmeg
Sea salt and pepper to taste
1 tbsp butter for frying

1. Gently fry the leek and garlic in the butter until soft.
2. Place the milk,115g butter and water in a pan and bring to the boil slowly until the butter has completely melted.
3. Add the flour and beat well to incorporate, it will come cleanly away from the sides of the pan and look glossy.

4. Add the leek mixture and the eggs one by one, beating continuously.
5. When all is smooth add the feta and nutmeg and season. Refrigerate for a couple of hours then form into balls and deep fry until golden brown

TURK TIP

You can add some chopped dill to the mixture for variation, but leave out the nutmeg.

BABA GANUSH

So many ways to produce this traditional aubergine delight.

3 large aubergines
3 fat cloves of garlic
3 tbsp tahini
1 lemon, juiced
2 glugs of olive oil
Sea salt
Pepper
Parsley plus extra olive oil for decoration

1. Scorch the aubergines on an open flame as in recipe page 00.
2. Once blackened and blistered, pierce the bottoms and leave to cool in a sieve or colander to drain away all the bitter juices.
3. Peel away the stems and the blistered skin, this can be a sticky job, but keep rinsing your hands and the job will go smoothly. Roughly chop into chunks and whizz in a large bowl along with the other ingredients (not the parsley).
4. When smooth, pop into a shallow dish or plate and drizzle with olive oil, sprinkle with parsley and, if you have them, some pomegranate seeds.

VERSION 2

1. Add a large tablespoonful of Turkish yogurt and some chopped parsley to above recipe.

VERSION 3

1. Add the yogurt and a handful of hulled walnuts, then whizz again.

All the above recipes benefit from being stood for a while in a cool place to bring out all the flavours.

WATERCRESS AND YOGURT

The watercress in Turkey is not like ours, it is bulkier and much more leafy, tasty and succulent. However, the leaves must be stripped from the stalks and the damn stuff goes off in what seems to be seconds! Just don't bank on keeping it for more than one day.

Large bunch of Turkish watercress or two packets of UK from supermarket
Large dollop of Turkish yoghurt
2 cloves Garlic, minced
Lemon juice to taste

1. Wash and strip the leaves, mix into Turkish yogurt with minced garlic and a squeeze of lemon juice. Add wild garlic in spring – delicious! Lovely as a refreshing salad with meat or fish.

CARAMELISED ONIONS AND YOGURT

I first had this in a lovely little artisan bar leaning over the hillside above Gumusluk. It was run by a group of friends from Istanbul, young and very enterprising. The wines and mezzes they served were impeccable. This dish was so yummy I had to replicate it, but I added a pinch of nutmeg to make it my own

4 or 5 brown onions
Olive oil for frying
A large cube of butter
Nutmeg – a pinch or ½ tsp
1 tsp of good balsamic vinegar
Sea Salt and pepper to taste
500ml Turkish yogurt

1. Peel and slice the onions, then chop, if you don't want tendrils of lush oily onion dripping down your chin when you eat (actually I love that!). In a large frying pan melt the butter with a small glug of olive oil and a pinch of salt. When hot enough add the onions and slowly, slowly caramelise, this bit does tax my patience, but if the heat is too high the onions crisp and go bitter.
2. After about 20 minutes the onions will soften and slowly but surely turn a deep caramel colour and become so sweet you could eat them by the spoonful.
3. At this point stir in the nutmeg, and mix well. Once caramelised and cooled you can add them to the yogurt with the salt and pepper.

If I have time I like to top this dish with crispy fried onions done in whole sliced rings on a high heat. This make a nice contrast of smooth, soft and crunchy. I also add crispy fries currants, try and get the small ones, it adds a bit of crunch too.

WHIPPED FETA AND DATES PLUS VARIATIONS

Some dates, some feta, whizz. Season. Drizzle with date molasses. Job done.

WHIPPED FETA AND SUMAC

200g feta
200g thick Turkish natural yogurt
½ lemon, juiced
2 glugs olive oil
1 tsp Sumac

1. Whizz the yogurt and the feta until creamy, add lemon juice, oil and sumac and stir..

WHIPPED FETA AND HERBS

200g feta
200g thick Turkish natural yogurt
½ lemon, juice and zest
Olive oil to serve
Pul biber to serve plus seeds
Herbs, e.g. dill or parsley and thyme

1. Whizz the yogurt and feta, add the juice AND zest of the lemon, plus whichever herbs you fancy. I suggest dill and parsley, with a sprinkling of thyme.

2. Season with salt and pepper. Serve drizzled with olive oil, pul biber and sesame/pumpkin/sunflower seeds .

You can make up your own recipes now, I'm sure. All of these Feta dips are delicious with fresh or toasted bread, crackers or freshly sliced carrots, celery anything you fancy.

ROASTED BUTTERNUT SQUASH WITH HAZELNUTS AND FETA CHEESE

This makes a lovely starter, a little bit more than a mezze, but not quite a main, or you can have it as a side dish to meat or fish.

- 1 whole butternut squash about 1kg in weight or equivalent in pumpkin
- 1 x 200g pack of feta or Gorgonzola, both work well
- Handful of hazelnuts, roasted
- A small bunch of fresh sage.
- 2 tbsp olive oil
- 1 tbsp honey
- Sea salt and black pepper
- Chicory leaves to serve

1. Peel and de-seed the squash and chop into bite-sized cubes.
2. Put in a roasting pan and cover with the olive oil so all sides are coated (I use my hands).
3. Drizzle over the honey, sprinkle with salt and pepper and some chopped sage leaves, reserving half a dozen for decoration.
4. Roast in a hot oven, 200° C fan until soft and the edges have started to brown and crisp.
5. Plate up by serving the squash on a few chicory leaves, dotted with the cheese and sprinkled with the crushed hazelnuts.
6. Drizzle the honey and oil juices from the pan as a dressing and top with sage leaves.

When I'm feeling flash I will deep fry large sage leaves and balance on the top. Delicious.

ROASTED RED PEPPERS

Pointy ones are best for this job. Roast on a medium heat 180°C for about an hour until a bit charred looking, but not black all over. Pop into a plastic bag, whilst still hot and the steam will help remove the skin. Once skinned, dress with olive oil and lemon juice. Or use in some of the other recipes below.

ROASTED RED PEPPERS WITH WALNUTS

- 6–8 roasted red peppers as above, or 1 x 200g jar of same. Home-roasted will be less watery
- 2 handfuls of fresh breadcrumbs
- 1 tbsp *nar* (pomegranate molasses)
- 2 fat cloves of garlic
- Juice of half a lemon
- 1 tsp cumin
- 1tsp paprika
- Pinch of pul biber
- 75g walnuts
- 3 glugs olive oil
- Pinch of salt

1. Whizz together in food processor or with a stick blender, that's it!

OR

MUHAMMARA

12 cloves garlic (FAT)
2 red peppers (pointy kind)
125g walnut pieces
I glug pomegranate molasses
2 tbsp sweet pepper paste
2–3 tsp pul biber
Glug of olive oil
Pinch of chilli or pul biber
2 tbsp water

1. Using tongs, hold garlic and peppers directly over a gas flame, turning until blackened all over. Transfer to a bowl, cool slightly, then rub off charred garlic and pepper skins.
2. Carefully cut open the peppers, discard seeds and chop flesh.
3. Place in a food processor with garlic, walnuts, pomegranate molasses, pul biber, chilli, oil and 2 tbsp water and process to a coarse paste.

Another nutty mezze or dippy starter

SPICY WALNUT SPREAD (*AYDIN CEMENI*)

Large handful of walnuts, pounded
1–2 garlic cloves
5–6 tbsp tomato paste
2 tbsp red pepper paste, sweet
1 tsp red pepper paste, hot
1/4 cup extra virgin olive oil
3/4 tsp cumin
1 tsp paprika
Salt
Pepper

Mix all the ingredients in a bowl. Serve with dried *yufka* or *pide* or any of the yummy Turkish breads.

ROASTED BEETROOTS, GOATS CHEESE AND FRESH THYME

3 medium-sized beets
6 cloves garlic, skins on
Glug of olive oil
Leaves stripped off bunch of fresh thyme.
250g soft goats cheese or curd cheese

1. Roast the beets in a hot oven (200°C/F400) Gas 6 in a covered tray with a glug of olive oil until cooked (about an hour). I usually add the garlic after about 25 minutes as if left longer it can easily go hard and bitter (not unlike humans, really!)
2. When cooked, slip the skins off the garlic and trim and peel the beets. Chop and whizz with the goats cheese together with the thyme. Season with sea salt and fresh black pepper. Job done.

Above the village

Still life in the garden

Turkish woman at Çomlekçi

Our shop musician

Rolling out the breakfast breads

Market pottery

The upper level with dining area

Carpet and cushions

She told me she was 93 and still looking for another husband!

Green pot with today's market finds

Wine under the pergola

Hamsi

Local fishing boats

Cooking Kaymak on the wood fire

MELON AND WHITE CHEESE

Another simple, but tip-top mezze is slices of peeled fresh melon and *beyaz peynir,* or white cheese. You can use feta, but get a good one, as the smoother the better.
Plate up with the slices of melon intermingled with the white cheese. This is a perfect summer mezze.

FRIED AUBERGINES WITH WHIPPED FETA AND WALNUT

- 2 aubergines cut lengthways and again into 8 pieces
- 150g feta
- Glug of olive oil
- 150 g semolina
- 50g plain flour
- Salt to taste
- 4 tbsp of date syrup, *pekniz* or equal parts of runny honey and treacle
- A sprinkling of fresh mint
- Oil for deep frying
- Pinch sugar
- 2 tbsp water

1. Slice the aubergines fairly thickly and soak in salted water for 15 mins to remove the bitter juices.
2. Cut the feta into chunks and whizz with the olive oil and 2 tbsp water. Leave aside.
3. Pat dry the aubergines and toss in a mixture of the flour, semolina and salt and fry in a deep pan until nice and crispy on the outside and soft inside. Serve drizzled with the whipped feta and date syrup with a sprinkling of the fresh mint.

AUBERGINE SALAD

There are loads of different aubergine salads and I love them all. I unswervingly will choose the aubergine mezze above all others when confronted with the '*tepsi*' (tray) of mezzes at a restaurant.

VERSION 1. *SAKSUKA* (SHAKSHUKA)

- 2 aubergines, diced
- 2–3 long green peppers – not the hot type – cut into thickish strips
- 3 tomatoes, grated
- 1 level tbsp tomato paste
- A few cloves of garlic
- Olive oil for frying
- ½ tsp of sugar
- Salt and pepper to taste

1. Gently fry the aubergines and the peppers in the oil in a shallow pan until soft and slightly coloured. Set aside to cool.
2. In the same pan add the grated tomato, sugar, paste, minced garlic and cook down to thicken.
3. When cool, cover the aubergines with the sauce and sprinkle with parsley.

Note: you can substitute pomegranate syrup for sugar, it's just to check the tomatoes.

AUBERGINE WITH YOGURT AND TAHINI

I absolutely love this dish, but you had better warn anyone in the house you are cooking it or they may call the fire brigade!

3–4 largish aubergines
3 tbsp yogurt
1 full dessert spoon tahini paste
2–3 plump garlic cloves
Squeeze of lemon juice
Salt and pepper to taste.

1. Prick your aubergines a couple of times to stop them exploding (I did warn you!)
2. Balance them over the largest burner on your hob and burn the skin, turning occasionally – don't use your fingers – until they turn black and the skin starts to crack and flake.
3. Only gas will do here, sorry you electric fans, you can put them into the oven on a high heat for 30 minutes or so, but to be honest the taste is far and away better on an open flame.
4. When thoroughly 'destroyed', I pick them up with tongs, slit their bases a bit so the juices run out and stand them upright in a colander.
5. When you feel you can touch them without screaming, peel off the blackened skin. This is a surprisingly sticky process, you may have to rinse your fingers. The skin should come off easily. If you find the flesh is attaching itself to the aubergine, then it wasn't burnt enough (you will know for next time).
6. Put the whole drained aubergines, minus stalks onto a chopping board and roughly chop up.
7. Add the tahini, yogurt and garlic and whizz. Salt and pepper and lemon juice can be added for your taste.
8. I find this is best left overnight for the flavours to really take a hold, but a few hours will suffice.

VERSION 2

1. Add walnut pieces and no tahini and then whizz. SO yummy, difficult to choose.

ANOTHER AUBERGINE SALAD

3 largish aubergines
2 cloves of garlic or as much as you see fit
2–3 long green peppers
2 large tomatoes
1 dessert spoon of tomato paste
Juice of ½ lemon
Glug of olive oil plus some for frying

1. Scorch your aubergines as before, but do not puree, just chop into bite–sized chunks.
2. Fry the onion and the green peppers until soft, add the chopped tomatoes and the tomato paste. Glug lots of good olive oil, minced garlic and freshly squeezed lemon juice on top and season with salt and pepper and fresh flat leaf parsley. This likes to sit for a couple of hours too.

CHOUX PASTRY PUFFS WITH FILLINGS

So easy to make, choux pastry is so versatile for savoury dishes that you can just pop into your mouth. Not just for profiteroles! An added bonus is that the dough can be made a couple of days in advance if stored in the freezer and once cooked they freeze well. A boon for me, I can assure you.

150g plain flour
1 tsp each sugar and salt
½ tsp paprika
100g unsalted butter
4 eggs
250ml water

1. Sieve the flour, sugar and salt onto baking paper. Put the butter and 250ml cold water into a saucepan. Bring to the boil, and then quickly slide the flour mixture off the paper and into the pan. Stir well.
2. Remove the saucepan from the heat. Using a wooden spoon, beat the mixture off the heat until it forms a ball and pulls away cleanly from the sides of the pan. This should take just a few minutes.
3. Beat the eggs together in a bowl. Still off the heat, beat the eggs into the mixture, a little at a time, until smooth. It will go a bit blobby at first, but keep beating and it will mix in smoothly.
4. Keep beating until all the egg mixture is used up and you have a paste that is thick and shiny. Spoon the mixture onto a greased baking tray with a dessert or soup spoon and bake at 200°C/fan180°C/gas 6 until golden brown.
5. Remove from the oven and make a small hole in the underside of each bun to release any steam. Set aside to cool on a wire rack.

These are now ready to fill with whatever you like. I suggest: mature cheese sauce with added flavourings; labneh and herbs; roasted pepper and cream cheese; whipped feta and date; mashed smoked aubergine (as in aubergine and tahini dip); smoked salmon and cream cheese with dill (smoked salmon surprisingly available in our local supermarket); puréed cauliflower and spicy yogurt. Pretty well anything actually. There are no rules.

ROASTED CAULIFLOWER DIP

1 large cauliflower (about 500g)
A teaspoon each of dried coriander, cumin, hot pul biber or chilli flakes
1 lemon, grated peel and juice
A handful parsley, chopped
2 cloves garlic
Large glug olive oil
200g Turkish yogurt
3 tbsp tahini paste
Sea salt and black pepper to taste

1. Pre-heat the oven to a high heat 200°C / 180 Fan / F400 Gas 6
2. Break up the cauliflower into florets, Save the central stalk for stock.
3. Place on a roasting tin, drizzle over the oil and turn to coat thoroughly. Roast for about 40 minutes until the florets turn colour and soften.
4. Put all the ingredients including the roasted cauliflower into a large bowl and whizz. Top with another drizzle of olive oil.
5. Refrigerate for a few hours then serve at room temperature.

ROASTED CAULIFLOWER WITH SESAME AND TAHINI

1 head of cauliflower leaves removed and cut into florets
Juice and rind of 1 lemon
1 tbsp tahini

- 1 dessert spoon of sesame seeds roasted in a hot pan for a couple of minutes
- 3 glugs of olive oil
- Salt and pepper to taste

1. Preheat oven to 200°C fan 180C 400F Gas 6
2. Toss the cauliflower florets in a glug of oil to coat
3. Roast in the oven for 30 minutes.
4. Make a sauce of tahini, lemon juice, seasoning and two glugs olive oil. Pour over the cooked cauli and scatter with roasted sesame seeds. Serve.

WITH CUMIN AND CORIANDER SEEDS

Prepare the cauli as before, sprinkle with the cumin and coriander seeds, roast as before. When cooked, dollop Turkish yogurt seasoned with salt and pepper and a little grated lemon rind. Scatter pomegranate seeds on top and serve.

VEGETABLE TAHINI DIPS: CARROT/BEETROOT

You can repeat this recipe with most vegetables (not potatoes) and get great results. I suggest carrot, beetroot, red peppers, onions or celeriac.

BLACK OLIVE TAPENADE

Usually tapenade has anchovies in it, but as I have never seen a can of anchovies in our local store, I make it without. Because the olives are so, so delicious and a bit salty, I don't miss the anchovies at all.

- 200g of the best black olives, I find the ones in brine a bit tasteless, so I go for the wrinkly ones stored in olive oil. Take out the stones.
- 35g almonds blanched, whole
- 2 cloves garlic
- 1–2 tbsp capers
- A handful of fresh thyme
- 2 glugs of good olive oil
- Black pepper to taste

1. Whizz it all up together. You can store in a jar in the fridge, but mine always disappears fast.

TURK TIP *See how to get the best out of your olives on page 134*

GRILLED /GRIDDLED VEGETABLES WITH YOGURT

Simple, but effective: slice lengthways aubergines and/or courgettes. Place on a griddle or skillet, brush with olive oil and cook until brown on each side.

Make a sauce with yogurt and garlic plus salt and pepper, drizzle over the vegetables, sprinkle with *pul biber*, green parsley and another drizzle of olive oil and Mustafa is your uncle!

CARROTS AND COURGETTES IN YOGURT

Grate carrots and courgettes into a large bowl and combine with oil, salt and pepper, fry quickly with garlic and cumin, turning over and over to make sure all is cooked. Add lemon juice and mix in with thick yogurt. Dad-ah!

VEGETABLES IN OLIVE OIL

I rather like to fry the veggies such as courgettes in a griddle and when charred smother with a garlic yogurt and sprinkle with parsley and a little *pul biber.* Frying in rosemary-infused oil makes it all the better.

You can also roast the veggies (peppers, courgettes, onions, pretty well anything) in the oven in lots of olive oil and garlic, then cover with the tomato sauce (see page 00) and pop back in the oven, stirring occasionally for another half hour. These make a lovely supper dish served with bulgur salad or couscous.

BARBUYA BEANS IN TOMATO SAUCE

360g dried barbuya beans (or 1kg of fresh barbuya beans, peeled)
2 onions, finely chopped
1 potato, cut into medium dice
1 carrot, cut into medium dice
3–4 cloves garlic, sliced
2 tomatoes, peeled, cut into medium dice (or 1 tbsp tomato paste)
Large glug olive oil
2 tsp salt
1 tsp sugar
1 bunch parsley leaves
1 lemon cut into 4 wedges

1. If using dried barbuya beans soak overnight. The next morning, boil the beans with a fresh batch of water for about 30 minutes.
2. Sauté the onions and garlic in olive oil until softened.
3. Add the tomatoes or tomato paste and continue sautéing for a few more minutes.
4. First add the carrots, then a little later add the potatoes and beans with enough water to fill the half the pot. Add the salt and sugar.
5. Cook over a low heat until the beans have softened, about 40 minutes. Serve with parsley leaves and lemon wedges.

BEETROOT WITH MINT

A very simple and deliciously Barbie pink mezze!

3–4 beetroot raw
Several dollops of yogurt
Dried or fresh mint
Olive oil
Salt and pepper

1. Wash and de-leaf the beetroot (you can use the leaves and stalks for salads if fresh enough).
2. Place in a pan of boiling water, cover and simmer for about 40 minutes, according to size – they may cook faster or slower, so test with a knife until it penetrates easily.

3. When cool, chop finely, you can whizz, but I like to have a bit of bite.
4. Mix together with the yogurt, the mint and a little oil, salt and pepper to taste.

Done.

STUFFED ARTICHOKES WITH FAVA OR POTATOES AND PEAS

I have often wondered who discovered that artichokes were delicious, they must have been pretty desperate for food to risk all those sharp leaves and that choke, As I have said earlier, the artichokes are sold already prepared, which makes producing this exotic looking dish very easy. Depending on what you want, they are usually in three different sizes, three different prices in three different plastic buckets. You can also buy them in large jars, or smaller ones in cans, but don't buy the ones with cones of pale leaves still intact. They taste fine, but you don't need the leaves.

However many artichoke hearts as you need, large ones will feed one person adequately,
Smaller ones may require two each.
Salt to taste
1 whole lemon cut into quarters
Olive oil to serve
Chopped dill to serve

1. Cook the artichoke hearts in a pan of boiling water, with salt and lemon quarters.
2. Simmer for around 20 to 40 minutes depending on the size, but please check as too soft an artichoke is difficult to handle and not so tasty. Leave to cool.
3. Stuff with Fava (see page 81), drizzle over some olive oil and sprinkle with chopped dill leaves.

ANOTHER WAY:

WITH PEAS, CARROTS AND POTATOES

In Turkey the peas are sold ready shelled and bagged up into kilos. Yes!

4 large artichoke hearts
2 carrots peeled and cubed
I large potato peeled and cubed
1 onion cubed
2 cloves of garlic
150g peas (frozen is fine)
1 dessert spoon flour
½ tsp sugar
A mug of chicken or vegetable stock
Sea salt and ground black pepper
Chopped dill to garnish
Glug of olive oil

1. In a large pan sautee the chopped onions and carrots over a medium heat and season.
2. Add a dessert spoon of flour and stir. Add a mug of chicken or veggie stock and stir around, still on the heat add the peas and potatoes plus the sugar and stir well.
3. Place your artichoke hearts on top of the mixture and add enough stock to cover the hearts. Season well then add the garlic. Cook for a further 30 minutes.
4. Pour over the olive oil and some lemon juice and leave to cool.
5. Stuff the hearts with the vegetable mix and serve at room temperature topped by fresh dill fronds.

TURK TIP *You can make this dish with fresh broad beans also, but you should remove the skins, sadly the market man doesn't do this bit! They also need longer to cook than peas.*

CACIK (CUCUMBER AND YOGURT WITH OLIVE OIL)

Again, a simple but so useful side dish or mezze.

1 large or three small Turkish cucumbers
Salt
Olive oil
Tbsp thick natural yogurt
1 fat clove garlic
Dessert spoon dried mint
Salt and black pepper

1. Chop or grate cucumber, salt and drain for about 10–15 minutes.
2. Mix together with a small glug of olive oil yogurt, salt, black pepper, crushed minced garlic and mint.

There you have it.

EZME

You can always find *ezme* on the menu in most Turkish *lokantas* or restaurants. The essence of this dish is the fine chopping of the ingredients. Once that has been successfully accomplished, it's plain sailing. It is not for the faint of heart. HOT!

4 medium tomatoes, peeled and seeds removed then finely chopped
1 large red onion finely chopped
Salt and pepper to taste
2 large green chillies (use peppers if you are getting frightened), finely chopped and seeds removed.
1 handful fresh mint, finely chopped
2 handfuls fresh parsley, finely chopped
1 tbsp *pul biber* or hot chilli flakes
1 tsp sumac
Olive oil
Juice of 1 lemon

1. Drain away all the excess juices from the tomatoes and put in a bowl along with the onion, chillies and herbs, add the spices and mix thoroughly.
2. Stir in the lemon juice and olive oil. Serve with a sprinkle of extra parsley.

TURK TIP *Just hold back on the chilli if you find it too much.*

LEEKS IN OLIVE OIL

4 large fat leeks, make sure they are fresh and firm. No one likes a floppy leek!
3 medium-sized carrots
1 large onion
2 tbsp long grain rice rinsed.
3 large glugs of olive oil
1 tbsp tomato puree
Boiling water to mix

1. Trim and wash the leeks, cut off the white parts and leave aside.
2. Split the green parts of the leeks in half and slice thinly.
3. Rinse again to get rid of any crunchy soil that may linger.
4. Peel and slice the carrots. Place the green leeks and carrots in a large pot with olive oil and sauté until the liquid is absorbed, stirring occasionally.
5. Finely chop the onion and add to the mixture, cook another few minutes until soft.
6. Add a mugful of boiling water mixed with the tomato paste and the rice and stir well.
7. Bring to the boil.
8. Slice the whites of the leeks into 2cm-thick pieces, put on top of the leek and tomato mixture, turn down the heat and simmer until soft. Leave to cool. I like to add extra olive oil and some lemon juice at this point.
9. Leave for a few hours to absorb the flavours and serve cool, not icy cold.

FRIED LIVER IN SPICES

In Turkish, the name of this dish is *'Arnavut cigeri,'* which means 'Albanian' liver. It's a popular dish served in taverna-style restaurants all around Istanbul. Wherever it may have originated, it's delicious. If you don't ordinarily like liver, this dish is sure to change your mind. I absolutely love it and order it as a mezze whenever I see it on the menu. I get the lion's share as most people won't give it a try. My evil plan works well.

600g of fresh calf or lamb liver
1 tsp salt
1 tsp black pepper
6 tbsp flour
½ –1 tsp paprika according to taste
4 tbsp butter
Glug of olive or vegetable oil for frying
1 large red onion (I prefer more)
Tbsp of chopped flat parsley
1 tsp ground sumac

1. Cut out the veins and straggly bits then cube the liver, rinse in water and pat dry with paper towel.
2. Mix the flour and spices, coat the livers with the flour mix, then fry in the combined oil and butter, turning around to brown evenly.
3. Finely slice the red onions and fry separately to a soft consistency. Pile the liver on top of the onions to serve and sprinkle with parsley. Turks prefer the onions raw, its yummy, but you can be a lonely person after dinner.

I also like to add some cumin. This dish is often served with dried spices to dip the chunks into, which in my opinion makes the dish.

MAINS

FISH DISHES

I don't make a lot of fish dishes at the house, It has to be cooked on the day, which makes storage a problem and the smell is not universally recognised as appetising after the event. However, I am hoping to prepare some decent barbecues once the outside kitchen is finished, and to be honest, nothing can beat the taste of plain unadulterated charcoal-grilled fish on the bone with a side salad and maybe…chips. There are not many fish dishes here as most Turkish folk like their fish fresh 'n fried. I can only agree, fried or charcoal grilled on the day of catching is best.

Here are the few dishes I do prepare regularly, the rest of the time I go down to my favourite harbour-side restaurant.

TURKISH 'TARTAR SAUCE'

I wonder if the word 'tartar' has anything to do with THE Tartars? This is a traditional recipe for a classic sauce served with seafood. I love it and the combo with grilled fish or fried calamari is superb. Another traditional accompaniment is garlic oil, but I prefer this recipe.

45g walnuts/pine nuts, ground
70g white breadcrumbs from day-old bread (you can use brown, but the colour of the sauce looks a bit muddy)
2 garlic cloves, minced
250g Turkish yogurt
2 tbsp good olive oil
Sea salt and white pepper to taste

1. Whizz all the ingredients except the yogurt together, then mix in the yogurt last. Put in the fridge for an hour before serving, so the flavours infuse.

ANOTHER ACCOMPANIMENT TO FISH:

SAMPHIRE WITH GARLIC AND LEMON OIL

150g samphire
1 tsp butter
1 tsp olive oil
1 clove garlic
Lemon juice to taste

1. Pick over the samphire and wash it thoroughly under running water in a colander.
2. Melt the butter in a wide pan and add the oil. Add the samphire and garlic and toss in the hot butter and oil mixture.
3. Cook over a low heat for 1–2 minutes, until hot through.
4. Remove the pan and serve the samphire in a warmed bowl, with a squeeze of lemon juice over the top.
5. As samphire grows in salty conditions it won't need more salt.

FISH IN TOMATO SAUCE WITH FETA

This recipe works with just shellfish or white fish alone, or a mix of both. Serves 8

Glug olive oil
Tomato sauce (see recipe on page 118)
1–2 large bulbs of fennel, diced into ½ inch pieces
¼ –½ glass Raki
Fennel seeds
Sea salt and freshly ground black pepper
Small handful basil or thyme, finely chopped
250g of feta cheese or *Beyaz Peynir* (which is creamier)
900–1350 grams of skinless fish, prawns and well, almost anything you fancy, You can judge how much you need for your own crew.
Crusty bread for serving

1. Preheat your oven to 425F, 220C Gas 7 and position a rack in the centre.
2. In a large oven proof skillet, heat 2 tablespoons of the olive oil over medium high heat.
3. Add the diced fennel and a pinch of salt and sauté, stirring occasionally until the fennel is slightly softened and lightly browned, 7 to 8 minutes.
4. Add the garlic and sauté until fragrant, 1 minute, stirring frequently and taking care not to let it burn.
5. Add the Raki, turn the temperature up a bit higher, and bring to a boil.
6. Add the tomato sauce, stir through and reduce to a medium heat until the consistency of thick cream, then remove from the heat.
7. Season with salt and pepper, although it should not need too much salt if using the salty feta. Pour into the skillet.
8. Arrange the fish and/or shellfish in a single layer on the tomato mixture, nestling it into the sauce, Then sprinkle over the chunks of feta.
9. Bake in the preheated oven until the fish is cooked through and the cheese is melting, about 15–18 minutes. Serve immediately.

Absolutely delicious and so easy, especially if you have the frozen pre-made tomato sauce. Told you!

GARLIC PRAWNS

Anything with garlic and prawns gets my vote.

1 kg uncooked prawns
1–2 large bulbs of garlic, cloves peeled and chopped
Large glug olive oil
4 red chillies, de-seeded and sliced, or a tsp of *aci biber* (hot pepper flakes)
I large bunch flat leaf parsley, chopped
Sea salt and pepper to taste
2 lemons

1. Peel and de-vein the prawns, leaving the tails on.
2. Heat the olive oil in a shallow pan, cook the garlic and chilli over a low heat until soft, but not browned (5 mins).
3. Add the prawns, season with salt and pepper and cook until they turn pink.

4. Stir in the parsley and a squeeze of lemon juice and serve hot with the other lemon cut into 4 wedges.

NOTE: You can substitute butter for oil in this dish, 300g should do it. I also think a splash of Raki flamed would not do any harm.

PRAWNS BAKED WITH VEGETABLES – *KARIDES GUVEC*

This is traditionally served as a mezze, usually before a fish main course, but I don't see any reason why it shouldn't take a star turn.

- 600g fresh raw prawns, de-veined and with the tails left on
- 1 large onion, peeled and chopped
- Half a bulb of garlic, cloves peeled and chopped
- 3 glugs olive oil
- 2–3 red peppers, sliced
- 1 green pepper, sliced
- 2–3 large tomatoes, peeled
- 200g button mushrooms
- 1 tbsp tomato paste
- 2–3 tsp *pul biber* (hot)
- Sea salt and pepper to taste
- 150g grated cheese

1. Heat the oil in a large pan and fry the onions.
2. After a few minutes add the garlic and a little salt, continue to cook until soft.
3. Add the peppers and cook further for a few minutes, then add the tomatoes, mushrooms, tomato paste and chilli flakes and simmer until reduced and most of the liquid has gone.
4. Add the prawns and then pop into a clay pot or terracotta dish, cover with grated cheese, any cheese will do, feta or even cheddar will give different, but equally good results.
5. Cook in a medium oven at 180°C until the cheese is bubbling and spotted with brown.

Serve hot with Turkish bread to mop up the juices.

FISH STEW

The Turks like nothing more than to suck as much protein out of one fish as they can, eyes, cheeks and all. It takes an age to eat one fish. Thus this fish stew is cooked all in one pot. For a more refined dish, I suggest first making a stock with the heads, onion, bay leaves, 2–3 carrots roughly chopped, parsley, garlic and lemon; once flavoursome, cook the filleted fish in it, add a dash of Raki, or brandy and maybe a swirl of cream and there you have it, but the following recipe is much quicker, easier and will take the whole evening for a Turk to eat. Happy days!

- 1 large onion, sliced into rings
- 2 bay leaves
- A handful of parsley, chopped
- 3 large tomatoes peeled and chopped
- 1 lemon juiced and 1 lemon peeled and sliced
- 2 cloves garlic
- 1kg mixed fish: mullet, bass, gurnard, etc, cleaned but leave the heads on
- Salt and pepper to season
- Glug of olive oil

1. In a large pan, place the onion rings on the bottom and dot with the garlic. Place the fish on top, scatter the peeled lemon over the fish and then the lemon juice. Top the lot with bay leaves, parsley including stalks and the chopped tomatoes. Pour on water to cover a couple of fingers above and finish with a large glug of good olive oil. Season to taste.
2. Put the whole she-bang on the hob at a medium heat and simmer for about 40 minutes until the flesh comes off the bones easily.
3. Spoon out the fish then add a glug of raki to the liquid, reduce down for a few minutes and serve with the sauce and lots of bread.

BAKED FISH WITH VEGETABLES

4 Sea bream, bass OR mullet, washed and cleaned
4 green peppers
4 red peppers
2 carrots
2 medium size potatoes
2 medium size onions
2 lemons, thinly sliced
2 glugs olive oil
Black pepper
Salt
1 tsp pul biber

1. Preheat oven to 200 degrees C. 180 Fan 400F Gas 6
2. Wash and clean the fish thoroughly, pat dry, season then set aside.
3. Chop all the vegetable into bite-sized portions. Place in a bowl and set aside.
4. Oil a baking tray as the fish skin may stick.
5. Reserving a few onions, green and red peppers for stuffing the fish place the chopped vegetables into the baking tray and season with salt, pepper and *pul biber.*
6. Drizzle over some olive oil and mix thoroughly with your hands making sure that all the vegetables have been salted and peppered.
7. Meanwhile, stuff each fish with the reserved veg. Then place a slice of lemon inside each fish and a small bay leaf as the final stuffing and sprinkle over some salt and pepper.
8. Place each stuffed fish carefully at the bottom of the baking tray (with all the chopped vegetables on top) and drizzle with the remaining olive oil. Garnish with the rest of the lemon slices.
9. Completely cover the dish with aluminium foil before finally placing the tray into the preheated oven.
10. Bake for about 40 minutes, but test after 30 to check on progress, as overdone fish is dry.

FISH WITH OLIVES

1kg fish fillets, something meaty, like snapper, is good
Bunch parsley, chopped
1 tsp *pul biber*
500g cherry tomatoes, halved
200g black olives, the wrinkly sort or Kalamata, stoned
6 garlic cloves, minced
Glug of olive oil

1. Heat olive oil in a heavy large pan over medium-high heat.
2. Sprinkle the fish with salt and pepper. Add half of the fish to the skillet and cook until just opaque

in the centre, about 3 minutes per side.

3. Transfer the fish to a warm dish. Repeat with the remaining fish.
4. Add parsley and *pul biber* to the same pan; sauté for 1 minute.
5. Add the tomatoes, olives and garlic; sauté until the tomatoes are soft and juicy, about 2 minutes.
6. Season sauce with salt and pepper; spoon over the fish.

SEAFOOD PASTA

Pasta in Turkish means 'cake', so when I first arrived I got a few surprises on ordering lunch! Actually, the word for pasta in turkey is *markana*, but they don't just have macaroni, lots of other pastas are available and very popular, the most common being the traditional *Manti*, which is a kind of ravioli, but more on that on page 159.

Turks make their seafood pasta with tomato sauce, so use the recipe on page 118 and then fry in oil your fish bits and prawns, add the sauce and then plop in some shellfish whilst the sauce is bubbling until the shells open, and you are done. However, sometimes I like to go the whole hog and use wine and spice and cheese, which isn't particularly Turkish, but I give it a twist by using Turkish spices; there is nothing a prawn likes more than garlic, butter and a little bit of heat.

500g spaghetti or pasta of your choice
250g fresh raw prawns
250g fish of choice
250g squid, cleaned and chopped into rings
Some fresh Dill, a handful should be fine
Glug of Wine
500ml Fish stock
Garlic to taste
Sea salt and black pepper
2 smallish leeks
Lemon
250g Labneh
1 tbsp Turkish yogurt
Pul biber
Olive oil
1 dessert spoon butter plus some for drizzle
1 tsp Sumac

1. Melt the butter and oil in a large pan, add the finely chopped leeks and a little salt and soften.
2. Add the garlic and *pul biber*, cook for a few minutes then add the seafood, toss and stir until the prawns start to turn pink and the fish has cooked.
3. Add the white wine and some stock, bring to a simmer reduce down a little and then add the *labneh* and yogurt and a squeeze of lemon. Stir until the sauce is creamy, add the chopped dill, salt and freshly ground black pepper to taste.
4. Serve stirred into the spaghetti or pasta of your choice and drizzle with lots of melted butter flavoured with sumac and *pul biber*. Scatter with more dill.

TURK TIP *Mushrooms also go well with this dish, but remember how much water they release, so adjust the amount of stock used accordingly.*

SEA BASS WITH ALMOND SAUCE (*BADEM TARATORLU LEVREK*)

This is a delicate dish and suitable for any occasion.

For the fish:
6 sea bass fillets
500ml fish stock or water
Sea salt
¼ tsp black peppercorns
1 large lemon, juiced
1 bay leaf
Bunch of parsley

For the sauce:
60g breadcrumbs
120g ground almonds
2 cloves garlic, minced
2 large lemons, juiced (approximately 3 tbsp)
4–6 tbsp water
4 glugs of olive oil
Sea salt and pepper to taste
Paprika

1. Rinse the fish and pat dry. In a large shallow pan, pour in the stock or if not available, the water, add the bay leaf, salt, peppercorns, lemon juice and parsley. Cover and bring to the boil, then simmer for 10 minutes so the flavours infuse.
2. Add the fish and simmer for 6–8 minutes until the fish is done (you can test with the point of a knife, it should flake easily).
3. For the sauce, whizz the breadcrumbs, almonds, garlic and lemon juice and add water until the sauce becomes a smooth creamy texture.
4. To serve, drain the fish well of all the liquor, place on warm plates and spoon over the hot almond sauce, sprinkle with paprika and a few chopped parsley leaves for colour.

MEAT

Actually, we get quite a few non-meat eaters on our holidays, so I try to make dishes that can easily be converted to be meatless.

KARNI YARIK MEAT IN A TRENCH (i.e. the trench formed in the aubergine)

4 aubergines (cut them crosswise if they are really big)
150g minced beef or lamb (if using lamb use less oil as lamb can be fatty)
2 large tomatoes, peeled and diced
1 onion, diced
4 garlic cloves, chopped
5 tbsp olive oil
1–2 tsp of *pul biber* /red pepper flakes
Salt
Ground black pepper
½ bunch parsley, finely chopped
1 cup water
1 tbsp pepper or tomato paste
2 glugs olive oil

For decoration:
1 green pepper cut into quarters
1 tomato quartered

1. Remove the stems and peel the aubergines using a potato peeler or sharp knife. Then make a slit along one side from stem to base without cutting in two. Place in a bowl of salted water for 20 minutes to get rid of the bitter juices. This also makes them easier to fry. Pat dry with paper or a tea towel.
2. Gently fry in 1 tablespoon of the olive oil in a large shallow pan, turning occasionally so all sides are softened and take on a golden brown colour on the peeled areas, you may need to do this in batches, set aside.
3. Heat 2 tablespoons of the olive oil in a pan and sauté the onion. Add minced beef, salt, black pepper, *pul biber* and garlic and stir. When the meat starts to colour add the diced tomatoes.
4. Continue stirring until the meat has absorbed all its own juices, then remove from the heat. Add the parsley and mix well.
5. Gently ease open the aubergines by using a spoon pushed into the slit, stuff the interior with the meat mixture and place them in an oven tray.
6. Slice 1 tomato and 2 peppers and place them on the stuffed aubergine bellies.
7. Mix 1 tbsp of the pepper or tomato paste with 1 mug of water. Pour it directly into the oven tray.
8. Drizzle little olive oil on each aubergine and bake at 200C 180 fan 400F Gas 6 until the tomatoes and green peppers are done (about 20–30 min).

I like to serve the aubergines on a circular Turkish '*Tepsi*' or tray, rather like the spokes of a wheel. I found a very large one in the kitchen when we moved in, it's perfect.

KÖFTE

Simple, I have honed my *köfte*-making into a freehand exercise, adding spices and herbs to the minced meat according to how the mood takes me, or what is available. I don't think there are any hard and fast rules. However, I can make two observations based on experience: you don't need an egg to bind the meatballs, just get your hands well into the mixture, and knead, knead, knead. This will bind the meat and other ingredients perfectly. Leave to sit for a few hours, even overnight, so all the flavours are infused. Job done.

BASIC KÖFTE

500g minced beef or lamb (lamb makes good *köfte* as you need the fat to keep them moist)
2 tbsp stale bread, soaked in water and squeezed out thoroughly
1 large onion, grated
1 heaped tsp cumin
1 heaped tsp cinnamon
1 heaped tsp coriander
1–2 tsp *pul biber.* You can cheat a bit by adding 'köfte spice' ready made, but it's nice to make them your own.
1 dessert spoon dried mint
Chilli flakes – it's up to you how much
2 cloves garlic, minced or pressed
Salt and pepper to taste
2 tbsp finely chopped parsley

1. Put all the ingredients in a large bowl, knead well for several minutes, form into golf ball sized balls in the palm of your hand then pat them down to make a patty shape.
2. Leave to infuse the flavours and then fry in oil until brown on both sides. You can grill or cook on a griddle, any which way is good.

OTHER OPTIONS

With courgettes

Make the meatballs as above, except form into balls rather than patties. Bake in a medium oven on a roasting tray for 15 minutes, remove and cool a little.

Meanwhile, slice the courgettes thinly into strips, brush with olive oil and griddle until scorched in places.

Place the courgette slices in the form of a cross with centres overlapping. Put one meatball in the centre and wrap the courgettes around so it looks like a parcel. Place face down on an oiled roasting tray and put back in the oven for about 10–15 minutes until everything is cooked.

With aubergines

Prepare the meatballs as before, pare slices of aubergine with a potato peeler, soak the slices in a bowl of salted water for 15 minutes, pat dry, brush with oil and griddle until scorched in places, wrap as with the courgettes and cook as before.

ICLI KÖFTE

A sort of Turkish Kinder egg; a firm shell of meat and bulgur surrounding the 'gift' of soft minced meat and crushed walnuts. The filling can be made in advance, which helps intensify the flavours.

Outside casing:
250g finely minced beef
2 onions, peeled and grated
250g fine or *köfte* bulgur
2 tbsp plain flour
125g semolina
1 egg
1 tsp cumin
I tsp *pul biber* /red pepper flakes
1 cup water
2 tbsp red pepper paste or tomato paste
Salt and pepper to taste

Filling:
250g minced lamb
2 onions, peeled and grated
2 glugs of olive oil
100g chopped walnut pieces
1–2 tsp red pepper flakes
A handful of chopped flat leaf parsley
Salt and pepper to taste

For the filling:

1. Heat the olive oil in a large pan and add the meat. Cook for about 3–5 minutes until the juices have evaporated.
2. Add the grated onion, salt, black pepper and red pepper flakes, and continue to cook for another 3–5 minutes until the onions have softened. Add the walnuts and chopped parsley last, mix, and turn the heat off. Allow to cool down.

For the dough casing:

1. Make the bulgur dough by adding red pepper paste, cumin, salt and red pepper flakes to the bulgur wheat in a large bowl. The bowl should be large enough that you have room to knead the contents.
2. Pour 1–1½ cups hot water over the mixture, thoroughly combine with your hands, and allow bulgur to sit absorbing the water for about 10 minutes.
3. In the meantime, put semolina in a separate bowl and stir ½ cup warm water over it. Mix until it forms very soft dough.
4. Wet your hands with cold water and knead the bulgur dough for about 5 minutes.
5. Add the semolina dough and knead to incorporate, don't be tempted to leave out the semolina, as it helps bind the bulgur dough.
6. Add the ground beef and continue to knead until combined, about 5 minutes, until you have a smooth, elastic dough.
7. With a bowl of cold water beside you, begin to shape the *köfte*. Take some dough into your hands and roll into an oval shape.
8. Using your thumb, hollow out the middle of the dough piece so that you can add about 1½ tbsp of meat filling. The bulgur should be about ¼ inch thick around the meat filling. Close and mend any cracks in the dough with wet fingers. Taper the ends for a classic lemon-shape.
9. Deep fry for a few minutes until golden brown and crispy.

If you really haven't the time or the patience, then I suggest you combine steps 1–3 and knead together to form the dough. Roll out portions of dough between two sheets of cling film then cut out circles using a cup or mug as a guide. Place the filling in the middle of a circle of dough and fold over to make a half-moon. Wet your fingers and press the sides together. Not the traditional shape but a bit quicker and tastes just as good. Trust me!.

POMEGRANATE AND YOGURT SAUCE

Good with *köfte* by way of a change

½ cup plain yogurt
1 tbsp pomegranate molasses; more for serving
2 tbsp chopped fresh mint
1 tsp ground sumac or ½ tsp fresh lemon juice

1. Combine all the ingredients and stir well.

ANOTHER WAY WITH *KÖFTE* AND AUBERGINE

This looks pretty good sitting in its serving pan and really simple to make.

Köfte made as above.
4 – 6 aubergines peeled with a potato peeler to make zebra stripes
Tomato sauce See P00

1. Take the peeled and de-stalked aubergines and soak in salted water for 15 minutes. Pat dry. Cut into thick slices about 5 cm.
2. Brush both sides with olive oil.
3. Take a circular tray (you can use square, but circular looks more professional somehow)
4. Starting at the centre take a raw meatball and sandwich on either side with the slices of aubergine. Carry on placing around the tray until all the meatballs are used. If there are any aubergine slices left just pop them where you see a space.
5. Drizzle with olive oil and the tomato sauce. Cover with foil.
6. Bake in a pre heated hot oven, 200C 180 fan. 400F Gas 6 for about 40 minutes until the meatballs are cooked through and the aubergines soft.

ADANA KEBAB

These kebabs are traditionally cooked over a large sink-like charcoal grill, but that may not be possible and even though we do have a large stone barbecue in our garden, I still use the grill plate.

500g (about 1lb 2oz) ground lamb
Sea salt
2 tsp ground cumin, 1 for the mix, 1 for cooking
2 tbsp ground sumac, 1 for the mix, 1 for cooking
2 tbsp ground Urfa pepper 1 for the mix, 1 for cooking
2 tbsp ice-cold water

To serve
1 red onion, thinly sliced
6 pieces _lavash_ or pita
1 cup fresh parsley leaves
2 medium tomatoes, thinly sliced
Pickled peppers

1. Combine the lamb with 7.5g (about 2 teaspoons) sea salt, 1 teaspoon cumin, 2 teaspoons sumac and 1 tablespoon pepper flakes.
2. Knead by hand or in a stand mixer fitted with a paddle attachment until the mixture turns tacky and starts sticking to the side of the bowl. Add water and continue kneading until incorporated. Place in refrigerator and chill well.
3. Meanwhile, combine the remaining teaspoon of cumin, 2 teaspoons of the sumac, the remaining tablespoon of pepper flakes, and 2 teaspoons of the salt in a small bowl. Set aside.
4. Combine the remaining 2 teaspoons of sumac and the red onions in a medium bowl. Season with salt to taste and set aside.
5. Using wet hands, divide the lamb mixture into 12 even balls. Then, form each ball into a long, flat kebab around a skewer.
6. Make sure it is smoking hot, oil it and then place the kebabs on the griddle, turning occasionally and sprinkling with the reserved spices until well browned and a bit charred on the crinkly bits.

7. During the last few minutes of cooking, place bread directly on top of the kebabs in batches until heated through.
8. Serve kebabs with warm bread, sumac, onions, parsley, tomatoes and pickled peppers.

MEAT-STUFFED PEPPERS/TOMATOES

I usually make both meat and veggie-filled stuffed vegetables, both are delicious, and you can use the veggie ones as a side dish or as a main. The type of peppers I use in Turkey are teeny tiny, sweet and very pretty on the plate. I find the thicker-skinned large peppers sold elsewhere a bit too hard, but have discovered that if you lightly fry them on all sides in olive oil before stuffing, the flavour is delicious and they are much softer. Depending on the size of the peppers I use between 12 and 20.

12–18 small green peppers or 8–10 large ones, the tops cut off and put aside and the white membrane cut away.
300g minced beef and lamb mixed
1 cup rice, washed and drained
2–3 large tomatoes, grated
2 large onions, grated
1 tsp cinnamon
1–2 tsp *pul biber*
1 tbsp dried mint
Small bunch parsley, chopped
Salt and black pepper to taste

Cooking liquor
Tomato paste
Large glug olive oil
Salt and black pepper to taste

1. The most important thing is to use a pan deep enough for the peppers to stand upright. If they topple over, just shave a bit off the bottom so they stand firm. The peppers should all fit snugly side by side, imagine a crowded tube train!
2. Once the leg work has been done – grating the tomatoes and onions – the rest is plain sailing. Don't worry when you grate them, you will always have a 'cheek' of onion left in your hand, just use it for flavouring stock or something later. The tomatoes, miraculously, just grate down beautifully until you are left with the whole empty skin.
3. Then combine all the stuffing ingredients I prefer to use my (clean) hands to do this, it's also very satisfying.
4. Stuff your peppers about ¾ full as the rice will expand, you can either then pop the 'lids' back on or you can go a step further and slice pieces of tomato with the skin uppermost and use instead of the pepper lid. Some Turkish ladies pop the tomato on top of the stuffing then remove the stem from the lid and place that on top so the red shows through the hole.
5. Once all the peppers are filled and sitting in the pan, pour over a mixture of tomato paste and a large glug of olive oil and season well.
6. The liquid should come up about 2/3 of the peppers, don't let it slosh over the stuffing mixture as it will then float away into the sauce, which is not a disaster, but doesn't look so good.
7. Pop onto a medium heat, bring to the boil clamp a lid on and simmer for about 30 minutes until the rice is cooked.
8. Serve at room temperature with *Cacik*, see page 95. Always tastes better the next day and also freezes surprisingly well.

SAVOURY STUFFED QUINCE

You can substitute rice for breadcrumbs as in stuffed peppers, they may need more liquid to plump up the rice.

Four large quinces
350g minced lamb
50g breadcrumbs
2 small red onions chopped, reserve one for the sauce
1 clove of garlic, crushed
Large pinch cumin
Large pinch Allspice
1 tsp cinnamon
A handful of pine nuts
6 dried apricots/figs, chopped
A few sprigs of fresh mint leaves, chopped
A handful of fresh flat leaf parsley chopped, reserve some for garnish
Some chilli flakes to taste

For the sauce:
Olive oil
500 ml chicken stock
Juice of 1 lemon
Pomegranate seeds for garnish
Salt and pepper

1. Peel and core the quinces but take out a little more of the flesh to make a larger hollow for the stuffing. You can use the left over quince in a pudding or another dish.
2. Mix together the meat and other ingredients, reserving the onion for the sauce, and stuff the quinces well.
3. In a pan soften the onion in olive oil and add the remaining quince flesh pulped in a hand blender or food processor, or if you don't have either, just finely chopped, then add the chicken stock, salt and pepper and lemon juice.
4. Poach the quinces gently in this mixture with the lid on for one hour, add a little water and some pomegranate molasses (*nar*) if necessary. The *nar* will add sweetness rather like balsamic vinegar.
5. Serve with a garnish of pomegranate seeds and mint.

Variations of this stuffing, with or without meat, can be used in chicken dishes. I add more breadcrumbs and some celery and leave out the cinnamon. Finely chopped quince flesh makes a lovely addition and served with saffron rice with almonds, it looks sensational!

MOUSSAKA TURKISH STYLE

As with many Greek dishes, there is a Turkish equivalent. The Turkish Moussaka, however, is quite different from the Greek inasmuch as it does not layer up and top off with a bechamel sauce. However, I do like the sauce, so I do a sort of combo of the two. Works for me and there is never any left over.

6–8 long aubergines, actually you can never have too many as they shrink down when fried, especially if you're like me and can't have enough of them
1 kg minced beef and lamb
1 tsp cinnamon
1 tsp nutmeg, freshly ground if possible
2 large onions, finely chopped
6 large tomatoes peeled and chopped or 2 cans chopped tomatoes

1 large green pepper chopped finely
A little dried thyme, it is quite strong so not too much. You can always add but you cannot take it away
1 tbsp chopped parsley
3–4 cloves garlic
1 tbsp tomato paste
1 tbsp sweet pepper paste
A generous amount of olive oil

Sauce:
1 large bay leaf
1 litre of milk heated in a pan with a bay leaf and a few peppercorns and left to steep for an hour
2 eggs, beaten
100g butter
200g flour
Pinch of grated nutmeg here too
Salt and black pepper to taste

1. Take off the stems and chop the aubergines into approximately 5cm cubes and soak in a bowl of salted water for 15 minutes.
2. In a large pan sautée the onions with a little salt to soften, then add the garlic and peppers, cook for a further minute or so then add the cinnamon and meat.
3. Cook for a further few minutes on a medium to high heat until the meat browns and starts to absorb its own juices. Stir thoroughly and then add the tomato and pepper pastes and the chopped tomatoes plus salt and pepper to taste. You may need to add a little water, up to 500ml, at this point and then reduce down until you get a thick meaty filling. Take off the heat and add the parsley. Stir.
4. Remove the aubergines from the salted water and dry thoroughly on kitchen towel. I press quite hard, to be sure there are no remaining juices.
5. In a large pan with plenty of space, fry the aubergines in a large glug of olive oil, aubergines are notorious for soaking up the oil, but hopefully the soaking will have done the trick. To my mind, you have to abandon all hope of an oil-free dish and we all know that the taste of the oil and the aubergines just make the dish that little bit better. If this is the only way I'm going to get rich, then I'm happy. You will probably need to fry them in batches and make sure they are well-coloured and a bit crispy on the edges. Set aside.
6. Now make the bechamel sauce, the usual way, but I like the added depth of flavour by steeping the milk first, also warm milk will thicken the sauce far more quickly than milk straight from the fridge.
7. Melt the butter in a large saucepan and then add the flour, stir around until it makes a roux, then slowly add the milk (extract the leaf and pepper first) to make a thickish sauce, the consistency of double cream. Once it has reached that stage, take off the heat and leave to cool a little while, then add the beaten eggs, grated nutmeg and seasoning, and stir thoroughly.
8. In a large oven-proof dish scoop all of the aubergine pieces onto the bottom, then spoon the meat over the top, then top over with the sauce, it should be enough to cover the meat by at least 5 cm or more so when you serve it cuts through.
9. Put into a medium oven 180°C 160 Fan 350F Gas 4 for half an hour or until the sauce bubbles and goes golden brown.

This is best served at room temperature with a good salad.

CHICKEN TRAY BAKE

Now I never make this the same way twice, but the principle is always the same: yogurt marinade.

10–12 chicken thighs (I don't like the legs, they irritate me, all stick and sinew)
3 large red onions, quartered

For the marinade:
250g Turkish or Greek natural yogurt
1 tbsp tomato paste
1 heaped tbsp honey
1–2 heaped tsp of each of: cumin, coriander, *pul biber* (sweet chilli flakes), sumac, *Harissa* mix
The grated rind and juice of 1 lemon
Salt and black pepper
6 cloves garlic, pressed
Glug of olive oil

1. In a large bowl, mix all the marinade ingredients together and thoroughly coat the chicken, use your hands, but don't forget to wash them afterwards (raw chicken!). Leave to marinade for at least 4 hours, preferably overnight.
2. Put the marinaded chicken in a large roasting pan with the quartered onions tucked in between. Spoon the rest of the marinade over the top.
3. Bake in the oven, 180°C for half an hour, then crank up the heat to 200°C FFF for a further 10–15 minutes until the chicken chars a little, it's actually the marinade catching, not the chicken, but it looks like it's been barbecued.

GUVEC

This is traditionally cooked in a stone/clay pot in the oven. It is usually shallow and either round or oval with a large surface for allowing maximum evaporation. These pots used to be taken to the bakery and left to cook in the wood-burning ovens. See p00 The essence is very slow cooking. You can use both meat and fish in a *guvec* and plenty of vegetables in season are added for flavour and colour.

CHICKEN *GUVEC*

800g chicken thighs de-boned (use the bones to make stock)
2 tomatoes
4 red peppers (pointy ones)
1 green pepper
1 aubergine
2 large onions or 12–18 small shallots
2–3 cloves garlic
I tbsp tomato paste
1 tbsp red pepper paste
2 tsp pul biber
2 tbsp butter
½ litre of chicken stock
Sea salt and black pepper to taste

1. Peel the aubergine in zebra stripes and soak in salted water for 15 minutes. Pat dry.
2. Chop the aubergine, peppers and tomatoes.
3. Melt the butter in a large pan and brown the chicken, then add the shallots, spice and garlic. Cook for 5 minutes.

4. Add the tomato and red pepper paste and cook for a further 5.
5. On top of the chicken layer first the aubergine, then the peppers and finally the tomatoes. Cover with the stock. Season well. Cover and bring to the boil over a medium heat.
6. Lower the heat and cook at a slow simmer for about 2 hours.
7. Remove from the heat and leave to rest for about 30 minutes before serving.

LAHMUCUN

So good for lunch, nothing better than to eat food with your fingers even those covered in paint! I will put my (painterly) hand up, I do buy frozen ones when short of time, but am racked with guilt because they are so easy to prepare. Lahmacun made with yufka as in this recipe, comes out looking more like what you find in Turkey.

To make homemade lahmacun *dough (*yufka*):*

1 pack of instant yeast (8g)
240ml warm water
1 tsp sugar
80g cup cornflour
155g plain flour
8 tbsp + 1 tbsp whole wheat flour (90g)
2 tbsp olive oil
½ tsp salt

1. In a large bowl, combine the yeast, warm water and sugar. Let sit for about 5 minutes until the yeast blooms.
2. In another bowl, mix together the 3 flours
3. Add olive oil and salt to the yeast mixture, then slowly incorporate the flour mixture into the yeast mixture.
4. Knead the dough for about 2 minutes, using additional flour as needed to keep it from getting too sticky. Try not to add too much flour as you don't want it to dry out the dough.
5. Allow the kneaded ball of dough to rest covered with a clean T towel in an oiled bowl for about 1 hour. It should at least double in size.
6. Pre heat the oven to ?????
7. Punch down the dough with floured hands, and split into 8 equally sized balls (approx. 70g each).
8. Use a rolling pin to roll the dough into thin, round circles or *yufka* (approx 2–3 mm thick).
9. Layer 2–3 pieces of *yufka* with some olive oil and water to keep them from separating.

For the topping

350g finely minced lamb
1 onion, grated
3 to 4 cloves garlic, minced
1 handful flat leaf parsley, finely chopped
2 large tomatoes, grated
1 green pepper, grated
1 tbsp red pepper paste
1 tbsp tomato paste
1 tbsp paprika
1 tbsp hot red pepper flakes
1tsp cumin
Sea salt and black pepper to taste

1. Preheat the oven to 230 C 210 fan 450 F. Gas 8
2. 230 C Turn the dough onto a flowered surface and divide into six balls. Roll out each ball into thin round shapes. Spread the topping onto the rounds and place on heated trays from the oven.

Bake for ten minutes until the dough is brown and the topping bubbling. Watch out these cook so quickly they may burn if you don't check them.

SPINACH RICE AND MINCED BEEF

1 kg fresh spinach thoroughly washed and chopped
300g minced beef or lamb
1 medium onion, chopped
2 cloves garlic, chopped
1 tbsp *biber salcasi* or tomato paste
1 tsp *pul biber*
250g rice
2 tbsp olive oil
Sea salt and black pepper

1. In a large pot slowly cook the minced meat in a little oil until it absorbs its own juices.
2. Add the onion, then after a few minutes the garlic, cook until the onion is tender.
3. Add the pepper paste or tomato puree and stir for 2–3 minutes.
4. Add the spinach and stir until it reduces in size and is wilted right down.
5. Add the rice and 175 ml boiling water and turn down the heat. Cover with a lid and simmer until the rice is cooked.
6. Season well, and add some chilli if you like a little heat. Serve warm with a dollop of yogurt.

OR IF VEGETARIAN OPTION REQUIRED:

SPINACH RICE AND EGGS.

Cook as above, but in a shallow pan omitting the meat, fry the onions and garlic, add the puree and the spinach, some *pul biber* and cumin and stir well for a few minutes. Next, add the rice and water, and when the rice is just about cooked, crack an egg into the mixture. Once the egg is cooked serve with bread and yogurt

SPICY CHICKEN CASSEROLE WITH SAFFRON AND DRIED FRUITS

Turkey has a surprising repertoire of meat and fruit dishes, I thought these were more North African, but I was pleasantly surprised. I have, however, made this dish a bit Fusion.

8 chicken thighs dusted in a little flour
2 large onions, sliced
1 fennel bulb, sliced
1 tbsp Ras al hanout or a mix of cinnamon, cumin, ginger and coriander
1 dessert spoon *pul biber*
Glug of olive oil
500 ml chicken stock
1 pinch saffron soaked in a little of the stock
1 handful of dried apricots and/or figs
Juice of ½ lemon

1. Fry off the chicken until browned. Set aside.

TURK TIP *You can also use lamb in this dish – watch out for fatty cuts though.*

2. In the same pan, fry the onions and fennel until softened, add the spice. Stir and cook for a couple of minutes.
3. Add the stock, saffron and chicken. Simmer until the chicken is thoroughly cooked.
4. Squeeze in the juice and mix. Serve with Almond Pilaf . *(see p00)*

LEMON CHICKEN

This an excellent chicken dish for the summer months. You need a few lemons, but for me at least, there's nothing easier than to saunter out into the garden and gather my own. Actually, now I come to think of it, it's quite dangerous as usually the fattest and juiciest lemons are the ones overhanging the swimming pool…

8 chicken breasts, quartered and dusted with flour
4 lemons, sliced thinly
1 litre stock (chicken or vegetable)
1 glass of white wine
1 tbsp parsley, chopped
1 tbsp dill, chopped
½ bulb garlic, cloves peeled and sliced thinly
2 onions, sliced
1 tsp Sumac
A handful of pitted green olives
Olive oil
1 tbsp *kaymak* (Turkish clotted cream)

1. In a pan fry the breasts turning them to seal the meat. Set aside.
2. In the same pan fry the onions and garlic, with some salt until soft, add the sumac and cook for a few minutes. Set aside.
3. De-glaze the pan with the white wine [explain?] and add the stock, reduce down a little and season well.
4. Put the chicken and the onions in an oven proof dish and layer up with the sliced lemons, sprinkling with the parsley, dill and olives as you go.
5. Pour over the reduced stock and cover with a lid or foil. Bake in the oven on a medium heat for 30 minutes.
6. When the chicken has cooked through, stir in the *kaymak* to slightly thicken the sauce.
7. Serve with rice pilaf, or crusty bread and a salad.

CHICKEN WITH CHICKPEAS

750g boneless, skinless chicken breasts, trimmed, cut into 1 inch (2.5cm) pieces
¼ cup lemon juice
1 tsp ground cumin
1 tsp paprika
1 tsp. *pul biber*
1 tsp sumac
½ tsp sugar
1 glug extra-virgin olive oil
1 large onion, chopped
3 tomatoes, peeled and chopped
400g chickpeas
Handful parsley, chopped

1. Mash the garlic and ½ teaspoon salt on a cutting board with the back of a fork until a paste forms. Transfer to a medium bowl and whisk in lemon juice, cumin, paprika and sumac. Add the chicken and stir to coat.

2. Heat the oil in a large cast-iron skillet over a medium-high heat. Add the onion and cook, stirring occasionally, until golden brown, 6 to 8 minutes.
3. Using a slotted spoon, transfer the chicken to the pan (reserve the marinade) and cook, stirring occasionally, until opaque on the outside, about 4 minutes.
4. Add the tomatoes with their juice, the chickpeas, the reserved marinade and the remaining ¼ teaspoon salt. Reduce the heat to medium and cook, stirring occasionally, until the chicken is cooked through, 5 to 7 minutes more.
5. Serve sprinkled with parsley.

LAMB WITH WHITE BEANS *GUVEC*

500g dry white beans soaked overnight, drained and cooked in boiling water until soft.
1 glug olive oil for cooking
1 large onion, chopped.
5 cloves of garlic
250g lamb cut into large chunks
1 tbsp tomato paste
1 tbsp red pepper paste
4 medium tomatoes peeled and chopped, or one 400g can chopped tomatoes.
1 orange, peeled and chopped
1 large sprig fresh thyme
1 bay leaf
1 tsp *pul biber*
1.5l lamb or chicken stock
Sea salt and black pepper to taste

1. Preheat the oven on 180°C 350 F Gas 4
2. Heat the olive oil and brown the lamb to seal. Set aside.
3. Fry the onion in the same oil until soft, add the whole cloves of garlic, the tomato paste and the diced tomatoes. Stir together, then stir in the beans, the chopped orange, the hot water, the *pul biber*, thyme, salt and pepper and the stock. Add the lamb and mix well, put into an oven proof dish and cook slowly for 2–3 hours. If it gets too dry you can add a little water.
4. Serve with bulgur or rice pilaf.

AUBERGINE STUFFED WITH CHICKEN BREAST OR QUAIL

Originally, for a family feast, I had tried to fit a whole quail into the 'jaws' of the aubergine, but discovered that I could not get the fat aubergines in the UK at Christmas, so I think it best to use a nice fat organic chicken breast instead. It will still taste just as good. In point of fact I suppose you could use lamb fillet as well, it goes really well with smoked aubergine. In fact, smoked aubergine is my staple combo with all meats. I don't use it with fish, somehow it's not so good.

4 large chicken breasts trimmed, skin on
4 large aubergines
Glug of olive oil
4 sprigs thyme
Toothpicks

For the glaze:
2 tbsp honey
1 tsp sherry or other fortified wine
3 tbsp water
4 cardamom pods, seeds crushed

½ tsp pink peppercorns crushed
1 dessert spoon orange flower water
Salt and pepper to taste

Preheat Oven to 200°C 180 Fan 350F Gas 6

1. Warm the honey with the sherry and water until dissolved. Remove from the heat. Add the cardamom seeds and peppercorns, then the orange blossom water .
2. Cut the aubergines in half lengthways, but still leaving the halves joined at the stem end by 10cm. Do not remove the stem.
3. Dust the inside flesh with salt and leave to drain in a colander for 20 minutes.
4. Rinse, pat dry and dredge with olive oil. Pop in the oven for 20 minutes, then set aside to cool.
5. Fry the chicken breasts on a medium /high heat for a few minutes, turning to brown on each side. Try to crisp the skin. Season well.
6. Place the chicken breast with a sprig of thyme inside the aubergine and secure with a toothpick.
7. Turn up the oven to 400°F / 200°C / 180° fan / Gas 4 and roast until the chicken is cooked through and the aubergines completely soft. Around 25 minutes, check after 15 minutes..
8. To serve, reheat the glaze and drizzle over the chicken and aubergine.

A simple salad works well with this dish, but you can always add a moulded pilaf with almonds to make it special.

SAC KAVURMA (BEEF ON AN IRON PLATE)

'SAC' is a large metal plate, iron to be precise (see p00), but you could substitute a wok. This dish is enjoyed by the Turkish people on the Eid holiday. See p00

1kg beef diced, beef fillet or a cut that does not require slow cooking
Olive oil for frying
2 large onions, roughly chopped.
2 green peppers de-seeded and sliced in rounds
1 red pepper de-seeded and sliced in rounds
4 large tomatoes, peeled and roughly chopped
1 tbsp butter
Large pinch of thyme or oregano
1 tbsp *pul biber*
Salt and pepper to taste

1. Fry the beef over a high heat in a large shallow pan to brown.
2. When the meat begins to absorb its own juices add the onions. Stir cook for a further few minutes.
3. Add the thyme, oregano and *pul biber*, stir and cook for a further minute or so.
4. Add the tomatoes and peppers and cook for a further ten minutes.
5. Plop the butter into the meat and stir through until it melts.

The traditional way of serving this is to make a pilaf, press it into a mould, make a hole in the middle of the meat mixture and then flip the rice upside down into it so that it sits centrally.

SULTAN'S DELIGHT (*HUNKAR BEGENDI*)

Hünkar Beğendi or Sultan's Delight, is an old Turkish recipe going back a few hundred years. There are a number of stories that explain the origin of this magnificently named Ottoman dish. In one, in the mid-19th century, Napoleon III and his wife, the Empress Eugenie, visited the sultan, this dish was prepared for the event, she liked the dish so much she asked for the recipe to be given to her chef, the sultan was very reluctant. I like this suggestion as I went to school in Hampshire in the old palace belonging to Napoleon III and his Empress, when they were exiled from France. From an early age I marched past their portraits in the refectory, which used to be their main grand salon. Needless to say, our school dinners were not as imaginative or tasty as this one.

The smoky flavour of the aubergine is essential to this dish, so I do hope you can char these beauties on an open flame.

For the stew:
1kg leg of lamb, diced
2 tbsp flour
1 tsp mild chilli powder
½ tsp salt
Freshly ground black pepper
3 tbsp olive oil
1 tsp sugar
2 medium onions, halved then sliced
1 green pepper, sliced into 1cm-strips
4 cloves garlic, finely chopped
4 medium tomatoes, roughly chopped, about 2.5cm/1 in
1tbsp tomato paste
1 tbsp red pepper paste
1 large sprig fresh thyme
1 tsp allspice
¼ tsp ground cloves
500ml/2 cups lamb/chicken stock

For the Begendi or aubergine sauce:
4 medium long aubergines
3 tbsp butter
3 tbsp flour
500ml/2 cups whole milk
60g/1 oz medium cheddar, grated
Salt and pepper to taste
A pinch of nutmeg
1 large handful fresh parsley, chopped

1. Prepare the aubergines as for Baba Ganus see page 85.
2. After they have been peeled, chop them finely, criss-crossing the knife to get as fine a mixture as possible. Set aside.
3. Coat the lamb pieces with the flour, the chilli powder and seasoning.
4. Heat the olive oil in a heavy-bottomed saucepan over a high heat, add the lamb and sugar and brown the lamb pieces for 5 minutes, turning the lamb frequently.
5. Lower the heat to medium, tip in the onion slices and fry, stirring, for a few more minutes.
6. Add the garlic, pepper and spices and cook for a further minute, stirring.
7. Now add the tomatoes, herbs, tomato and red pepper pastes and mix everything thoroughly.
8. Add the stock and bring to boil.
9. Lower the heat right down, add half the parsley and cover and leave to simmer for 1–1½ hours, until the lamb is cooked and tender and the sauce is thick and a rich red brown.
10. Melt the butter in a medium saucepan over medium heat.
11. Add the flour and whisk with a small whisk or wooden spoon for 2 minutes until the roux has

thickened; slowly, add the milk, whisking continuously.

12. Cook the béchamel sauce for 4–5 minutes until it thickens to the consistency of thick double cream.
13. Remove from the heat and stir in the cheese until melted.
14. Add the smoky aubergine to the béchamel sauce with a pinch of salt, the nutmeg and some freshly ground black pepper until it's all completely mixed in and you have a beautiful aubergine cheese sauce. Check for seasoning.
15. Spoon some aubergine sauce onto each plate, make a dip in each portion like a nest and fill it with the meat.
16. Sprinkle with the remaining parsley. Well worth the effort, sublime!

ALI NAZIK

Minced beef with smoked aubergine and yogurt, similar to, but not the same as the Sultan's Delight, using yogurt instead of bechamel sauce but I'm quite sure he'd have been pretty pleased with this recipe too.

For the stew:
300g minced lamb or beef
2 cloves garlic, chopped
1 large green pepper, chopped
1 large onion, chopped
2 tomatoes, peeled and chopped
50g butter
1 tbsp red pepper paste
1 tsp red pepper flakes
A handful of fresh parsley
Sea salt and pepper to taste

For the aubergine puree:
4 charred aubergines (as previous recipe)
3–4 tbsp Turkish yogurt
2 cloves garlic, minced
Sea salt and pepper to taste
1 tbsp butter
½ tsp paprika

1. Melt the butter in a large pan and add the minced beef or lamb. Fry until the colour changes and it starts to absorb its own juices, then add the spices, Stir.
2. Add the onions and peppers and cook for a further 5 minutes.
3. Add the tomatoes and paste, stir and cook for a further 10 minutes. Stir frequently. Season.
4. Add half the chopped parsley. Cook for a further 10–15 minutes then remove from the heat. Leave to stand.
5. For the aubergine base, after charring, cooling and peeling the aubergines, mash with a fork until almost a puree, but still retaining some texture. Put into a pan and cook again until browner and sweeter. Cool a little. Add the garlic and yogurt and season well.
6. To assemble, take a large dish and spread the aubergine mixture on the bottom, ladle the mince on the top. Melt the remaining butter in a pan and sprinkle in some paprika. Drizzle over the whole and sprinkle with fresh parsley.
7. Serve with chunks of crusty bred to capture all the juices.

Finally. Trumpets sound and drum roll!

KESKEK

That celebration dish that needs to be understood… You need to add extra 24 hours to soak the wheat overnight (serves: 6–8) but you can double up to any quantity, to as many as 3,000 servings!

500g chicken, thigh or breast meat
2 bay leaves
500g wheat (soaked overnight)
1 tbsp pepper paste or red pepper flakes
6–7 peppercorns
10 cups water
Salt to taste
Ground black pepper to taste
15 g butter

1. Fill a large pot with water. Add the meat, bay leaves and the peppercorns and boil, covered for 3 hours on medium heat until the meat starts to soften and separate. Drain, reserving a cup or two of the liquid and some of the chicken for shredding later.
2. Drain the wheat and add to the meat. Add salt and the black pepper. Cover and cook for 2 hours and stir every 15 minutes with a wooden spoon. The *keskek* should be finished when the wheat swells and starts to dissolve. If needed, cook longer to attain the right consistency. The texture should be soft and creamy.
3. For its sauce, heat the butter and add 1 cup meat broth (the water in which you boiled the chicken) and pepper paste or pepper flakes.
4. For serving, dollop some *keskek* into a bowl and pour the sauce on it, sprinkle some black pepper and add some extra shredded chicken on the top.

VEGETARIAN

Some of these recipes could just as easily sit within the mezze section, it is all a matter of portion size, you can choose, but whatever you call them, they are all equally delicious and simple to prepare.

First and foremost – the staple sauce.

TOMATO SAUCE

I am quoting enough sauce so you can freeze in 500ml cartons to use as and when required. Then you can add extra flavourings depending on the recipe.

1kg of tomatoes, skins removed in boiling water, and roughly chopped. It doesn't matter if they go a bit mushy this time
3 large white or yellow onions, they need to be strongly flavoured.
3–4 cloves of garlic, pressed, peeled and chopped finely
Dessert spoon of tomato puree
1–2 sugar cubes give g equivalent
Generous pinch of chilli flakes or *pul biber*
Sea Salt and black pepper to taste
Olive oil for frying
1.5 litres water

1. Chop the onions and fry gently in a large heavy bottomed pan in the olive oil; they need to be thoroughly soft, add a little sea salt after a couple of minutes to help this along.
2. When completely soft, add the garlic, cook for a couple of minutes more then add the tomatoes, there should be lots of juice so try and get all of it in the pot.
3. Add the water and bring to the boil, add the puree, chilli flakes, sugar cubes and pepper, there is salt already in the onions so adjust the salt at the end of the process.
4. Lower the heat and simmer gently until all the contents have merged and the tomatoes have pulped down. You may need to add more water if the mix appears too thick. The whole process should take about an hour, the more it cooks, the deeper the flavour.

This is a basis for many of the dishes I mention here, I just add extra flavours – for example, the *Manti* (ravioli) sauce has extra dried tomatoes added and some parsley. *Menemem* requires peppers to be added. I can use this sauce in my moussakas and *Imam Beyeldi*, too. I can't tell you how useful it is to have these tomato sauces available straight from the freezer,

AROMATIC RICE-STUFFED PEPPERS, TOMATOES AUBERGINES

The same stuffing can be used in many vegetables.

12 small, thin-skinned green peppers
400g rice
2 small or 1 large onion
2 large beef tomatoes
1 medium tomato for decoration
100g *Kus uzumu* ('birds grapes') tiny currants will do
100g pine nuts toasted in a hot pan
A handful of parsley
1 small tsp allspice and cinnamon
Handful Dill
Large handful Dried mint

For the sauce:
3 tomatoes, grated
I tbsp tomato puree or a mix of pepper paste and tomato puree
Olive oil
Tsp *pul biber* or chilli flakes
Boiling water

1. Wash the peppers and take off the tops, rather like a boiled egg. You may need to shave a little from the bottom so they stand straight in the pan.
2. In a large bowl, grate the onion and tomatoes and mix in with the rice and all the other ingredients. Mix well. I use my hands for this, far better and more satisfying, somehow.
3. Now stuff each pepper until ¾ full (the rice will expand on cooking). When all are full, place upright in a pan with the pepper lids back on. Depending on your time and inclination, you can leave like this with jaunty lids and stalks on top rather like a Frenchman's beret, OR you can go the whole Turkish hog and cut 'cheeks' out of the tomato and place on top of the stuffing, then pull out the stem of the pepper leaving a hole and replace so the red of the tomato shows through.
4. Make a simple sauce with a tablespoon of tomato puree, a large glug of olive oil, some more grated tomatoes and a dash of *pul biber.* Top up with boiling water and pour over the peppers so it reaches about two thirds of the way up. Cover and cook on the hob for about 30 minutes.

They will then need to cool down a little as they are best served when the rice has had time to firm up a little. Serve with yogurt and mint sauce. As with most dishes, this tastes better the next day.

IMAM BEYELDI (AUBERGINE WITH TOMATOES AND PEPPERS)

I usually cook this alongside the *Karniyark* (aubergine with meat stuffing) so both veggies and carnivores are happy. Lots of good olive oil required.

- 4 long aubergines, not the fat ones if possible
- 2 large onions, sliced into half moons
- 6 tomatoes peeled and chopped
- 2 medium or one large green pepper, sliced
- Half a bulb of garlic, chopped – don't panic it will be fine
- A handful of fresh parsley
- 6–8 tbsp olive oil (told you!)
- Juice of 1 lemon
- 2 sugar cubes or 2 tsp sugar
- 1 tbsp dried mint
- 1 dessert spoon tomato paste
- Sea salt and pepper to taste

1. Remove the stems and peel the aubergines in strips with a potato peeler or sharp knife. Then make a slit along one side from stem to base without cutting in two.
2. Place in a bowl of salted water for 20 minutes to get rid of the bitter juices. This also makes them easier to fry. Pat dry with paper or a tea towel.
3. Gently fry in 1 tbsp olive oil in a large shallow pan, turning occasionally so all sides are softened and acquire a golden brown colour on the peeled areas, you may need to do this in batches, set aside.
4. Fry onions in another 2 tbsp olive oil with some salt then after a few minutes add the chopped garlic and cook on a low heat until softened, 10–12 minutes.
5. Add the peppers, cook for another few minutes then add the tomatoes, and season well. Cook for a further minute or so, then add a handful of fresh parsley and mint. Stir well, take off the heat and leave to cool.
6. Take the cooled aubergines and gently open up where the split was made and push aside to make a boat shape. Sprinkle the interior flesh with a little salt and some sugar. Stuff as much of the mixture as you can into the 'boats'. If there is any left over you can add to the cooking liquid later.
7. Make the cooking sauce from tomato paste, seasoned with salt and pepper, some hot water and the remaining olive oil. At this point if you have any left-over filling, whizz it all in together. Transfer the boats to a baking dish and surround with the liquid up to a third of the depth of the boats. If not enough cooking liquid add some extra water with a dash of tomato puree
8. Loosely cover with foil and place in a medium oven 150–180° C. 130–40 Fan 300F Gas 2–3 for 30–35 minutes.
9. When cooked, allow to cool, cover with foil and put in the fridge overnight. This allows all the flavours to permeate.

Serve at room temperature drizzled with the last olive oil and some freshly chopped parsley.

PIYAZ (WHITE BEANS WITH HARD-BOILED EGGS AND OLIVES)

Piyaz without the egg is served as a traditional accompaniment to *köfte* in our local *Köfteci*, to me it's the best part. Serves 4–6

- 500g dried haricot/cannellini beans soaked overnight and simmered for about 30 minutes, they must be soft, but don't over boil or the skins will drift off.
- 1 red onion sliced into rings
- A handful of flat leaf parsley
- 3–4 tbsp black olives, stoned (I like the large wrinkly ones)
- 2 roasted red peppers, peeled and sliced
- 3 medium tomatoes, peeled and chopped
- 6 hard-boiled eggs, peeled and quartered
- Juice of 1 lemon
- 1 tsp sumac
- 1 tsp *pul biber* or if adventurous, *kirmizi biber* (hotter) or chilli flakes
- 2 large glugs of good olive oil
- Sea salt and black pepper to taste

1. Drain the beans and allow to cool. Rub salt and sumac into the onions until the onions are softened. Use your hands for this.
2. Add the onions, tomatoes olives, parsley and *pul biber* into a large salad bowl, with the bean mixture then pour over a dressing made with lots of olive oil and lemon juice, and season to taste. Lastly surround the piled-up beans with the quartered eggs.

It all tastes much better after the oil dressing has had time to soak into the beans, so you can make in advance and refrigerate for a few hours. Best served at room temperature though.

SARAMSAK KÖFTE – GARLIC *KÖFTE*

These *köfte* are not fried, but boiled rather like dumplings. They are made with semolina and fine bulgur wheat and served in a tasty tomato sauce.

- 2 water glasses of fine bulgur
- 2 water glasses of hot water
- 1 water glass of flour
- 1 tea glass of semolina
- 1 dessert spoon of *biber salcasi* (hot pepper paste)
- 1 dessert spoon of cumin

For the Sauce:

- 4–6 garlic cloves, chopped
- 2 large tomatoes
- Parsley
- Lots of salt and black pepper

1. Put a pan of water on to boil.
2. Combine the semolina and bulgur with the water and hot pepper paste.
3. Add the garlic, mix together and wait until the water has been absorbed by the semolina and bulgur.
4. Add the flour and knead until it has a pliable consistency. Roll out into little balls and with one resting in the palm of your hand, slightly press and flatten one side of it with a small indentation.
5. When the water has boiled, drop in the balls and simmer for 10–15 minutes. Drain and serve in a tomato sauce (See P.00) with extra garlic. Or make this sauce as below. To avoid the boiled kofete getting cold have the sauce ready in advance.

6. Fry the garlic gently in the oil, add the rest of the ingredients (except for the water and parsley) and allow to simmer gently for ten minutes.
7. Check the taste and if it is too rich and thick add as much of the cooking water from the *köfte* to the sauce as is needed to thin it out a bit.
8. Add ½ a bunch of finely chopped parsley to the sauce and mix and then add the *köfte*. Serve hot.

SPINACH AND CHICKPEAS

This is a great veggie standby and freezes well – although I do perk up the spice once it has thawed. I use dried, soaked, par-cooked chickpeas for this dish as I think the pulse takes on the flavour of the spices better than the canned whilst cooking. You can use one of the frozen tomato sauces here as I have previously suggested, which cuts out most of the prep time.

- 300g chickpeas, soaked for 12 hours and par cooked for 30 minutes.
- 1kg fresh spinach thoroughly washed and chopped, or frozen spinach, about 4–5 blocks
- 2 onions
- 3 cloves fat garlic
- 2 cans of tomatoes
- 1 tbsp tomato paste
- 2 tsp *pul biber*
- 2 tsp cumin powder
- Sea salt and black pepper to taste
- Olive oil
- Sometimes I add a couple of large chopped carrots as well

1. In a large pan soften the onions and garlic in some oil and a little salt.
2. Add in the cumin and the *pul biber* and stir for a couple of minutes.
3. Add the tomatoes and carrots, if you are using them, and then the half-cooked chickpeas.
4. Simmer for another half hour until the chickpeas are thoroughly cooked and the sauce has amalgamated nicely.
5. Finally add the spinach, if using fresh spinach add in large handfuls and slowly press down with a wooden spoon until it has all wilted and mixed well into the sauce.
6. I would mention at this point to make sure your spinach is well chopped up or you will end up with long tendrils of soft spinach that will be difficult to eat as they have a tendency to ping tomato sauce all over you if you're not careful. Bitter experience!
7. Cook again for a further 10 minutes, adjust the seasoning and serve with a drizzle of oil and yogurt with mint.

MAQLUBA (THIS MEANS 'UPSIDE DOWN')

You'll need a big, heavy-based pot with a 5-litre capacity (23–25cm in diameter, 12cm, or less, deep) and a plate or platter big enough to cover the pot – the plate will be used for unmoulding the rice, much as you do with a pudding.

- 200ml vegetable oil for frying
- 1 large aubergine, cut lengthways into 0.5cm thick slices
- 2 medium potatoes, peeled and cut into 0.5cm slices
- 1 small cauliflower, cut into large florets

2 medium carrots, cut lengthways into 0.5cm thick slices
2 large tomatoes, cut into 1cm thick slices
4 garlic cloves, peeled and sliced
200g short-grain rice (risotto or paella rice), washed and drained
3 pieces of chicken, thighs or breasts cooked and flaked

For the liquid:
400–500ml vegetable stock or water
½ tsp ground turmeric
1 tsp paprika
1 tsp allspice
½ tsp cinnamon
1 tsp ground nutmeg
3 or 4 cardamom pods
1 tsp black pepper
2 tsp salt
Toasted almonds and chopped parsley for decoration

1. Pour the oil into a wide frying pan and place over a high heat. When hot, fry the aubergine in batches for a minute a side, until coloured. Transfer to paper towel.
2. Repeat with the potato and then the cauliflower and carrot, but for only about 30 seconds a side – these vegetables need to take on some colour but stay crunchy.
3. To the cooking pot first add the olive oil followed by a thin layer of rice. Arrange the chicken on top of it and fill the gaps with rice. Add a layer of vegetables then top with the remaining rice.
4. Sprinkle the salt, allspice, cinnamon and cardamom on top
5. Mix the boiling water or stock with the spices and seasoning.
6. Gently pour the mix over the rice, making sure it covers the rice by 1–2cm.
7. Put the pot on the hob and bring gently to a simmer (you don't want it to boil as that will spoil the layers).
8. Once simmering, reduce the heat to its lowest point, cover the pot and cook for 20–40 minutes. You can apply a plate over the top layer to keep it in place.
9. Remove from the heat, lift off the lid, place a clean tea towel over the pan, put the lid back on and leave to rest for 20 minutes.
10. Place the serving dish on top of the uncovered pot and flip it over, you may need to tap the pot to release all the *Maqluba*.
11. Decorate the top with toasted almonds, chopped parsley and more flaked chicken if you wish.

Serve with a simple tahini yogurt side dish. Nothing should distract from the intricate flavours of the *Maqluba*.

MENEMEN

This has to be served whilst singing the Muppet's theme tune. Me neh meh nemen, toot too to doo doo, meh neh menem too toot too too! Maybe you have to be there…

6 eggs beaten
1 large onion, chopped
1large green pepper, chopped
1 large red pepper, chopped
6 large tomatoes, peeled and chopped
1 tsp of *pul biber*
Sea salt and black pepper to taste
Glug of olive oil

1. In a large shallow pan fry the onions in the oil with a little salt until softened, add the peppers and the tomatoes and cook on a low heat until the juices from the tomatoes draw out and the whole becomes a sloppy sauce.
2. Add the beaten eggs and seasoning and continue cooking on a low heat until the eggs cook and thicken the sauce to a thick custardy consistency.

Serve sprinkled with parsley and chunks of bread either as part of a Turkish breakfast or as I do, as part of a buffet lunch.

ALMOND AND POTATO *KÖFTE*

This does have a long ingredient list, but is easy to prepare.

500g baked potatoes. Do not boil the potatoes as this will make the mixture too wet to fry
50 g plain flour
40g butter
A good handful each of fresh dill and flat leaf parsley, chopped
A small handful of coriander and spring onions, chopped. I use a little less coriander as the strong flavour can drown out the subtle parsley and dill.)
1 green chilli, chopped
1 tsp turmeric
1 tsp paprika/pul biber
100g feta, crumbled
½ tsp sugar

Salt and pepper to taste
For coating to fry
1–2 eggs
50g plain flour
100g flaked almonds
2 tsp dhukka
Oil

1. Bake the potatoes until thoroughly soft. Scoop out the flesh and mix with all the other ingredients in a large bowl.
2. Knead a bit to combine and form into sausage shapes about 5cm long.
3. Once they are all formed, dip the, first into the flour, then the beaten egg and then the Dhukka and flaked almonds. Fry for a few minutes until golden brown.

You can serve this with a yogurt sauce or on their own.
NOTE: should fresh herbs not be available, use ½ tsp each of powdered cumin, coriander and cardamom with the turmeric, *pul biber* and green chilli, which will produce a different, but equally delicious veggie *köfte*.

AUBERGINE CIGARS

As usual the versatile aubergine makes an outstanding dish. Surprisingly, the smoked aubergine freezes well and can be taken out, as with all the dishes, as required. For my part, it saves the house and indeed me, smelling of charred aubergine for days. I must get an extractor fan.

4–5 medium aubergines, fat or thin
250g floury potatoes, peeled
200g *beyaz peynir* or feta cheese, crumbled
1 large egg, beaten

1. Prepare the aubergines as before, page 85. Scorch them on your gas hob flame or, if using electricity, prick and roast in the oven, or grill. This won't give the same smoky flavour, but that's the price you pay for cleanliness, as charring on the open flame can be very messy.
2. Chop the peeled aubergine and leave to one side in a colander to drain.
3. Meanwhile, boil the potatoes until soft, drain and mash roughly. If you are roasting your aubergines it may be an idea to bake the potatoes at the same time – saves on fuel and also the mash will be less wet, which is a good thing.
4. Once all have cooled, add the feta cheese, egg, seasoning and mix. Add about half the breadcrumbs until the mixture can be shaped into fat cigars.
5. Coat them in the remaining breadcrumbs and fry in oil on a medium heat until golden brown and crispy.

Drain and serve either hot or cold.

SIDES AND SALADS

KISIR

My Turkish husband taught me to make this. I think I have improved on his recipe.

This is a brilliant salad, but a word of warning: unless like me you are catering for 10 people or more, beware of how much bulgur wheat you start with. Do not be fooled into thinking 'this won't be nearly enough for 4/5/6. I will add more.' Once you have added all the other ingredients suggested and some I have not (be brave) the dish will have expanded hugely and you will find yourself eating kisir for the next millennium, and besides which, the fresh herbs go soggy. Not a good look, or taste. This recipe should serve 6.

500g coarse bulgur wheat
2 tbsp red pepper paste or if unavailable, tomato paste (but add some *pul biber* or chilli flakes too)
About 1 litre of boiled water
1 tsp ground cumin
2 large red onions, peeled and finely chopped
4 tomatoes, peeled and chopped
½ large cucumber or 2–3 small Turkish ones
4 pointy green peppers
6 tbsp chopped parsley
Small bunch of spring onions, finely shredded, plus an extra one to garnish
2 garlic cloves, crushed
1 large handful of mint leaves roughly chopped

1. In a very large bowl, soak the bulgur wheat in boiling water to cover easily.
2. Add the red pepper paste or tomato puree, the cumin and if using tomato puree, the pepper flakes, and some salt and stir well until thoroughly mixed so the pepper paste is not lumpy (I use my hands).
3. Cover with a plate and leave to cool 15 minutes, if not soft enough at this point you can add more boiling water, a little at a time. Fluff up with a fork.

4. Chop up all the vegetables and herbs finely and add to the cooled bulgur.
5. Make a dressing with the olive oil, lemon juice, molasses, garlic, salt and pepper. Stir into the bulgur mix. Just before serving, add the toasted pine nuts and pomegranate seeds. Drizzle more olive oil on top.

Perfect as a side or even as part of a vegetarian main.

PILAFS

With rice pilafs a general rule of thumb is twice as much liquid as rice and try not to lift the lid too often, never stir after the first twist of the spoon. Never.

BULGUR WHEAT PILAF

Use the coarser bulgur wheat for pilaf; the finer is used for *köfte*. Luckily in Turkey the labels say, '*köfte* bulgur' or '*pilaf* bulgur' so no excuse to get it wrong. Here too, almost twice as much liquid to bulgur is required, but add it slowly, you don't want it to be soggy.

2 cups bulgur wheat
2 tbsp butter
1 tbsp extra virgin olive oil
1 medium onion, diced
1 large tomato, diced
3½ cups water
1 tbsp tomato paste (sometimes I add sweet red pepper paste by way of a change from tomato)
1 tsp of *pul biber*
Salt and black pepper to taste

1. Melt the butter with olive oil in a saucepan. Then add the diced onions and stir until soft.
2. Add the diced tomato, tomato paste, *pul biber*, salt and black pepper and stir well.
3. Add the bulgur and stir until well combined and then add the water and bring the mixture to a boil.
4. Simmer on a low heat with the lid on for 10–20 minutes until all the liquid has gone.
5. Remove the saucepan from the heat and take off the lid. Put a clean tea towel over the saucepan and close the lid again. Let it rest for 5 minutes. Serve.

BULGUR WHEAT PILAF WITH SAUTÉED ALMONDS

350g coarse bulgur wheat
75g flaked almonds or whole blanched
600ml boiling water
Handful *kus uzumu* (tiny currants)
2 glugs olive oil
Handful fresh herbs, such as mint, parsley, dill, chopped
Sea salt and black pepper to taste

1. Heat 1 glug of olive oil in a large pan and stir in the bulgur, coating it thoroughly, Pour on the boiling water, season and stir well. Bring to a simmer and cook for about 15 minutes until all the liquid has been absorbed.
2. Add the currants then cover with a tea towel. Set aside.

3. Fry the almonds in a shallow pan until golden brown.

Serve the pilaf sprinkled with the herbs and fried almonds.

RICE PILAF WITH ORZO

For years I wondered what the little oval seed like things in my rice were, when served pilaf in Turkish restaurants or homes. Then I finally realised…Orzo! Turkish pilafs are cooked with lots, and lots of butter, always a winner for the taste buds, but not necessarily for the waistline. Hey, ho, you don't have to have it every day….

125g butter
1 glug olive oil
2 tbsp orzo pasta
I cup rice (*baldo* is best, a short-grained fat rice rather like arborio or pudding rice)
2 cups of stock (chicken or vegetable)

1. In a shallow saucepan, melt the butter and oil together. Once melted, add the orzo pasta and stir continuously over medium heat until the pasta turns a dark golden colour. Be careful and keep stirring so the butter and orzo don't burn.
2. Add the uncooked rice and stir thoroughly until the oil has worked its way through all the grains.
3. Add your stock and spices and bring to a boil. Cover and reduce the heat. Let the rice slowly simmer until the liquid disappears. Check after about 20 minutes. When all absorbed take the pan from the heat, take off the lid, place a tea towel over the top of the pan and clamp the lid back on and put it aside to cool down. Keep the top on at all times while the rice cools.
4. Before serving, open the lid and gently stir the rice to loosen the bottom and separate the grains.
5. To serve, press some of the pilaf into a large cup or small bowl, quickly upturn onto the serving plate and it should retain this pleasing shape.

The type of rice used will decide the cooking time. Always check the labels. Sometimes to ring the changes it's an idea to add sautéed softened onion or leek to the mix before adding the rice.

RICE PILAF WITH CHICKPEAS AND CRUNCHY ONIONS

1. Make the pilaf as before, and then stir in 250g of cooked chickpeas.
2. In a shallow pan fry thinly sliced brown onions until they crisp up and are a deep golden brown, they should be brittle at this point.
3. Turn out the pilaf-like sand 'castles' and top with the crunchy fried onions.

PUMPKIN AND SPINACH KIBBEH

For the dough:
1kg pumpkin or butternut squash
1 cup of *köfte* (fine) bulgur
3 tbsp semolina
3–4 tsp cornstarch
1 onion
1 tbsp butter
Sea salt and pepper to taste

For the filling:
350g fresh spinach thoroughly washed and finely chopped
1 cup walnuts coarsely chopped
1 tbsp small currants (*kus uzumu*)
½ lemon zested and juiced
½ tsp sumac
Pinch of sugar (optional)
Olive oil

1. Rinse and drain the pumpkin and cut into cubes. Put in a large saucepan. Set to boil with some salt.
2. Grate the onion and gently squeeze out any excess moisture into kitchen paper or a tea towel. Place in a bowl and add the bulgur and the semolina. Add salt and pepper and coarsely chopped butter
3. When the pumpkin water has started to boil, take out a ladleful of the water and then cook for a further 20–25 minutes with a lid on, until the pumpkin is tender.
4. Pour the reserved pumpkin water onto the bulgur and semolina mix, stir well. Cover the bowl with a plate and set aside for about 20 minutes, stirring occasionally.
5. For the filling, put the chopped spinach into a large shallow pan, heat up the olive oil over a medium heat, add the chopped onion, season well and fry until soft.
6. Add the currants, sumac then the chickpeas, stir well, then gradually add the spinach in batches so it wilts and reduces in volume, add a pinch of sugar.
7. Cook until thoroughly tender, then add the lemon juice.
8. Cook until it sizzles and add the walnuts, remove from the heat and leave to cool.
9. Drain the cooked pumpkin thoroughly in a sieve and then mash or whizz to a puree.
10. As with the onion, squeeze out any excess water and put back into the bowl, add the bulgur mixture and mix well.
11. Season well, then knead well for at least five minutes, whilst gradually adding the cornflour until it forms a soft dough that holds well.
12. Pre-heat the oven to 180°C/350°F/gas mark 4
13. Oil an oven-proof round or square baking dish, approximately 24cm diameter.
14. Divide the dough into two and press one half into the dish so that it completely covers the base and runs halfway up the sides. Spread the filling evenly over the base layer. Then cover with the second layer, this can be a messy job. Try placing the dough between two sheets of cling film, roll out to the approximate size of the dish, then remove the top layer and flop over the filling, then tidy up by hand. With a sharp knife.
15. Mark out diamond shapes on the top and place a walnut half in the middle of each diamond.
16. Drizzle with olive oil and bake in the oven for 35–40 minutes until golden brown. Cool for 20 minutes and serve in the diamond shapes.

TURK TIP *It occurred to me that this would make a great coating for a veggie scotch egg. And it did. Give that a try.*

VEGGIE 'MOUSSAKA'

I usually serve this when presenting the meaty version to our painters. It has been known for the carnivores to tuck into this so hard that the poor vegetarians are left with no 'seconds'.

180g green lentils
2 large, long aubergines, skin peeled in stripes, cut in half and soaked in salted water for 15 minutes, then dried
2 large onions, chopped
4 cloves garlic, finely chopped
1 red pepper, thinly sliced
500g fresh tomatoes peeled and chopped or 1 400g can
3 glugs of olive oil for frying the aubergines
1 extra glug of olive oil for the mix.
1 tsp sugar
1 dessert spoon of dried mint
1 tsp cinnamon
1 tsp cumin
1 bay leaf
Sea salt and black pepper to taste
250 ml water/veggie stock

1. Put the lentils in a pan of boiling water with the bay leaf, stir and cover. Turn down the heat and simmer for 15 minutes. Drain and set aside.
2. Chop the aubergines into chunks. Put the olive oil in a large pan and fry the chunks turning them until they start to go soft and colour up.
3. In a large bowl combine the half-cooked lentils, onion, garlic, peppers, tomatoes, sugar, mint and spices, season well.
4. In an oven proof dish layer up the aubergines and lentil mixture, finishing with the lentils.
5. Pour over the stock, cover and cook in a medium oven for around 40 minutes. Make sure it doesn't dry out.

Serve with a salad and a dollop of *cakik (p00)*

LENTILS AND RICE

This is jolly useful dish to put together when I have leftovers of both ingredients, although it is always easy to make from scratch.

120g butter
4 onions sliced into rounds
200g green lentils rinsed
2 tsp cumin seeds
4 tsp coriander seeds
Glug of olive oil
200g long grain rice rinsed
Sea salt and pepper

1. In a large pan, melt the butter over a low heat and cook the onion until golden brown. Add some salt at this time as it helps to soften the onion without burning.
2. 40 minutes should do the trick.
3. Cook the lentils in boiling water for 10 minutes, drain and set aside.
4. Add the cumin and the coriander seeds to the onions and cook for a couple of minutes until aromatic, then add the oil and the rice. Stir to coat the rice then add the lentils and 350ml water. Cook for about 15 minutes on a low heat.
5. Season generously. Serve hot.

BULGUR WHEAT WITH TOMATOES AND FETA CHEESE

2 red peppers cut into thick strips
300g small or cherry tomatoes
4 cloves garlic
2 glugs olive oil
50g pine nuts
200g coarse bulgur wheat
400ml stock (chicken or veggie)
100g feta cheese
Handful of flat leaf parsley, or purple basil leaves

1. Pre-heat the over to 200C / F 180 Fan 400F Gas 6
2. Drizzle the peppers and tomatoes with the oil and season well.
3. Roast in a large roasting tin and after ten minutes add the garlic cloves. After another 5 minutes add the pine nuts to colour. Return to the oven for a further 5 minutes or so.
4. Pour in the bulgur wheat and stir until coated, add the stock and cover the pan with tin foil. Return to the oven to cook for another 10–15 minutes.
5. Remove from the heat when the bulgur wheat is cooked and can be fluffed up.
6. Scatter with feta cheese and parsley and serve hot.

ROAST CELERIAC AND PUY LENTIL SALAD WITH HAZELNUTS, PRESERVED LEMON AND MINT

With thanks to Ottolenghi

60g whole hazelnuts (skin on)
200g puy lentils
700ml water
2 bay leaves
4 thyme sprigs
1 small celeriac (650g), peeled and diced
4 tbsp olive oil
1 preserved lemon, finely chopped
3 tbsp hazelnut oil
3 tbsp good-quality red wine vinegar
4 tbsp chopped mint
Salt and black pepper

1. Preheat the oven to 200 C 180 Fan 425F. Gas 6
2. Place the diced celeriac on a baking sheet, sprinkle with olive oil and a little salt and roast until tender, approximately 20 minutes. When done, set aside to cool.
3. Put the lentils, broth/water, bay leaves and thyme sprigs in a small saucepan. Bring to a boil, then simmer for 15–20 minutes, or until the lentils are soft but not falling apart. Drain in a sieve.
4. Remove and discard the bay leaves and the woody sprigs.
5. In a large bowl, mix the hot lentils (make sure they don't cool – lentils soak up flavours much better when they're hot) with the remainder of the oil, vinegar, a few grinds of black pepper and plenty of salt (at least ½ tsp.). Add the celeriac, stir, taste and adjust the seasoning as necessary.
6. If you're serving this straight away, stir in half the mint, the preserved lemon and the hazelnuts, then pile in a big heap on to a suitable serving dish.
7. Drizzle the remaining hazelnut oil over the top,.then garnish with the rest of the mint and nuts.
8. If you're planning on serving it cold, wait for the lentil and celeriac mixture to cool down, taste again, then make a final adjustment to the seasoning. Add the rest of the hazelnut oil, the mint and the nuts just as you do when serving it hot.

YESIL *FASULIYE*

I learned that the secret of *Yesil fasuliye* – or fresh beans stew is to cook the beans a long time, as if we were living in 1950s Britain. Contrary to our idea of *al dente* beans, we want these to thoroughly soften and absorb the flavours of the oil and tomato. They don't taste over cooked, honestly!

This goes perfectly with *köfte*, but my caretaker's wife will have it as a main dish with lots of bread. I use fresh tomatoes because I'm a purist and slightly mad.

1kg long green beans topped and tailed and cut in half
500g tomatoes or two cans chopped tomatoes
1 large onion chopped
2 fat cloves garlic
1 dessert spoon tomato puree
Salt and pepper to taste
Pinch of *pul biber* or not–too–hot chilli powder
½ litre water (or more, you be the judge)
Olive oil for frying plus a glug for finishing
Squeeze of lemon juice

1. Soften the onions in the olive oil with a little salt, then add the garlic. Cook for a couple of minutes then add the peeled and chopped tomatoes and the water.
2. Bring to the boil then add the puree and simmer.
3. Add the beans and more water to cover well. (Remember that these beans will be cooking a long time and we don't want them to dry out.)
4. Simmer with a lid on the pan for about 45 minutes to an hour so all the flavours combine.
5. When cooked, adjust the seasoning, and add a further glug of olive oil and a squeeze of lemon juice.

This can be served hot or cold, as a side dish or as a vegetarian main on a bed of rice.

OKRA IN TOMATO SAUCE

I can almost feel the breeze as the page is hurriedly turned over, YES I know okra can be beastly and slimy and well, not nice, but here is a foolproof way of cooking it. Izzet, the boatman, serves okra to us when we go on one of his manic boat trips around the islands off the Yalikavak coast. I didn't try it at first, but on realising the marauding guests had consumed pretty much everything else, hunger pangs forced my hand. It was delicious! So I asked Izzet how he made it and why it wasn't at all slimy. Here is his recipe, plus a few tips.

Buy firm okra this is essential advice, They should be small and snap easily, as would a fresh green bean, never should they bend. Don't buy out of season.

500g okra
2 large tomatoes peeled and chopped
1 large onion sliced
1 red pepper de–seeded and chopped
3–4 cloves of garlic (I suspect Izzet used far more than that, but this should be enough)
2 generous glugs of olive oil

1 tsp sugar
1 tsp paprika or *pul biber* or both if you like it a bit edgy
Juice of ½ a lemon
Sea salt and pepper to taste

1. Wash and trim the okra – see Turk Tip below. Fry the onions in the olive oil until softened. Add the okra and stir well to coat it.
2. Add the peppers and cook for a further few minutes before adding the tomatoes, garlic, spices and sugar.
3. Pour in enough water to cover the okra. Simmer for 30 minutes, add a further glug of olive oil and season. Leave to cool.

Best served at room temperature.

TURK TIP *To avoid the dreaded creature from the black lagoon-style slime, cut off the stems but leave the cap on the okra, never cut up the okra.*

TOMATO AND POMEGRANATE SALAD

There is never enough of this salad when I serve it to my painters. The flavour of the fresh tomatoes and the onions with the pomegranate molasses is just sublime. Sometimes I add chopped parsley and black olives, it looks very colourful.

As many tomatoes as you think will serve your numbers
2 red onions per kilo of tomatoes
1 tsp sugar
A large glug of virgin olive oil
A good spirited shake of pomegranate molasses, about 30 seconds' worth
Sea salt
Black pepper
Handful of parsley, chopped
Black olives – as many as you like to see scattered amongst the tomatoes

1. Skin and slice the tomatoes across from the stem end.
2. In a large bowl mix the olive oil, pomegranate molasses, salt and pepper and a half teaspoon of the sugar.
3. Pile up the tomatoes in a large bowl. Shake together the dressing ingredients plus the sugar. Pour over the tomatoes, dig your clean hands into the lot and turn the fruits in the dressing. Salt and pepper to taste. Serve sprinkled with parsley and the black olives (optional).

SHEPHERD'S SALAD

As you would expect, this salad has sheep's cheese in it! A very simple mixed salad of finely chopped lettuce, cucumber, grated carrot, red onion, tomatoes, black olives, parsley and sheep's cheese cubed. Smother with a dressing of olive oil, lemon juice and salt and pepper. It's the freshness that makes it so delicious. Never keep a salad.

TAHINI SPINACH SALAD

Young fresh spinach tastes so sophisticated with this dressing

- 500g young spinach leaves
- 1 red onion sliced
- A handful of pumpkin seeds
- 1 cup / 240ml tahini paste
- 60 ml each water and white wine vinegar
- 2 large glugs olive oil
- 1 tbsp honey
- Pinch cumin
- Salt and pepper to taste

1. Whoosh up the spinach leaves and onion in a large bowl,
2. Whisk up the dressing ingredients separately, season to taste then drizzle over the spinach leaves.
3. Serve with a handful of pumpkin seeds for crunch.

You can use this tahini dressing on roasted chunks of sweet potatoes, chickpeas, roasted aubergine or anything that you fancy really. It jazzes up the dullest veg.

POTATO SALAD

I tend to change the ingredients for this depending on what I have to hand, but potatoes are always in it!

- 1kg decent waxy potatoes, you don't want them to 'go over' and crumble
- 2 small red onions
- 1 tbsp of capers
- Grated zest of 1 lemon
- I tbsp mayonnaise
- 1 tbsp Turkish yogurt
- Salt and pepper to taste
- Pinch of sumac

1. Peel and halve or quarter if large, the potatoes
2. Put to boil in salted water until you can just pierce easily with a knife point. About 20 minutes.
3. Drain and cool a little.
4. Mix together the mayonnaise, yogurt, capers and red onion with the lemon zest until it forms a smooth dressing. Season with salt and pepper to taste.
5. Mix together with the potatoes in a large bowl.

Serve sprinkled with a little red sumac.

ROASTED POTATOES WITH GARLIC ROSEMARY AND LEMON PEEL

Sandra loves these! The secret of a decent roastie is very hot fat. Olive oil does not get as hot as sunflower oil or dripping but you can't fault it for taste, So I parboil the potatoes, fluff them up, and make sure they don't overlap whilst cooking.

- 1kg NON waxy potatoes
- Lots of garlic cloves
- 2–3 tbsp olive oil (or 2 large glugs)
- Salt and pepper
- A few sprigs of rosemary
- Lemon peel from 1 lemon

1. Heat the oven to 220C 200°C Fan. 425F Gas 7

2. Put a tray with a tablespoon of olive oil into the oven for 5 minutes.
3. Peel and chop the potatoes into bite size chunks (for big mouths).
4. Parboil the potatoes in boiling salted water for about15+ minutes depending on the size of the chunks.
5. Drain and shake about to rough up the edges. Pop them back in the cooking pan and pour on the rest of the olive oil, salt and pepper and lemon rind.
6. Pop onto the heated tray and arrange so they are separate; scatter the unpeeled garlic cloves and roughly break up the rosemary sprigs and jam them around and under the potatoes.
7. Roast in the oven until golden brown and a little dark on the corners.

It is so yummy to eat the potatoes with the squeezed-out garlic cloves.

GREEN OLIVE SALAD WITH WALNUTS

The olives in the *pazar* are delicious and the choice can sometimes be overwhelming, however, everything is made easy as one is allowed to sample them all before purchase. There is a small box provided for discarded stones. The stall holder proffers the suggested olives on a long-handled perforated spoon. You take one or two, maybe offering one to your associate ,and taste. Too salty? Too bland? Too hard? Too soft? Just like Goldilocks, you will discover the one that you want. A kilo should do it. One of green, one of red. Phil always wants the stuffed ones (almonds, peppers, garlic) as he continues to forget that there will be stones, shoves a handful in his mouth and Hey Presto! the local dentist is off to the Seychelles for his holidays.

I was particularly touched to be given a 5 kilo jar of green olives in brine by Dursan from Stratonikea. So only black olives will be bought by me for at least a year.

The recipe is really up to you. A ratio of 3–1 olives to walnuts. Add chopped parsley, spring onions and chopped garlic and make a dressing from red pepper paste, olive oil, lemon juice and salt and pepper to taste. By now you will have got the idea regarding quantities. Frankly there are no rules. Always taste though.

SCORCHED BROCCOLI

This is so simple and effective as an alternative to salad and looks gorgeous. Add some crumbled goats cheese for a more substantial salad.

500g broccoli heads
2 red peppers (pointy kind)
Handful of walnut pieces
Large glug olive oil
Juice of one lemon
2 cloves garlic
Char-grilled peel of two lemons, chopped
1 tsp *pul biber*

1. Chop the broccoli into large chunks then coat with some of the olive oil and season well.
2. Cut the peppers into thick strips, coat with oil and season.
3. Place both onto a hot griddle or skillet (a barbecue works really well) and on a high heat turn until both are blackened and scorched in places. This should take about 10 minutes, the broccoli should not cook, it is a salad after all.

4. Place in a large salad bowl or plate and leave to cool.
5. Make a dressing from the rest of the oil, lemon juice and garlic and season with salt, pepper and a teaspoon of *pul biber*. Drizzle over the broccoli and peppers and serve.

BUTTERNUT SQUASH SALAD

You can substitute mint for the rosemary for a fresher salad. You'll need a handful.

1 large butternut squash
I red onion sliced thinly into half moons
400g of chickpeas cooked or from a can
A few sprigs of fresh rosemary stripped (reserve 1 for serving)
Blanched almonds, roasted in a pan until golden brown
1 sharp-tasting apple such as Granny Smith
2 glugs of olive oil
Juice of 1 lemon
Salt and pepper to taste

1. Pre-heat the oven to 190°C 170 Fan 375F Gas 5
2. Peel, de-seed and chop the squash into half-moons, coat with some of the oil and roast in a hot oven for 30 minutes resting on the sprigs of rosemary.
3. When the squash has started to soften, blacken and crisp at the edges, remove from the oven and leave to cool.
4. Peel and chop the apple and place in lemon juice so as not to go brown.
5. Mix up a dressing from the oil and lemon juice and season well.
6. Put the squash in a large bowl, mix in the chickpeas, apple and sliced onion. Scatter with rosemary leaves and roasted almonds.

Again, you could add some feta cheese to turn this into a main dish.

CARROT AND LENTIL SALAD

600g carrots, peeled and quartered lengthways
2 red onions, in quarters
4 tbsp olive oil
250g green lentils, cooked
100g spinach
1 tbsp sumac
75g almonds chopped
Handful each of fresh mint and parsley
2 tbsp pomegranate seeds
Salt and pepper to taste

1. Preheat the oven to 200C 180 Fan 400F Gas 6
2. Toss together the carrots, onions, olive oil and sumac and season.
3. Place on a roasting tray and roast for 20 minutes, turning occasionally until caramelised and coloured.
4. Mix the spinach and lentils together and place on a large serving dish. Cover with the roasted vegetables, and sprinkle over the herbs, almonds and pomegranate seeds.

Refrigerate and serve with *cakik* (yogurt, mint, garlic and olive oil) See page 95.

FATTOUCHE

This is a great way of using up stale bread (by Turkish standards, that means over half a day old.)

1 large red onion sliced into rings
4 crispy lettuce leaves (cos or iceberg)
Some radishes (if using the Turkish ones they are ENORMOUS and very peppery so 1 or even ½ will be fine)
2 large tomatoes, roughly chopped
1 cucumber, roughly chopped
2 tsp sumac
½ tsp allspice (*yenibahar*)
A few grinds of fresh black pepper
A handful of mint leaves roughly torn
A handful of flat leaf parsley roughly chopped
1 Turkish flatbread or leftover flatbreads
60g butter
One large and one small glug of olive oil
2 garlic cloves mashed with salt
Juice of a lemon
½ tbsp vinegar (cider, balsamic or pomegranate molasses)

1. Rub the sumac into the red onion along with the allspice and the pepper.
2. Cut up the lettuce into strips and place in a large salad bowl along with the radishes, cucumber, tomatoes and herbs.
3. Split the bread as you would for Melba toast (i.e. slice it in half to make super-thin pieces) and fry briskly in the melted butter and oil until golden brown and crispy.
4. Make a dressing with the garlic paste, lemon juice, oil and vinegar.

Serve with the spiced onion tossed in at the last moment. Season with salt and pour over the dressing. Top with the crispy fried bread.

DAKOS

Another stale(ish) bread recipe. Serves four

6 large tomatoes, cut into 1cm dice
½ red onion, peeled and cut into 0.5cm dice
1 tbsp red-wine vinegar
2 tbsp olive oil, plus 1 tbsp extra
½ tsp ground allspice
Salt and black pepper
70g feta, roughly crumbled
40g black olives, pitted and halved
30g capers, whole or very roughly chopped
150g Cretan dakos (or other rusks)
5g chopped parsley, to serve

1. Slice a loaf of bread into half-inch pieces, sprinkle with olive oil and a little bit of salt.
2. Bake in a preheated 180C 160 Fan 350° F Gas 4 oven for 10–15 minutes.
3. Put the tomatoes, onion, vinegar, two tablespoons of oil and the allspice in a bowl, add a third of a teaspoon of salt and a good grind of black pepper, stir gently and set aside.
4. Spread out the *dakos* on a large platter and spoon the tomato mixture on top.
5. Sprinkle over the feta, olives and capers, and top with parsley and the remaining olive oil.
6. Wait for the bread to soften and eat them before someone else does!

FIG AND GREEN BEAN SALAD WITH POMEGRANATE MOLASSES AND TOASTED ALMONDS

This looks so colourful on the serving dish, it really is a work of art. Get out your paintbrushes!

400g fine green beans topped and tailed
3 glugs of olive oil
1 tbsp red wine vinegar
Sea salt and black pepper to taste
3 tbsp molasses
12 fresh purple figs quartered
80g flaked almonds toasted

1. Boil the beans in water for about 5 minutes until they are 'al dente'.
2. Plunge straight into iced water to prevent further cooking. Drain when cool and set aside.
3. Make a dressing of oil, vinegar and molasses well combined.
4. Arrange the figs and the beans on a flat serving plate, drizzle over the dressing and top with the golden toasted almonds. Take a picture.

DESSERTS

DRIED FRUIT COMPOTE WITH GINGER

Equal amounts of: dried raisins, prunes, apricots, unbleached if possible, figs, apples and pears
A small handful of crystallised ginger
Small cinnamon stick

1. In a large bowl soak the dried fruit overnight in boiled Earl Grey tea. I just shove a couple of tea bags into the bowl, cover in boiling water and leave to steep. You can fish the bags out the following day.
2. In a pan simmer (not boil or it will disintegrate) the fruit with a small cinnamon stick for about an hour. You could add some honey at this point, but the fruit should have enough of its own sweetness.
3. Leave to cool, pop in the ginger and mix. Once cold for crunch you could add some blanched almonds.

I serve with Turkish ice cream, or a scoop of *kaymak* and perhaps a homemade ginger snap.

DATES WITH *KAYMAK*

The simplest dessert possible. Stone the dates or apricots or figs, fill the hole with *kaymak* and press a half walnut into the cream. Voila! Finger food heaven. You can use dried apricots and figs too.

STUFFED QUINCE WITH NUTS

These are oven baked as you would a Bramley apple, but they take longer to cook.

- 120g almonds
- 180g pistachios finely chopped
- Pinch of green cardamom seeds ground in a pestle and mortar, no husks
- 112g brown sugar
- 180g softened butter
- 2 large or 4 small quinces (large is better, more stuffing)
- 2 tbsp honey
- 3 tbsp butter
- Juice and zest of 1 orange
- Zest of a small lemon
- 1 small vanilla pod or a tsp of real vanilla essence

1. Pre-heat the oven to 170° C 150° fan 325F Gas 3
2. Mix together the nuts, butter and sugar with the ground cardamom.
3. Place the peeled and cored quinces upside down in a buttered oven proof dish. Drizzle with the honey and sprinkle on the zest and juice and dab with the butter, this will produce a lovely sticky flavoured sauce when cooked. Sticky flavoured? Sticky not really a flavour as such…..
4. Bake for 1–2 hours until tender. Place the stuffing in the quinces when just al dente, then crank up the heat to 400°F or 200°C to brown up the stuffing. Serve with *kaymak*, or full fat Turkish yogurt.

SUTLAC (RICE PUDDING)

This is a very simple and satisfying recipe. It also happens to be one of the classic desserts, cherished all over Turkey. I would like to note that many recipes add rice flour or corn starch to help thicken the pudding. I do not care for this style as to my mind it results in a rather heavier texture and the taste is a little blancmangey.

If the rice is first boiled in water it will release its own starch. The rice pudding made this way will thicken in the fridge and – topped with a blob of *kaymak* and an almond – looks delightful. You could also try it with some saffron or rose water in the milk.

My only problem with this dessert is as in the chocolate mousse, they take up so much room in my fridge in their individual pots. Making it in one large bowl is not a good idea in my case as there is always one painter who does not exercise caution when helping themselves and the person at the end of the line gets only a scraping. Usually me!

- ½ cup short grain rice
- 4 cups milk
- 2 cups water
- 2/3 cup sugar
- 1/4 stick vanilla

1. Boil two cups of water and add the rice. Reduce the heat and simmer for 30 minutes.
2. Add the milk and the vanilla, raise the heat and bring the mixture to a boil. As soon as it begins to boil, reduce the heat and simmer for 30 minutes.
3. Add the sugar and simmer for another 10 minutes.
4. Pour into serving bowls, sprinkle with cinnamon, but not if using rose or saffron flavourings, just a little too much gilding.
5. Refrigerate before serving.

FRANGIPANE TARTS

I could not find ground almonds anywhere in the local shops and supermarkets, so my ideas for puddings were going out the window. Then, as I was passing a new cake shop in Yalikavak, I noticed the macaroons. As a long shot I asked the owner where he got his ground almonds. He told me they came from the bakers in the next village, and offered to get me some. The next day I collected a huge plastic bag full of this marvellous ingredient, softly tumbling out of the bag into my hand, about half a kilo of sweet success; it was a deeper yellowy green than my UK shop-bought variety, a larger grind, but so fresh the smell was wonderful. I vowed to go home and start work immediately.

115g melted butter,
90g plain flour
1 tsp baking powder
50g ground almonds
40g ground hazelnuts
40g ground pistachios
190g icing sugar
5 egg whites (plan your recipes so you have an idea about what to do with the yolks, custard is always good, or extra-rich *menemen* for breakfast)
2 tsp vanilla extract (not essence)

For the topping:
50g chopped pistachios and some fresh raspberries or other berries.

1. Preheat oven to 180°C 160°C fan 350F Gas 4
2. Whizz all the main ingredients together until foamy, spoon into greased muffin cases, top with the fruit and nuts and bake 15–20 minutes.

HOSMERIN (baked ricotta cheese cake from the Aegean region)

'Hoş mu Erim?' in Turkish means, 'Is it good, my husband?' – which has been corrupted to its present name. Perhaps. The real McCoy requires the Turkish housewife to make her own cheese. No wonder she was anxious for praise. You can be the recipient of plenty of accolades for this recipe without going that extra mile, I promise you.

Equal quantities of milk, semolina, water and sugar. I suggest using a mug, the same one each time…
2 tbsp icing sugar
50g butter
150g ricotta cheese
A few saffron threads dissolved in water.
Peeled whole almonds to decorate

1. Preheat the oven to 180°C 160°C fan 350F Gas 4
2. Grease and line a 20 x10cm loaf tin or equivalent in size
3. Melt the butter in a pan, then add the semolina, cook until it toasts and changes colour to a golden yellow. Set aside.
4. In another pan boil the milk together with the saffron, sugar and water.
5. Pour this over the semolina, add the cheese and cook until the cheese melts and completely combines.
6. Pour into the tin, decorate with almonds and bake for 20 minutes or until golden brown.

Serve with strawberries cooked with sugar and pureed or any other fruit coulis and *kaymak*.

BREAD AND BUTTER PUDDING MADE WITH DRIED FIGS

Another use for day-old bread, believe me I have lots of it.

- 100g sugar
- 1 tsp ground cinnamon
- 5–6 slices of any THICKLY SLICED bread, crusts removed
- Lots of butter
- About 8–10 dried figs, stalks removed and chopped
- 500ml milk
- 6 eggs
- Zest of one lemon

1. Grease a 1 litre pie dish with butter.
2. Spread each slice of bread both sides with butter, and then cut into triangles.
3. Arrange a layer of bread in the bottom of the dish, and then add a layer of figs. Sprinkle with a little cinnamon, then repeat the layers of bread and sultanas, sprinkling with cinnamon, until you have used up all of the bread. Finish with a layer of the buttered bread, and then set aside.
4. Gently warm the milk in a pan over a low heat to scalding point. Don't let it boil.
5. Crack the eggs into a bowl, add three quarters of the sugar and lightly whisk until pale.
6. Add the warm milk and stir well, then strain the custard into a bowl, add the lemon zest.
7. Pour the custard over the prepared bread layers and sprinkle with nutmeg and the remaining sugar and leave to stand for 30 minutes.
8. Preheat the oven to 180C 160 fan 355F Gas 4
9. Place the dish into the oven and bake for 30–40 minutes, or until the custard has set and the top is golden-brown.

Of course if I were in the UK I would use half milk, half double cream, but Turkey has no equivalent on sale, so I splurge on the butter. 'Needs must as the devil drives' as my mother used to say.

FIGS BAKED IN HONEY WITH ROSE YOGURT

This is so easy, there are no hard and fast rules, so I won't even give ingredient quantities. All you need are lots of purple figs, cut in half with stalks removed, lots of honey and a hot grill. Yogurt and rose water for a topping.

1. In a large oven proof tray, place the figs, cut side up they can snuggle up, the more the merrier.
2. Drizzle with loads of golden liquid honey, shove it under a hot grill and wait for the honey to bubble, the fig juices to run out and the tops of the figs to start to caramelise. Sooooooo good

Serve with fresh Turkish yogurt mixed with however much or little rose water you want. It's the simple things in life, isn't it?

STRAWBERRY YOGURT FREEZER CAKE

From May until September strawberries are everywhere in the market. Much smaller and sweeter than those in the UK, the best ones come from neighbouring Gumusluk However, they don't keep well, a day will see them go soft, so using the soft ones to make a puree makes sense.

400g strawberries, washed and chopped
1 tsp vanilla essence
115g honey
560g Turkish yogurt

For the base:
80g whole almonds
20g desiccated coconut
1 tbsp unsalted butter
100g fresh dates, stoned

1. In a saucepan, put the strawberries, vanilla and honey in a pan over a medium heat and cook for about 10 minutes, stirring occasionally.
2. Remove from the heat and set aside to cool, then whizz to a smooth puree. Set aside a tablespoon of the puree and add the yogurt to the rest, stirring well to combine.
3. To make the base, melt the butter in a small pan, process the almonds, coconut and dates for a few minutes, gradually adding the melted butter until it comes together. Press down firmly onto the bottom of a baking tin (20cm) – a loose-bottomed or spring-form is best for turning out the finished cake easily.
4. Pour over the yogurt mixture, spoon over the reserved puree and gently swirl it in with the point of a knife to make a ripple pattern.

Freeze for at least 4 hours or overnight. Take out 15 minutes before serving.

PISTACHIO ICE CREAM

Strictly speaking this is difficult to make in Turkey, as the double cream we would use is not available, but why let that stop us? We are international here! An ice cream maker would be useful, but you can just whip the mixture and freeze.

1 cup unsalted whole pistachios, roughly chopped
2/3 cup sugar
1 ½ cups milk
1 ½ cups double cream
4 egg yolks
Pinch of salt
½ tsp almond extract NOT flavouring, which can taste metallic

1. Preheat an oven to 180C 160 Fan 350°F. Gas 4
2. Arrange the pistachios in a single layer on a baking sheet and bake, shaking the pan occasionally, until the nuts are lightly golden and toasted, 5 to 7 minutes. Let cool to room temperature.
3. In a mini-food processor or standard-size food processor, combine ½ cup of the pistachios with the sugar and process until finely chopped and well blended. Reserve the remaining ½ cup pistachios. In my case you bash it all up in a freezer bag with a rolling pin. Gets rid of all that pent up aggression.
4. In a saucepan, combine the milk, cream and the pistachio-sugar mixture and stir to blend. Set the pan over medium-low heat and warm the mixture, stirring occasionally, until the sugar is dissolved and steam begins to rise from the surface, 3 to 4 minutes. Remove from the heat and let the mixture steep for 10 to 15 minutes.
5. In a bowl, whisk together the egg yolks and salt until blended. Form a kitchen towel into a ring and place the bowl on top to prevent it from moving. Whisk in ½ cup of the pistachio-cream until smooth and blended, then pour the egg mixture back into the pan.

6. Cook over medium-low heat, stirring slowly and continuously with a wooden spoon or spatula, until the custard thickens and a finger drawn across the back of the spoon leaves a path, 8 to 10 minutes; do not allow the custard to boil.
7. Pour the custard through a fine-mesh sieve set over a clean bowl; discard the pistachios. Nestle the bowl in a larger one filled halfway with ice and water and cool the custard to room temperature, stirring occasionally. Refrigerate until chilled, at least 1 hour.
8. Stir the almond extract into the custard, transfer to an ice cream maker and freeze according to the manufacturer's instructions. At the end of the freezing stage, add the remaining ½ cup pistachios and continue processing just until they are blended into the ice cream. Transfer the ice cream to a chilled container, cover and freeze until firm, at least 3 hours or up to 3 days, before serving.

CHOCOLATE POTS

I discovered that you can buy these frozen and ready made in our local cash and carry, I bought them, I served them, I hate myself!

300g dark chocolate 70% cocoa or over
200g salted butter
300g caster sugar
5 large organic eggs

For the topping sauce:
8 *manalins* or if in the UK, clementines
2 tbsp caster sugar
12 tsp crème fraiche / Turkish yogurt or *Labneh*

1. Preheat the oven 180°C 160 Fan 350F Gas 4
2. Break the chocolate into pieces and put in a large bowl. Add the butter and place over a pan of simmering water, the bowl should not touch the water. Stir occasionally until completely melted. Remove from the heat and leave to cool.
3. In a separate bowl whisk the sugar and the egg together until pale, thick and fluffy, then gradually, gradually add the cooled chocolate, whisking all the time to incorporate.
4. Divide between 12 ramekins then place in a large roasting tin, pop into the oven and fill the tray with boiling water until it reaches halfway up the ramekins. Bake for 25 minutes. Remove from the pan and leave to sit for about 15 minutes before serving.
5. While the pots are in the oven make the sauce by adding sugar to the clementine juice and bringing to the boil. Reduce to a gentle simmer for 15 minutes until the sauce thickens. Take off the heat and leave to cool.

Serve the pots at room temperature with a drizzle of the sauce and a dollop of *kaymak*.

CHOCOLATE HELVA CAKE WITH ALMONDS AND ROSE PETALS.

This is otherwise known amongst our painters as 'OH MY GOD THIS IS AMAZING! cake.'

6 egg whites
1 cup (220g) caster sugar
1 cup (125g) ground almonds
500g chocolate helva, chopped

150g pitted dates, chopped
Grated zest of 2 oranges
120g dark chocolate, finely chopped
1/4 cup (60ml) brandy
2 tbsp edible dried rose petals
2 tbsp slivered pistachios (see note)
2 tbsp pomegranate seeds
Small mint sprigs, to serve

Chocolate glaze
100ml cream or a little unsalted butter
150g dark chocolate, roughly chopped

1. Preheat the oven to 170°C. Grease and line a 24cm spring-form cake pan with baking paper.
2. Beat the egg whites with electric beaters until stiff peaks form.
3. Gradually add the sugar, beating constantly, then beat for 5 minutes more or until thick and glossy.
4. Fold in the almonds, helva, dates, zest and chocolate until just combined.
5. Spoon the mixture into the cake pan, then bake for 1 hour 20 minutes or until dry and firm to the touch (the cake will still be moist in the centre when tested with a skewer).
6. While it is still hot, poke several holes in the top of the cake with a skewer. Pour brandy over the cake, then cool completely in the pan.
7. Meanwhile, for the glaze, place the cream and chocolate in a pan over low heat, stirring until smooth. Remove from the heat and stand for 30 minutes or until it is a thick pouring consistency.
8. Remove the cooled cake from the pan, transfer to a platter and pour over the chocolate glaze, allowing it to drip down the sides. Decorate with rose petals, nuts, pomegranate seeds and mint.

TEA TIME

When you are invited for tea, don't expect a 'cuppa' as we have here, supplemented if you are lucky with a digestive biscuit. You will receive all sorts of sweet and savoury pastries and salads, some of which I show below. You won't need anything else at all after tea, I promise you!

REVANI

Makes 12 to 15 servings, perfect for one hungry group of painters.

For the syrup:
3 cups sugar
3 cups water
Juice of ½ lemon

For the cake:
3 eggs
200g caster sugar
3/4 cup vegetable oil
Zest of 1 lemon
1 tsp vanilla
1 cup plain yogurt
3 tbsp flour
1 cup uncooked semolina
1/4 cup finely ground hazelnuts
½ tsp baking soda
2 tsp baking powder
Coconut flakes and ground nuts for garnish

1. Preheat the oven to 350 F 175 C 160 Fan Gas 4 and grease a 23 x 33 baking tin.

2. Before you start making the cake, prepare the syrup to give it time to cool down.
3. Begin by mixing the sugar and water in a medium saucepan. Turn the heat on high and bring the mixture to a boil while continuously stirring it. Once it boils, reduce the heat to low and let the syrup boil gently for about 10 minutes with the lid off. Add the lemon juice toward the end. Turn off the heat and let the syrup cool down while you make the rest of the recipe.
4. In a large mixing bowl, whisk together the eggs and sugar – do this briskly for several minutes until the sugar dissolves. The more you whisk, the better your *revani* will turn out.
5. Add the oil, lemon zest, vanilla and yogurt and whisk for several minutes more.
6. Add the dry ingredients and mix together well until you have a smooth batter.
7. Pour the batter into the greased baking pan. Bake until the top is nicely browned and a toothpick inserted in the centre comes out clean, 30 to 40 minutes. Once you remove the pan from the oven, let it rest for about 5 minutes.
8. Cut the cake into portion-sized squares or rectangles while still in the pan.
9. Using a large spoon, slowly drizzle all of the cooled syrup over the cake and let it soak in. Cover the cake with foil and refrigerate it for several hours or overnight.
10. Before serving, garnish each square of cake with a pinch of coconut and ground nuts.

You can also make orange-flavoured *revani* by substituting the lemon zest and juice with orange zest and juice. Or, you can eliminate the lemon altogether and use rose water instead to give the cake a wonderful rose aroma.

A VARIATION WITH BUTTER

For the syrup:
450g caster sugar
2 tbsp lemon or orange juice

For the cake:
110g butter, melted, plus extra for greasing
280ml full-fat Greek yogurt
200g caster sugar
240g semolina
1 tbsp baking powder

You'll also need
28cm x 18cm cake tin at least 6cm deep, greased with butter and lined with non-stick baking paper

1. To make the syrup, put the sugar and 340ml cold water into a pan over a medium heat and let the sugar dissolve. Add the lemon or orange juice and bring to a boil. Once the syrup begins to boil, reduce the heat to low and simmer gently for 8–10 minutes. Remove from the heat.
2. Heat the oven to 180°C/160°C fan/ gas 4.
3. In a mixing bowl, combine the butter, yogurt and sugar using a metal spoon.
4. In a separate large bowl, combine the semolina and baking powder. Carefully fold the butter mixture into the semolina until just combined.
5. Pour the batter into the tin and bake for 25 minutes until golden and a skewer pushed into the middle comes out clean.
6. Slowly pour the syrup over the cake until no more can be absorbed. Cool, then turn out onto a large plate or board. Cut into diamond shapes to serve.

MACAROONS

In Turkey, you can find these confections in practically every bakery. If there is one Turkish biscuit, this is it. They are traditionally baked with bitter and sweet almonds as in the almond soup recipe, but as these are hard to find, it is easier to substitute almond extract in their place.

Every time we go to Gumusluk, the charming, protected fishing village just down the coast from us, I drag people down to press our noses against the windows of one of the best bakers and patisseries in the area. Their macaroons are enormous. Why does that sound like something out of a *Carry On* film? I digress, those macaroons would satisfy the cravings of two people. A deep beige in colour with cracks and wrinkles, their soft yet crunchy domes are topped with a single almond. Highly prized by me, I can never leave without a few stuffed into my carrier bag, or indeed stuffed inside me.

140g almonds
140g oz sugar
½ tsp almond extract
⅓ cup egg whites (from 2 eggs)
½ tsp lemon juice
18–20 whole blanched almonds

Makes about 10 macaroons

1. Preheat the oven to 140C 120 C fan 275F Gas 1
2. I recommend using baking parchment, or even as my mother used to use, rice paper. If you do not have any, you can use baking sheets but you have to be careful when you pull the macaroons off the paper as they are very delicate.
3. If you are beginning with whole blanched almonds, grind them finely in your food processor. You can also use raw almonds with their brown skins, the cookies will be a little darker but you may even like that. Alternatively, you can use ground almonds.
4. Combine the almonds, almond extract, sugar and egg whites in a non-stick pan.
5. At very, very, very low heat, allow the sugar to melt while mixing the batter continuously with a wooden spoon. Approximately 10 minutes should be sufficient to reach the desired consistency. In this step, the temperature is very critical, we do not want to cook the egg whites.
6. Pour the mixture onto a cold surface and let it cool down to room temperature. You have to be patient here! The batter hardens as it cools down and this is essential for the macaroons to preserve their shapes when you drop them onto the baking tray one by one.
7. When cool add the lemon juice to the mixture and mix well.
8. Transfer to a piping bag. and pipe 3.5–5cm mounds onto the baking sheet. If the mixture is too dry for piping, add a teaspoon or two of egg whites. If the mixture is too runny, add ground almonds. When dropped, the cookies should not spread on the baking sheet easily. Achieving this consistency is the most important thing you will have to learn.
9. Optional: Place a whole blanched almond on each cookie – the original recipe calls for half an almond on each cookie – probably so as to reduce the weight of the almond so the cookie can rise freely.
10. Bake on the middle rack of the oven for 30–35 minutes.

11. After 30 minutes move the tray to the upper rack of the oven and set the temperature to low broil (if your oven has this feature). Otherwise pop them under a low grill until they have turned a golden brown.

Do not over bake, they will harden fairly quickly – they are supposed to have a thin crust with a chewy middle. When ready, take them off the hot baking tray immediately, This is easier if you bake them on baking parchment and not directly in the tin.

CHOCOLATE MACAROONS WITH COCONUT

2 medium egg whites
1 tsp cream of tartar
200g caster sugar
200g desiccated coconut\60g??? 70%or more cocoa chocolate
Vinegar for wiping

1. Preheat oven to 140°C 120 Fan 275 F Gas1 Fan
2. Line a baking tray with greased baking parchment or rice paper if you can find any.
3. Wipe out your large mixing bowl with a little vinegar.
4. Whisk egg whites until they start to get frothy, then add the cream of tartar. Whilst whisking, slowly add the sugar. The egg whites will start to turn glossy and look firmer.
5. When the whites are standing in soft peaks, add the coconut and mix well.
6. Place on the baking tray in tablespoon-full batches.
7. Bake for 25 minutes until light golden in colour. Leave to cool.
8. Meanwhile, melt the chocolate in a bain marie over boiling water. I am not tempted to use a microwave as I think the chocolate cooks as well as melts that way and seems to behave differently. Once the macaroons are cool, dip half of each one in the melted chocolate and leave to set.

SEKERPARE (SEMOLINA BISCUITS IN SYRUP)

Zest of 1 small lemon
115g sugar
125g unsalted butter
300g plain flour
95g fine semolina
2 eggs
1 tbsp baking powder
2 tbsp light olive oil (and a little extra to grease the baking tray)
20 blanched almonds or hazelnuts
Small bowl of cold water (to help shape the biscuits)

For the syrup:
Juice of 1 small lemon
345 g sugar
480ml water

1. Preheat the oven to 180 C/ 350 F/ Gas mark 4
2. First make the syrup. Grate the lemon zest into a bowl and set aside.
3. In a heavy pan place sugar and water over a medium heat and bring to the boil. Stir until the sugar dissolves.

4. Add the lemon juice, reduce the heat and simmer for a further 15 minutes for the syrup to thicken slightly. Turn the heat off and set the syrup aside to cool.
5. Melt the butter in a small saucepan over a low heat; do not let it burn.
6. Sift the flour into a large mixing bowl and stir in the semolina. Make a well in the middle and pour in the butter. Stir in the 2 eggs, the sugar, lemon zest, the olive oil and the baking powder.
7. Knead for 5 minutes until you get a soft dough. Cover with a damp cloth and set aside to rest for 15 minutes.
8. Have a small bowl of cold water nearby. Knead the dough again for 5 minutes. Then wet your hands lightly with cold water, divide the dough and shape into 20 spheres the size of golf balls.
9. Grease a baking tray with a little butter and place the balls in rows, making sure you leave extra space between them to expand. Slightly flatten the rounds gently with the palm of your hand.
10. Push an almond or hazelnut into the centre of each biscuit.
11. Bake in the preheated oven for 20–25 minutes, until they start to turn light brown.
12. Remove and pour the cooled syrup over the hot biscuits whilst they sit in their tray.
13. Leave to cool and let the biscuits absorb the syrup for 15 minutes.
14. When cooled down take out and place on a serving platter.

TURK TIP *These will keep for up to 3 days as the sugar syrup will preserve the moistness.*

APPLE AND WALNUT BISCUITS

Kurabiye is the general term for biscuit in Kars in Eastern Anatolia. The apples and walnuts used for the filling are grown in that area. Traditionally, the dough encircles the filling rather like a croissant, in a crescent shape, but the method below works just as well and saved me a lot of time when I had 14 mouths to feed. You can use unbleached flour as this is what would have been used in the region.

Large square baking tin or just form into a square shape on baking parchment. They are supposed to be rustic.
4 large sharp-tasting apples (Granny Smiths, for example), peeled, cored and grated
55g caster sugar
1 level tsp cinnamon
½ tsp vanilla extract
400g plain flour
40g icing sugar
1 tsp baking powder
250g salted butter, melted
2 tbsp Turkish yogurt
100g walnuts chopped

1. Preheat oven to 200°C 180 Fan 400F Gas 6
2. In a large pan place the apples and sugar over a medium-low heat, stirring frequently. Cook for about 15 minutes until the apples are soft, but not too broken down.
3. Add the cinnamon, vanilla and walnuts and stir. Remove from the heat. Set aside.
4. Sift together the flour, baking powder and icing sugar, add the butter and the yogurt and stir to combine. Do not overwork at this point.
5. Divide the dough in half and press it with your fingers over the base and sides of the baking tin, Spread the apple mixture on top.

6. Place the remaining dough on a sheet of baking parchment and press into a square the same size as the tin. (It may be helpful to trace the shape onto the paper so you get it right.) Invert the paper over the tin so the dough flops on top of the apple and walnut mixture. Try and get the dough to reach the edges of the tin and pinch together.
7. Bake the biscuit slab for 30 minutes until golden brown and crispy.

Serve dusted with icing sugar whilst still warm.

BAKLAVA

There is absolutely no point in giving a recipe for *baklava*, the shop or Pazar-bought confection will be far superior. I once laboured for hours making a tray of walnut *baklava* to surprise my then husband. He solemnly ate a plateful and told me not to bother again. Nuff said.

LOKMA

Lokma is a fried sweet dough that is covered in a simple syrup. Served as a dessert, lokma is a popular coffee accompaniment

1¼ cups warm water
1 tsp sugar
1 tsp active dry yeast
2 cups all purpose flour plus 2 tablespoons
1 tspn salt
Vegetable oil

For the syrup
3 cups sugar
1⅓ cups water
2 tbsp lemon juice

1. In a measuring cup, add the yeast and sugar to warm water. Stir until dissolved. Allow to sit for 5–10 minutes.
2. In a medium bowl, combine the flour and salt. Add the yeast water and stir with an oiled wooden spoon until it has a dough-like consistency.
3. Cover and place in a warm area and allow to rise for 1 ½ hours, or until doubled in size.
4. Preheat vegetable oil to 375. If you don't have a thermometer the easiest and safest method is to stick the end of a wooden spoon into the oil. If you see many bubbles form around the wood and they start to float up, your oil is ready for frying. If it is bubbling hard, the oil is too hot; let it cool a bit and check the temperature again.
5. Spoon the dough by the tablespoon into the vegetable oil and allow to cook for about 2 minutes on each side, until each side is a golden brown colour. Repeat with the remaining dough. Drain on paper towels.
6. About 20 minutes prior to frying the dough, make the syrup. Mix all the ingredients in a saucepan until the sugar is dissolved over a medium heat. Bring to a boil, then allow to simmer on low for about 10–15 minutes, until it become a syrup consistency. Do not stir frequently because the sugar will make the syrup cloudy.

Drizzle the syrup over the fried dough and serve immediately.

SEMOLINA *HELVA*

Serves 6–8

110g butter
Small glug light olive oil
450g coarse semolina
900ml milk (whole milk preferred)
335g sugar
1 tbsp pine nuts plus an optional 1 tbsp toasted to decorate
2 tsp ground cinnamon to decorate

1. Melt the butter and olive oil in a heavy pan, stir in the pine nuts and semolina and cook over a medium heat, stirring all the time, until lightly browned.
2. At the same time, warm the milk in a separate pan and stir in the sugar, mix well and let the sugar dissolve. Turn the heat off once the milk is hot (but not boiling) and the sugar has dissolved.
3. Pour the milk and sugar mixture into the semolina and pine nuts mixture and lower the heat. Mix well and cook over a low heat until the milk has been absorbed, stirring continuously for about 10–15 minutes. Turn the heat off.
4. Place a paper towel over the pan and cover with the lid, let the *helva* rest for about 10 minutes – the paper towel will absorb all the excess moisture.
5. If you like, sauté 1 tablespoon pine nuts in a drizzle of olive oil for a few minutes. Spoon the semolina *helva* into individual bowls, and serve with a dust of cinnamon and a few sautéed pine nuts over them.

WHOLE LEMON CAKE

This is a sure-fire winner for a dessert or with tea whilst on a break, sharp yet sweet and really moist. This recipe makes enough for 12 people. Happy days.

2–4 lemons, depending on size, I err on the side of largesse
250g caster sugar (I like it tangy, but you can add more)
6 organic eggs, separated
300g ground almonds
A couple of handfuls of flaked almonds
Icing sugar to dust

1. In a large saucepan put the whole unpeeled fruit and cover with cold water. Cover with a lid and bring to the boil. Lower the heat and gently simmer for 1–2 hours until very soft. Leave to cool.
2. You must allow enough time to let the lemons cool or you'll be hopping about blowing on your hands whilst you try to extract any pips from the hot innards.
3. Heat the oven to 160°C fan or 180° non fan FFF and grease and line a 23cm baking tin (loose bottomed if you have one).
4. When the lemons have cooled enough, drain them, reserving the flavoured water, and remove any woody ends. Chop finely, taking out any seeds as you go. Whizz up to a puree.
5. In a large bowl, whisk the egg whites with a pinch of salt until they are forming stiff peaks.
6. Then whisk the yolks in a separate bowl with the sugar until pale and thick.
7. Whisk in the lemon puree and ground almonds and finally, gently fold in the egg whites.
8. Pour the batter into the lined tin, scatter with the flaked almonds and bake in the centre of the oven for about an hour. You should test if it's ready by using a skewer at around 50 minutes; if it comes out clean it's done. Leave to cool on a rack.

9. Make a lemon syrup by boiling together 250ml lemon water and 250 ml lemon juice with 250g sugar. Boil until the syrup thickens and goes darker in colour. Prick the cake all over and drizzle the syrup all over so it seeps into the holes. You can repeat this a couple of times until the cake is saturated.

Serve with *kaymak* or yogurt flavoured with a little rosewater. Because of the syrup I suspect this cake will keep for a few days, but I have never had it hang around long enough to find out.

TURK TIP *Sometimes I add extra flavouring to the syrup. Try adding a clove or a cardamom pod or two whilst boiling*

YOGURT CAKE WITH PISTACHIOS

The ubiquitous yogurt rears its head again!

3 large organic eggs separated
70g caster sugar
1 tsp vanilla extract
350g Turkish yogurt
Grated zest and juice of 1 lemon
Grated zest of ½ orange
20g plain flour

30 shelled unsalted pistachios chopped
Handful of pomegranate seeds to decorate

1. Grease and line a 25cm round or square baking tin.
2. Preheat the oven to 180° C 160Fan 350F Gas 4
3. Warm a bain marie of water on the middle shelf, make sure it is big enough to hold the tin!.
4. In a large bowl beat the egg yolks with ¾ of the sugar until pale and thick.
5. Add the vanilla essence, the yogurt, lemon and orange zest, lemon juice and flour. Mix well.
6. In a separate bowl whisk the egg whites with the remaining sugar until they form soft peaks.
7. Fold the egg whites gently into the yogurt mixture and pour into the baking tin.
8. Place the tin into the bain marie, making sure the water comes halfway up the tin, and bake for about 40 minutes until golden brown in colour.
9. Tip out of the tin when slightly cooled and place on a cake rack. When completely cool, put on the serving plate and scatter with pistachios and pomegranate seeds.

POMEGRANATE AND APRICOT MERINGUE CAKES

Simple to make, the almond flakes and pomegranate seeds make these little cakes look very impressive.

100g room temperature butter, plus extra for greasing the tins
100g caster sugar
100g self raising flour
2 large organic eggs
1 tsp vanilla extract/paste
For the meringues:
2 large egg whites
50g caster sugar
Vinegar for wiping

To decorate:
Apricot jam
2 tbsp flaked almonds
A handful of pomegranate seeds

1. Preheat the oven to 180 C 160° C Fan 350 F Gas 4
2. Grease well 6 shallow tart tins, about 10cm in diameter.
3. In a large bowl whisk the butter, sugar, flour and eggs plus the vanilla extract for 2 minutes or so until light in colour and creamy.
4. Divide the batter evenly between the tart tins and bake for 10–12 minutes. You can test if they are done by inserting a skewer, if it comes out clean they are ready.
5. Set aside to cool on a rack.
6. Once cooled, spread apricot jam over the top of each tart, not too thickly.
7. Now make the meringue: in a large bowl (make sure it's clean by wiping around with a vinegar-damp paper towel) whisk the egg whites until they form soft peaks, gradually add the sugar until the mixture looks glossy.
8. Put the meringue mixture on top of the apricot-coated bases, you could pipe it, but to my mind it's going to be covered in almonds and pomegranate seeds, so it may be unnecessary.
9. Sprinkle with flaked almonds and pop back into the oven to cook for about 15 minutes until firm and slightly coloured.
10. Cool and serve scattered with the jewel-like pomegranate seeds.

QUINCE CRUMBLE CAKE

2 large quinces, (approximately 300–400g each) peeled, quartered and cored
1l water
440g caster sugar
140ml sweet Marsala wine
2 cinnamon sticks, halved
1 vanilla pod, split lengthways
Parchment paper

For the crumble:
25g plain flour
35g soft brown muscovado sugar
40gb walnuts, chopped
35g unsalted butter, chopped

For the cake:
185g self-raising flour
1 tsp mixed spice
½ tsp baking powder
100g ground almonds
250g unsalted butter, softened, plus extra to grease the tin
220g soft brown muscovado sugar
220g tinned chestnut purée, unsweetened
3 large eggs
60ml whole milk
24cm spring-form cake tin

1. To begin, prepare the quince. Place the water, caster sugar, Marsala, cinnamon sticks and vanilla pod in a medium pan over a low heat. Stir continually until all the sugar has dissolved.
2. Add the quince quarters to the syrup and cover with a round of parchment paper shaped to fit with a small hole cut in the middle to allow steam to escape. Simmer for 2 hours or until the fruit is deep red and tender. The syrup should be nicely reduced.
3. Remove the fruit with a slotted spoon and transfer to a bowl to cool, reserving the syrup.

4. When cool, cut the quince quarters in half.
5. Preheat the oven to 180°C/160 Fan 350F Gas 4. Grease and line a 24cm spring-form cake tin with baking paper.
6. Make the crumble topping by combining the flour, sugar, walnuts and cubed butter in a bowl. Rub the butter into the mixture until it forms coarse crumbs then set aside.
7. Sieve the flour, mixed spice and baking powder into a bowl and add the almonds. Set aside.
8. Place the butter and sugar into a bowl and beat until the mix is pale and fluffy. Obviously an electric beater is quicker, but think of the arm muscles. Add the chestnut purée and beat until just smooth.
9. Add the eggs, one at a time, and beat until just combined. Gently fold in the flour mixture and milk until just combined.
10. Spoon the batter into the prepared tin and spread until level. Arrange 12 quince slices in a circular pattern on top, then 4 slices in the centre. Sprinkle the crumble evenly over the top.
11. Place in the oven and bake for 1 hour to 1 hour 15 minutes, or until a skewer inserted into the centre of the cake comes out clean.
12. Remove from the oven and allow to sit in the tin for 10 minutes before transferring to a wire rack to cool.
13. Serve warm or cool, drizzled with the reserved syrup. The cake is best eaten on the day of making.

JAM RECIPES FOR HIGH SUMMER

AUBERGINE JAM

Absolutely the bees knees!

500g aubergine, peeled and cut into chunks
6 cloves
400ml boiling water
1 lemon
450g sugar

1. Cook the aubergine for 10 minutes in boiling salted water. Drain well.
2. Wash the lemon and press the cloves into the skin.
3. Put in a pan with the sugar. Pour over the boiling water and stir until the sugar has dissolved.
4. Add the drained cooked aubergine and stir until well mixed. Cool and leave overnight.
5. Wash and warm two jars. Bring the mixture to the boil and boil steadily to 105C. The aubergine will become almost translucent and the liquid thick and syrupy.
6. Gently press the lemon with the back of a spoon and then remove and discard, before potting the aubergine in the jars. Seal and cool before labelling and storing in a dark, dry, cool place.

CHILLI JAM

Also completely yummy, who'd have thought it? This is a recipe from Mehmet Ali's wife, Fatma Ozince. Known as Fatos, she is the steely eye and hand that runs the Breakfast Place close to our house. No weights or numbers are included, but it is very straightforward. 1kg of apples to one large chilli and two green ones should do the trick, although I reckon you should not exceed two red chillies as they can be very hot. Give it a go, but start early!

This is what she told me, as I said, Turkish cooking is not an applied science!

Red chillies, de-seeded and chopped
Hot green peppers, chopped
Red apples, cored and chopped
Sugar

1. Put the chillies, peppers and apples into a large pan and cover with water.
2. Add a couple of tablespoons of sugar and bring to boil.
3. Simmer for EIGHT hours!.
4. Pour the jam into sterilised jars and seal. Don't worry if it's a little runny as Turkish jam tends to be

According to the taste and structure you can add more sugar/chilli/water and boil for *another* eight hours. Hope you were not planning a day out!

ROSE JAM

120g of washes red or pink perfumed rose petals (no pesticides)
800g sugar
2 tbsp lemon juice

1. Thoroughly wash the rose petals, then drain on paper towel.
2. Combine the rose petals with 200g of the sugar and rub with your hands until they form a paste.
3. Dissolve the remaining sugar in 450 ml water in a large stainless steel saucepan over low heat. Stir in the rose petal mixture and bring to the boil. Boil for 20 minutes, or until the jam is thickened but still slightly runny. Stir in the lemon juice, then remove from the heat.
4. Pour the jam into sterilised jars and seal.

BREADS AND OTHER FLOUR-BASED RECIPES

If there is one thing I cannot avoid writing about, nor indeed do I want to, it is any sort of Turkish bread. It is obligatory in Turkish life. No apologies, and no concerns about getting fat. Just eat!

BAZLAMA BREAD

These can be circular or oval, the diameter you prefer, about 2cmm thick, but of course, always flat!

500g plain flour
2 tsp salt
1 tsp sugar
I sachet dried yeast
1 dessert spoon olive oil
300 ml hand-hot water (if it's comfortable to your hand it's fine, if it feels too hot it is not)

1. Put all the dry ingredients into a large bowl and mix, make a well and add the olive oil then slowly add the water whilst pulling the mix together. Knead until no longer sticky.
2. Cover with a clean tea towel and leave at room temperature for about an hour and a half.
3. Cut the dough into 10–12 equal pieces, shape into rounds and flatten. Cover again and leave for another 15 minutes.
4. Heat griddle pan or skillet on a high heat, place one dough piece onto the griddle and cook until brown spots appear on the top. Turn over and bake for a further minute or two. Repeat until all the pieces are cooked.
5. Serve warm with soup or mezzes. These breads will keep for a few days.

RYE AND THYME FLATBREAD

These are crispy, not soft like *bazlama*. You can replace the thyme with rosemary for equal effect.

300g plain flour
300g rye flour
1 large handful fresh thyme, the leaves stripped from the thicker stalks and roughly chopped
4 tsp sea salt plus some for finish
330 ml water
2 large glugs of olive oil

1. Heat oven to 220°C fan /240° non fan FFF
2. Put all the dry ingredients, including the thyme, into a large bowl and mix and knead as for *bazlama*
3. Wrap with a clean cloth or cling film roll it into a cylinder shape and leave for ½ hour at room temperature.
4. Take a quarter of the dough and roll out thinly between sheets of baking parchment. It should be paper thin.
5. Remove the top paper and slide the dough onto a baking tray, brush with olive oil and sprinkle with sea salt and a few thyme leaves. Bake for 6–8 minutes until golden brown.
6. Repeat until all batches are baked to crispy perfection.

Once cool they can be broken into fragments and eaten with soups, mezzes or as a sort of home made crisp with drinks or with cheese.

PIDE WITH CHEESE AND PEPPERS

You can improvise on all fillings, use different types of cheese, minced meat and any combo of vegetables you fancy. You can even crack an egg onto the *pide* halfway through the cooking process.

Makes 2 *pides*, enough for 4 hungry painters

For the dough:

300g + 2 tbsp all-purpose plain flour
14g/4 tsp dried yeast (2 packs of 7g dried yeast)
8fl oz. /ml 1 cup warm water
45ml/3 tbsp olive oil

For the topping:

1 medium onion, finely chopped
200g spinach leaves, washed and pat dried
200g feta cheese, crumbled
1 red bell pepper, de-seeded and cut in half lengthways and thinly sliced
15 ml/1 tbsp Turkish red pepper paste (option, you can use ½ tsp if you prefer less spicy or omit)
15 ml/1 tbsp olive oil
Salt (optional, as feta cheese may be quite salty too) and freshly ground black pepper to taste
1 egg + 15 ml/1 tbsp olive oil to brush the *pide*

1. Preheat the oven to 180 C/160 Fan 350 F Gas 4
2. Stir the dried yeast into a small bowl and pour in ½ cup warm water. Dissolve the yeast in the water, mixing with your fingers. Set aside for 5 minutes for the yeast mixture to get frothy.
3. Combine the flour and salt in a large bowl. Make a well in the middle and pour in 2 tbsp olive oil and the yeast mixture.
4. Pour in the remaining warm water. Using your hands, draw in the flour from the sides and work the mixture into a dough.
5. Knead for 3–5 minutes, until you achieve a soft, smooth dough. The dough gets sticky as you knead, so use a tablespoon of olive oil and stir in the additional 2 tablespoons of flour to help shape into a soft dough.
6. Place the dough in a large bowl and cover with cling film. Leave it in a warm place for minimum 1 hour; it will double in size.
7. In the meantime, prepare your filling. Heat 15ml/1tbsp olive oil in a wide heavy pan and stir in the onions and peppers. Sauté the onions and peppers for 3–5 minutes over medium heat until they start to soften.
8. Turn the heat off and stir in the spinach, red pepper paste (if using) and feta cheese, combine well. Season with salt and freshly ground black pepper.
9. Once the dough is risen, place it on a lightly floured surface. Knead for a minute then divide into two pieces and roll into two balls.
10. On a lightly floured surface, roll the dough balls into 2 oval shapes of 20 cm x 40 cm (about 8'x16'), with ½ cm (0.2') thickness.
11. Line a large baking tray with baking paper and place the 2 flat bread ovals on the tray.
12. Spread the filling evenly over the flat breads, leaving 2 cm at the edges as a border with no filling (I've found it's easier to spread the filling while the oval dough is in the tray).
13. Fold in the sides to act as a border to keep the filling in situ. Squeeze the oval dough at each end to make it pointy.
14. Beat an egg in a small bowl and mix it with the last tbsp olive oil. Brush the edges of dough with this mixture.
15. Bake for 25 minutes, until the *pides* are golden brown and crispy at the edges.

Once cool, cut into slices and serve.

SIMPLEST FLAT BREAD RECIPE

Take flour then add half its quantity in yogurt (Turkish full fat), add some salt and mix well. Form into rounds, roll out and cook on a dry griddle until spotted with brown. Done!

SIMIT Makes 8

300ml water
7g fresh yeast or 1 tsp dried active yeast
1 tsp salt
500g flour, plus extra for dusting
140g sesame seeds
60g grape molasses (*pekmez*)
60ml water

1. Pour the water into a large mixing bowl and dissolve the yeast. Add the salt and one third of the flour and stir into a runny pancake-like batter.
2. Continue adding the flour gradually, stirring the thickening batter with the spoon.
3. When about one third of the flour is left, dust a clean surface with some of it and transfer the dough to the surface.
4. Knead slowly, incorporating the remaining flour about 10 minutes. The resulting dough will be a bit stiff. Put it in a large bowl, cover with cling film and leave to rise in the fridge overnight.
5. In the morning, dust the work surface with flour. Knead the dough gently a few times to deflate. Divide into 8 equal pieces, shaping each piece into a neat ball. Cover these dough balls with a tea towel and let them rest for 10–15 minutes.
6. Put the sesame seeds in a frying pan over a medium heat. Toss every 2–3 minutes to ensure even browning: after 7–10 minutes, the seeds should pick up a light-brown colour, but make sure they don't turn caramel-brown (as they will taste bitter). Transfer the toasted seeds to a small deep tray.
7. Whisk together the grape molasses and water in a deep wide plate, then take one dough ball and roll it into a long rope – start rolling in the middle and work outwards. If you dusted the dough balls while dividing, you don't need to dust the working surface with the flour: too much flour makes rolling tricky.
8. When the rope is about 60cm long, lift it from the middle and swing a bit to extend it. Now holding the middle in one hand and both ends in the other twist the rope a couple of times. Put the ends into the loop to make a ring.
9. Set aside on a lightly floured surface, cover with kitchen paper and repeat with the rest of the dough.
10. Dip each *simit* into the molasses and then transfer to a colander/sieve to drain any excess liquid. Once all the *simits* are dipped, one by one place them in the tray with the toasted sesame seeds and coat well. Arrange the coated *simits* on two baking trays lined with baking paper and shape each bread ring into a neat round. Leave to prove for 30 minutes, then preheat the oven to high – 240C/475F/gas mark 9.
11. Put a metal tray with boiling water in the bottom of the oven and splash about 60ml water around the interior of the oven: you want a bit of steam in there to ensure dramatic 'oven spring' (rising of the bread rings during the initial stages of baking dough). Bake the *simits* for 10 minutes.

Remove the water tray carefully and let the *simits* bake for 10 minutes more until the tops and bottoms are reddish brown. *Simit* is best within just a few hours of coming out of the oven. You can cool it down and freeze the baked ones and then warm them up in a high oven.

HOW TO MAKE *GOZLEME*

The name *Gozleme* originates from the word 'eye' (in Turkish *goz* means eye). When you start to cook it, you will see some little brown round shaped spots on it, which look like eyes, this also shows when it is time to turn the *Gozleme* over.

The hard work is the rolling, not quite as thinly as in *Yufka* but it is made easier if you have the thin rolling pin that is traditionally used. Makes about 5 *Gozleme*

3 cups / 16 oz/ 1lb.ggg plain flour
8g sachet instant dried yeast
Pinch of salt
45 ml/3 tbsp olive oil
30 ml/2 tbsp plain natural full fat Greek-style yoghurt
10 fl oz /ml 1 ½ cups water

1. Sift the flour into a large bowl. Make a well in the middle and pour in the yeast mixture, olive oil, yoghurt and the water.
2. Using your hand, draw in the flour from the sides and work the mixture into a dough. Knead thoroughly to form a soft dough. Divide the dough into 5 pieces, knead them and roll into balls.
3. Place the balls on a floured surface, cover with a damp cloth and leave them to rest for about 30 minutes, or until the dough doubles in size.

Whilst you are waiting for the dough to prove make the fillings.

CHEESE FILLING

½ cup feta cheese (*cokolek* if you have it), crumbled
1/4 cup parsley, chopped
I like to add some chopped spring onions

You can also make *Gozleme* with beef, spinach, potato or aubergine filling. Makes 2 servings

BEEF FILLING

150g lean ground beef
1 small onion, chopped
Salt
Pepper

1. Fry the onions until soft, (add salt to make that quicker) add the meat stir and turn until well browned add pepper or pul biber and more salt if required and sprinkle some chopped parsley on top.

SPINACH FILLING

500g of fresh washed spinach, chopped so as not to get stringy when eaten.
1 small onion, chopped
1 tbsp olive oil

1/4 cup of *cokerme* or feta cheese, crumbled
1 pinch crushed pepper
Salt and pepper

1. Sauté the onion with olive oil. Add all the ingredients except the feta cheese, cook for about 4–5 minutes. Turn the heat off, add feta cheese and stir.

POTATO FILLING

1 potato, boiled, peeled and mashed
1 small onion, chopped
1 ½ tbsp olive oil or butter
1/4 cup feta cheese, crumbled
1 pinch crushed pepper
Salt and pepper

1. Sauté the onion with olive oil, then add the rest of the ingredients.

ROASTED EGGPLANT FILLING

1 medium eggplant, roasted, peeled and drained
1/4 cup cheese, grated
1 tbsp olive oil
1 pinch crushed pepper
Salt and pepper

Serve *Gozleme* while it is still warm. It is traditionally eaten with the salted yogurt drink, *ayran*. Perfect for lunch on a hot summer day.

POGACA

Easy recipe For Home-style Turkish '*Pogaca*', a traditional Turkish pastry usually served at breakfast.

2 cups plain yogurt
3/4 cup melted butter (or margarine)
½ tsp salt
2 ½ tsp baking powder
1/4 tsp sugar
2 cups flour (plus as much flour as the mixture can take in)
1/3 cup feta or goat's cheese (crumbled)
1 tbsp fresh parsley (finely chopped) this is optional, but if you have it, why not?
1/4 cup fresh herbs (finely chopped) ditto
2 egg yolks
2 tbsp sesame seeds (or poppy seeds or black cumin seeds, for garnish)

1. First, prepare the filling. Crumble the feta or goat's cheese with a fork. Add about 1 tablespoon of finely chopped parsley. If you're adding herbs to the dough, omit the parsley in the filling.
2. In a large mixing bowl, starting with about 2 cups of flour, combine all the ingredients and work them together with your hands. Keep kneading the mixture and adding flour gradually until you have a smooth, firm dough about as firm as an earlobe.
3. If you are using fresh herbs in the dough, knead them in thoroughly. Decide what size you wish to make your rolls. For breakfast rolls, make balls of dough about the size of a small plum. For bite-sized *pogaca*, make them about the size of an apricot.
4. Take a ball of dough and press it down on a lightly floured surface to flatten it.

5. Put a small amount of your chosen filling in the centre. Fold the circle in half over the filling so the edges come together and pinch them closed very gently.
6. On a baking tray lined with grease-proof baking paper, place the *pogaca*, seam side down and tuck the ends under gently as you go. Your roll should be an oval that is wider and rounder in the centre and narrower at the ends.
7. Repeat this with all the dough balls, leaving about one inch (2.5cm) between each roll.
8. With a pastry brush, coat the top of each roll with egg yolk. Sprinkle the sesame, poppy or black cumin seeds on top of each roll.
9. Bake in a 180C 160 Fan 350F Gas 4 oven until the rolls puff up and the tops turn a golden brown.

Serve the *pogaca* while still warm.

TURKISH BREAD RAVIOLI (*BAYAT EKMEK MANTISI*)

If you buy too much bread as I often do, tending to get carried away, you may find yourself with a surfeit of not quite the freshest bread, this recipe will use it up.

For the bread balls
250g /9ox stale bread
2 medium onions minced or grated
3 cloves garlic put through a crusher
1 egg
Handful fresh parsley
Salt to taste
½ cup water
Black pepper
Cumin
Pul Biber (red pepper flakes)
Dried mint leaves
Dried thyme
Dried basil

For the yogurt sauce
5 tablespoons of thick plain yogurt
Salt
Garlic if you want it especially garlicky

For the dressing
1 tsp tomato paste
2 tbsp olive oil
Dried mint
Paprika (I like the smoked variety)

1. Whizz up the stale bread to crumbs in a large bowl, then add onions, garlic, and all the herbs and spices, plus one egg. Mix together to form a stiff-ish dough add water to get the right consistency.
2. Form the mixture into balls, then roll them in flour so they are completely coated.
3. Heat sunflower oil in a deep pan and fry the balls turning to get every side crispy and golden.
4. Put in a large platter and cover with the garlic yogurt sauce.
5. For the dressing heat up 2 tbsp of olive oil in a pan add the tomato paste and mint and spice. Trickle on top of the yogurt to make the bread balls look glamorous!

PICKLES, PASTES & SAUCES

TOMATO SAUCE

I am quoting enough sauce so you can freeze in 500ml cartons to use as and when required. Then you can add extra flavourings depending on the recipe.

- 1 kg of tomatoes, skinned by putting into boiling water, and roughly chopped
- 3 large white or yellow onions, they need to be strongly flavoured.
- 3–4 cloves of garlic, pressed, peeled and chopped finely
- 1 Dessert spoon of tomato puree
- 1–2 sugar cubes
- Generous pinch of chilli flakes or *pul biber*
- Sea salt and black pepper to taste
- Olive oil for frying
- 1.5 litres water

1. Chop the onions and fry gently in a large heavy bottomed pan in the olive oil, they need to be thoroughly soft, adding a little sea salt after a couple of minutes helps this along.
2. When completely soft, add the garlic cook for a couple of minutes more then add the tomatoes, there should be lots of juice so try and get all of it in the pot.
3. Add the water and bring to the boil, then add the puree, chilli flakes, sugar cubes and pepper. There is salt already in the onions so adjust the seasoning at the end of the process.
4. Lower the heat and simmer gently until all the contents have merged and the tomatoes have pulped down.
5. You may need to add more water if the sauce appears too thick. The whole process should take about an hour, the more it cooks the deeper the flavour.

This is a basis for many of the dishes I mention here, I just add extra flavours – for example, the *Manti* (ravioli) sauce [pp00] has extra dried tomatoes and some parsley. *Menemem* requires peppers to be added.

I can use this sauce in my *moussakas* and imam beyeldi too. I can't tell you how useful it is to have it available straight from the freezer. It is best to defrost naturally and not use the microwave. Also don't forget to re season after freezing.

TAHINI SAUCE

This is lovely with many roasted vegetable mezzes or side dishes.

- 4–5 tbsp tahini.
- Zest and juice of 1 lemon
- 2 chunky garlic cloves, peeled and chopped
- Salt and pepper to taste
- Drizzle of grape molasses, or honey
- A pinch of za'atar

1. Combine all the ingredients in a bowl and slowly add 4–6 tbsp cold water, whizzing with a whisk or a stick blender until it gets pale and fluffy.

You can leave out the za'atar if you prefer a purer sesame taste. You can also add yogurt instead of water for a variation.

RED PEPPER PASTE

4 red peppers
4 red chillies
40ml water
1tsp salt
1tsp sugar
20ml olive oil
1tsp cumin

1. Cut the peppers into large chunks, discarding the seed core.
2. Slice the chillies in half (discarding the seeds for if you require a milder paste) and trim any stems.
3. Place the peppers, chillies, water, salt, sugar and olive oil into a food processor until smooth.
4. Transfer the mixture to a saucepan and simmer gently until it has reduced to a thick paste (about 1 hour), stirring frequently.
5. Keep stirring frequently to take care that the mixture doesn't stick to the bottom of the pan.
6. Allow to cool then use as desired in Turkish recipes or any time that you want a little 'heat' in your cooking.

This mixture can be kept in a refrigerator or up to a week in a sealable container. Or, it can be frozen in a small sealable plastic container. You can also buy in jars at some UK supermarkets.

ANOTHER WAY

500g red peppers (any kind), discard seeds and cut in half
Extra virgin olive oil
Spicy red pepper (optional)
Salt

1. Boil the red peppers with water for about 15–20 minutes to soften them.
2. Leave them in a paper bag for 10 minutes so you can peel them easily.
3. Puree them in the blender.
4. Pour them into a pot, add salt and simmer until all the water evaporates. Spread on a tray and [if possible?] leave under the sun all day. Then put in a jar, cover with some olive oil and refrigerate.

You should make this in the summer. I did it a bit earlier this year. When you leave the paste under the sun, its colour will darken and it will be a bit thicker.

PICKLED VEGETABLES

The Turks will pickle pretty well anything. You can make your own, or buy in a jar or can, or from large plastic tubs in the market. You can get cabbage, carrots, peppers, chillies, cauliflower, tomatoes, turnips, green beans, the list goes on, or any combo of the list.

You will need some 1 or 2 litre glass or plastic jars with screw lids or a Kilner type jars. Note that autumn vegetables are good to use as they are stronger in flavour.

- 1 small cauliflower in florets
- 3 largish or 6 baby carrots, cut into chunks
- 3 small white onions cut into quarters
- 3 largish Turkish cucumbers (they are the small [???] ones that look a bit like courgettes), cut into quarters and pricked with a fork
- 1 handful of fresh green chillies, pierced with a fork or tip of a knife then boiled in a little water. Reserve the water.
- Half a white cabbage chopped into chunks
- Six or so garlic cloves, peeled
- 8 coriander seeds
- 1 small handful of black peppercorns (I also use the pink ones from our tree for colour)
- 1 lemon sliced
- Dill, parsley, or mint
- 125g rock salt
- Dessert spoon of sugar; brown is best, if you are adding more chillies then sugar softens the heat
- 1.5l good apple or wine vinegar
- 2–3l water

1. Add the chilli water to the water and bring to the boil, then mix the salt vinegar into the water. Allow to cool.
2. Fill the jar with the vegetables, stuffing them in as hard as you can and making sure you disperse the garlic, some lemon slices, herbs of choice, cardamom and pepper throughout.
3. Fill up the jars with the cooled vinegar mixture, making sure every part is well-covered with the liquid.
4. Stand the jar in a COOL place for a month. You could turn upside down initially to make sure the contents are soaked with the vinegar. Make sure the cap is sealed properly!

TURK TIP *Some people swear by adding a small handful of dried chickpeas to the bottom of the jars before the veg. This is supposed to aid the pickling process. You can use pretty much any vegetable or fruit (tomatoes) as you wish. Red peppers and garlic make great pickles. Grill and skin the peppers beforehand.*

WINES, SPIRITS & OTHER DRINKS

I should give a short dissertation on the drinks that can be taken with the food or as an aperitif.

Although many Muslims do not drink – Sazili, Sema and most of the villagers are teetotal – most of my Turkish friends do like to drink, they enjoy every drop, especially raki.

Turkey is divided over alcohol consumption. Some Turks, mostly in the eastern and central areas are against it, for many reasons – religious, and economic. The national drink was *raki* (rather like pastis or Ouzo) and for the most part, on the Western side still is, but the government would prefer it to be *ayran*, the yogurt drink with salt, so perfect for summer snacks and lunches.

In between there is a wonderful selection of uncelebrated Turkish wines that would rival any from France. Turkish lager-type beer is also delicious and considered one of the best ever, Efes, named after the ancient city being my favourite and available in the UK, although I have to say it never tastes the same there.

The biggest problem is the cost: once, we could buy a decent plonk for around £1.50 and a beer for about 50 pence, but the government taxes have put pay to that and dedicated drinkers now have to pay Euro prices for a bottle of wine, £4–7 for a table wine and £2 for a beer. *Raki* and other spirits are now about 300TL a bottle and rising. To be honest I can't keep up with Turkish prices for alcohol, it's not only the taxes, but also the mercurial movement of the Lira. All my Turkish friends beg me to bring alcohol in for them, when I come in from the UK. My priority, though, is my gin for the early evening drinkies for my painters, so mostly, I'm afraid my Turkish pals will have to wait – or join us for the evening.

We used to be able to buy Turkish gin about 25 years ago and it wasn't half bad, and also half the price of, say a Gordon's. Also back then and if you were lucky, in some out of the way bars nobody seemed to know how to pour a spirit, we would be handed half a tumbler full of gin, vodka or rum, with the merest sprinkle of a mixer. No wonder our holidays were such a success in the 80s!

I did not develop a taste for *raki* for several years, but now find it a wonderful clean tasting drink, perfect as an accompaniment for fish in any shape or form. A '*duble*' costs around 30TK (£4) and all depending on the amount of water and ice you add, it can last the dinner through. Two of these cloudy relaxers and you could be asking yourself if YOU can last the dinner through!

Regardless of the taxation and the ban on advertising wines and spirits, my friends from the coastal resorts and the major cities will still enjoy a drink, and very good those drinks are too.

I must also mention that it is possible (surprisingly) to buy raw basic alcohol in the supermarkets. My next door neighbour, Behice, an imposing woman of great intellect, makes the most superb Limoncella with her own lemons. Phil had several glasses, albeit small, and still glazes over at the thought of those delicious digestifs. He has also been the victim of our neighbour's home made Raki, after three glasses, he had lost the feeling in his legs and sadly when trying to stroke the lovely dog opposite our house, fell on top of her and had to be hauled up by his arms. No damage to the dog, or indeed to Phil as he had not the expected hangover the next day.

Another friend of mine suggested adding peeled ginger root and limes or lemons (or indeed any other fruit) to cheap Turkish gin (*cin*) leave it for a month she told me, and there you have one of those fancy Botanicals so cool amongst the hipsters of Shoreditch and for a fraction of the price. I intend to give that a go this year.

I have heard on the grapevine (haha) that the new vineyard up near the carpet village produces some very fine wines indeed and as a plus point will conduct tours of their establishment, culminating, naturally, in a sale of the produce. I intend to give it a shot (again haha) and buy a dozen bottles, just in case we get a run on the refreshments this year.*

COMFORTING *SAHLEP* DRINK WITH CINNAMON AND PISTACHIO NUTS

Serves 2

16fl oz./ml 2 cups of cold whole milk
10ml/1 tbsp *Sahlep* powder, this can be found in Turkish or Indian grocery shops or online.
Sugar to your taste
5ml/1 tsp ground cinnamon for garnish
5ml/1 tsp ground pistachios for garnish – optional

1. Place the cold milk, *sahlep* powder and sugar in a small pan and bring to a gentle boil.
2. Stir continuously for 2–3 minutes over a gentle heat until it starts to thicken.
3. Turn the heat off and pour the hot drink into two cups.
4. Sprinkle the ground cinnamon and crushed pistachios (if using) over the top and serve immediately.

* I have since been and they were right, the wine was fabulous and I ordered three cases!

AUTHOR'S NOTE

FUNCTION OVER FORM

Now don't get me wrong, I love the people and the landscapes, the history and of course the food of Turkey, but one thing that does please me less, at least in our neck of the woods is that function most definitely takes precedence over form. Style and the 'look' of a house, municipal building or anything that does actually have a function, definitely takes second place to the use for which is was intended.

It is hard to argue sometimes and I am still getting those quizzical looks when I suggest that perhaps using up that old tin of peach paint when the rest of the room is turquoise, may not be a good idea. Nailing a picture to a wall, absolutely nothing being level, that sort of thing.

I really cannot, ever, not ever, leave my Turkish gardener, builder, electrician, plumber to their own devices, Lord alone knows what I would come back to, well actually I do, because I have and it's pretty dispiriting. I ordered brand spanking new air conditioning for the annexe we lovingly call 'The Cottage'. Not only was the unit at a crazy angle, but the connecting wires ran across the wall from the floor to the opposite ceiling at 45°. Go fathom. The electrician was incredulous when I suggested that he should rewire the lot by following the corners of the room and going neatly across the rear of the wall where it meets the ceiling. It worked didn't it? No, there is no such thing as 'chasing in' around here.

I see fluorescent light fittings fitted with daylight bulbs searing my eyeballs; 'No Nails' plastic mousse used at every opportunity; chairs mended with electrical insulation tape (Sazili's preferred modus operandi for most problems); fences cobbled together with old pieces of plastic, maybe a radiator and discarded doors. They keep the chickens out, but I reckon it's because the chickens have been reading Ideal Home *magazine and fear the consequences of their actions may impinge on their sense of elan.*

Sazili – eager to please on listening to my exasperated yelps, when I realised my neighbour's dog was using my front garden flower bed as a bunkhouse, with the inherent consequence of mangled plants and dug up earth – built a shanti town type barricade in front of said flower bed. Bright orange, ex gas company plastic fencing and all tied together with copious amounts of hairy string. I didn't have the heart to explain my painters were aesthetes and may find their first view of the house a little less than compelling, so I kept it for a few days, but it had to go and I felt a real traitor ripping it out.

I am not suggesting everyone is the same, there are people in the village who have beautifully tended gardens, salons and outhouses, and I know that money is short for some folk, but even in such extremis surely a screw is better than a nail. I reckon Sazili has the measure of me now and I am sure there is much eye rolling behind my back, but even he shouts out 'TEMIZ' ('Tidy') to the workman who come to the house, and they obey.

So maybe I am fighting a one-woman battle against the ramshackle, but at least it seems to be having an effect in my own back yard.

I hope by now you are more understanding of the Turkish ways of life, least ways in our own locality. So much has already changed in the thirty odd years I have been popping back and forth from London to Yalikavak, that I do worry it will be spoiled, sometimes to the extent that I grit my teeth on the way up Ceviz Sokak towards the house. But there is so much that is left unspoiled, so much history to still be unearthed, and so many wonderful people who I am glad to call friends that I know all will be the same, especially the hospitality and, of course that wonderful food.

ADDENDUM

So now the book is finished and I feel as if I could ramble on for hours or more telling new silly stories and observations of my half (yarim yarim) sisters and brothers in Turkey. I returned to the village a couple of weeks ago before my final results on my brain tumour came through and was overwhelmed by the love and happiness that greeted me on my first walk down the village street. It was as if I had been away for a life time and equally only ten minutes. What a lovely welcome and at least six invites to come and eat! Now given an 'all clear' I intend to return again, this time for a long, long time, there's a lot of food to eat!